CRIMINAL LAW AND THE AUTHORITY OF THE STATE

How does the state, as a public authority, relate to those under its jurisdiction through the criminal law? Connecting the ways in which criminal lawyers, legal theorists, public lawyers and criminologists address questions of the criminal law's legitimacy, contributors to this collection explore issues such as criminal law-making and jurisdiction; the political-ethical underpinnings of legitimate criminal law enforcement; the offence of treason; the importance of doctrinal guidance in the application of criminal law; the interface between tort and crime; and the purposes and mechanisms of state punishment. Overall, the collection aims to enhance and deepen our understanding of criminal law by conceiving of the practices of criminal justice as explicitly and distinctly embedded in the project of liberal self-governance.

Studies in Penal Theory and Penal Ethics: Volume 6

Studies in Penal Theory and Penal Ethics

A Series Published for the Centre for
Penal Theory and Penal Ethics
Institute of Criminology, University of Cambridge

FOUNDING EDITOR: ANDREW VON HIRSCH

GENERAL EDITORS:
ANTHONY E BOTTOMS, ANTJE DU BOIS-PEDAIN

Ethical and Social Perspectives on Situational Crime Prevention
edited by Andrew von Hirsch, David Garland and Alison Wakefield

Restorative Justice and Criminal Justice: Competing or Reconcilable Paradigms?
edited by Andrew von Hirsch, Julian Roberts, Anthony E Bottoms, Kent Roach and Mara Schiff

Incivilities: Regulating Offensive Behaviour
edited by Andrew von Hirsch and AP Simester

Previous Convictions at Sentencing: Theoretical and Applied Perspectives
edited by Julian V Roberts and Andrew von Hirsch

Setting the Watch: Privacy and the Ethics of CCTV Surveillance
Beatrice von Silva-Tarouca Larsen

Criminal Law and the Authority of the State

Edited by

Antje du Bois-Pedain, Magnus Ulväng and Petter Asp

HART PUBLISHING

OXFORD AND PORTLAND, OREGON

2017

Hart Publishing
An imprint of Bloomsbury Publishing Plc

Hart Publishing Ltd
Kemp House
Chawley Park
Cumnor Hill
Oxford OX2 9PH
UK

Bloomsbury Publishing Plc
50 Bedford Square
London
WC1B 3DP
UK

www.hartpub.co.uk
www.bloomsbury.com

Published in North America (US and Canada) by
Hart Publishing
c/o International Specialized Book Services
920 NE 58th Avenue, Suite 300
Portland, OR 97213-3786
USA

www.isbs.com

HART PUBLISHING, the Hart/Stag logo, BLOOMSBURY and the Diana logo are trademarks of Bloomsbury Publishing Plc

First published 2017

British Library Cataloguing-in-Publication Data
A catalogue record for this book is available from the British Library.

ISBN: HB: 978-1-50990-513-3
ePDF: 978-1-50990-515-7
ePub: 978-1-50990-514-0

Library of Congress Cataloging-in-Publication Data

Names: Du Bois-Pedain, Antje, editor. | Ulväng, Magnus, 1970- editor. | Asp, Petter, editor.

Title: Criminal law and the authority of the state / Antje du Bois-Pedain, Magnus Ulväng and Petter Asp.

Description: Oxford ; Portland, Oregon : Hart Publishing, an imprint of Bloomsbury Publishing Plc, 2017. | Series: Studies in penal theory and penal ethics ; volume 6 | Includes bibliographical references and index.

Identifiers: LCCN 2016054441 | ISBN 9781509905133 (hardback : alk. paper)

Subjects: LCSH: Criminal justice, Administration of.

Classification: LCC K5001 .C753 2017 | DDC 364—dc23

LC record available at https://lccn.loc.gov/2016054441

Typeset by Compuscript Ltd, Shannon
Printed and bound in Great Britain by TJ International Ltd, Padstow, Cornwall

Contents

Contributors

Petter Asp, Professor of Criminal Law, Stockholm University.

Anthony E Bottoms, Wolfson Professor of Criminology Emeritus, Director of the Centre for Penal Theory and Penal Ethics, Institute of Criminology, University of Cambridge; Fellow of Fitzwilliam College, Cambridge.

Iain Cameron, Professor of Public International Law, Uppsala University.

Antje du Bois-Pedain, University Senior Lecturer, Faculty of Law, Deputy Director of the Centre for Penal Theory and Penal Ethics, Institute of Criminology, University of Cambridge; Fellow of Magdalene College, Cambridge.

Matthew Dyson, Associate Professor, Faculty of Law, University of Oxford and Tutorial Fellow of Corpus Christi College, Oxford.

Alon Harel, Phillip and Estelle Mizock Chair in Administrative and Criminal Law, The Hebrew University, Jerusalem.

Anat Scolnicov, Professor of Public Law, Winchester University.

Erik Svensson, Lecturer in Law, Uppsala University.

Justice Tankebe, University Lecturer in Criminology, University of Cambridge.

Malcolm Thorburn, Associate Professor, University of Toronto.

Magnus Ulväng, Professor of Criminal Law, Uppsala University.

Lucia Zedner, Senior Research Fellow at All Souls College and Professor in the Faculty of Law, University of Oxford; Conjoint Professor in the Faculty of Law, University of New South Wales, Sydney.

Introduction

ANTJE DU BOIS-PEDAIN, MAGNUS ULVÄNG AND PETTER ASP

THE QUESTION THAT animates this collection of essays is how the state, as a public authority, relates to those under its jurisdiction through the criminal law. The book brings together criminal lawyers, criminologists, legal theorists and public lawyers who, from a shared acceptance of broadly liberal political foundations for state authority, address specific aspects of this relationship, such as questions of criminal law-making and jurisdiction; the use of criminal law to suppress challenges to state authority; the purposes and mechanisms of state punishment; the interface between tort and crime; and the political-ethical underpinnings of legitimate criminal law enforcement.

There has been surprisingly little exchange between criminal lawyers and public lawyers on what is clearly an area of overlapping concern—given that the criminal justice system engages in what is often seen as the most invasive, and most problematic, use of the coercive power of the state. For much of the time, the position has simply been that public (and particularly constitutional) lawyers have one understanding of what legitimates the exercise of power by the state, including through its criminal law, whereas criminal lawyers traditionally approach the legitimacy conditions of criminal law in other ways. These are not necessarily incompatible with public lawyers' conception of the foundations of state authority, but certainly place the emphasis on different questions and concerns. The perspectives of criminologists and criminal law theorists on what matters to the justification of criminal justice practice also often betray a degree of disconnection.

The separation of different discourses on the legitimacy of criminal law in, respectively, public law, criminal law theory, and sociologically oriented criminal justice scholarship, is however problematic. Each of these specialised approaches risks missing out on dimensions of criminal legal practice that would have to be addressed to provide a full account and justification. As Alice Ristroph perceptively notes:

> State punishment claims distinctive normative status precisely because it is a kind of *state* action, produced by trained, authorized and regulated officials rather than vigilantes. Whether those officials comply with their training, or act within the scope of their authority, is central to the legitimacy of the criminal justice process. Moreover, we should view the criminal justice process holistically rather than as a series of isolated, discrete episodes. … We authorize police forces as mechanisms

> to make punishment possible. The legitimacy of punishment depends, in part, on the policing that provides the targets of punishment.[1]

Ristroph therefore quite rightly takes penal theorists to task for 'focus[ing] nearly exclusively on the target of punishment—the wrongdoer—and neglect[ing] the various persons and groups that authorize, impose and administer punishment'.[2] (Similar accusations of myopia can, of course, also be directed at approaches which reduce criminal justice to a form of regulatory guidance that is not, as such, concerned with wrongdoing or blame.)

Ristroph goes on to identify four conditions for legitimate state punishment: (1) the existence of a legitimate state, (2) fair substantive criminal laws, (3) legitimate policing, and (4) a determination that the state's violence does not inflict unacceptably high levels of collateral damage on those subject to investigation and punishment and on third parties.[3]

The chapters in this collection address these conditions. Moreover, the spotlight is very much on the agent of punishment: 'the state', when identified in the abstract-impersonal mode, and police officers, prosecutors, judges and prison staff, when we turn to the institutions and individuals through which the state acts.

Of course, a collection of this kind cannot in and of itself lay the foundations for each of the key concepts invoked in its title. Some of the essays bring conceptual questions to the fore—for instance, Thorburn's chapter does so in respect of the concept of state authority, and Svensson's chapter does so as regards the concept of criminal law. Other contributors work (expressly or by implication) with a range of possible conceptions of 'criminal law' and 'state authority'. 'Criminal law' is used in the title of this book in a very wide sense that spans socio-legal and doctrinal understandings. The socio-legal perspective encompasses the practices and outcomes of law-creation and law enforcement that we understand as potentially oriented towards the imposition of reprobative sanctions by the institutions of government. The doctrinal perspective captures other distinctive features: it conceives of criminal law as a normative system rationally oriented towards behavioural guidance and responsibility assessment for violations of conduct norms potentially subject to state punishment. As a sense-making activity, it treats legal norms as (if they were) an integrated system of behavioural guidance supported by a coherent conceptual architecture. Similarly, other contributors do not necessarily share the notion of 'robust state authority' that

[1] A Ristroph, 'Conditions of Legitimate Punishment' in C Flanders and Z Hoskins (eds), *The New Philosophy of Criminal Law* (London and New York, Rowman and Littlefield, 2016) 79 at 87–88.

[2] Ibid at 81. There are, of course, exceptions, eg, Nicola Lacey, Vincent Chiao and many of the scholars working in Kantian, Hegelian and contractarian traditions.

[3] Ibid at 81.

Thorburn develops and defends in the opening chapter of this book. State authority is, again, taken in a broad sense, as identifying a concern with legitimate rule in the specific mode of governance invoked by the notion of the state.[4]

The chapters also differ in scholarly approach. Some tackle the justification of state punishment at an abstract, theoretical level. Others are 'theoretical' only in that what stands behind the argument is a normative concern with the ideal way of conceptualising the role of the state in respect of the issue under discussion. In keeping with the continental tradition of bringing theory to bear on questions concerning the operation of a legal system, philosophical positions about the foundations of the state, theoretical perspectives on legal reasoning, etc may be used to explain the underlying structure of a problem, or to defend conclusions, but engagement with theoretical issues is not pushed beyond a point where academics who define themselves as criminal lawyers or public lawyers, as opposed to political or legal philosophers, will find these arguments directly relevant to the issues that concern them. While a number of chapters draw on examples from different legal systems, the aim is not to provide information about different legal systems, as such. Where a comparative angle becomes prominent, this is so because the comparison best illuminates the point under discussion.

I. THE INDIVIDUAL CONTRIBUTIONS

The opening chapter by Malcolm Thorburn[5] firmly sets the justification of criminal justice institutions into the context of the justification of state authority. Thorburn argues that it is a mistake to try and make sense of criminal punishment as a practice that emerges from relations between individuals taken simply as natural persons, none answerable to any other. The institution of criminal punishment—as Thomas Aquinas pointed out many centuries ago[6]—has its place only within a relationship of robust public authority. To justify the institution of criminal punishment, we must therefore first make clear how it fits into the relationship of robust public authority. Once this step is in place, we can then consider how such a relationship of

[4] On the theoretical conception of the state, including the historical development of the concept, see, eg, D Runciman, 'The Concept of the State' in Q Skinner and B Strath (eds), *States and Citizens* (Cambridge, Cambridge University Press, 2003) 28; Q Skinner, 'The Sovereign State: A Genealogy' in H Kalmo and Q Skinner (eds), *Sovereignty in Fragments: The Past, Present and Future of a Contested Concept* (Cambridge, Cambridge University Press, 2010) 26. On the historical evolution of the mode of governance referenced by the term, see M van Crefeld, *The Rise and Decline of the State* (Cambridge, Cambridge University Press, 1999).

[5] M Thorburn, 'Punishment and Public Authority', ch 1 in this collection.

[6] St Thomas Aquinas *Summa Theologica* I-II Q 90 a 3 ad 2 in *Introduction to St Thomas Aquinas* edited by A Pegis (New York, Modern Library, 1948) 614: 'this coercive power is vested in the whole people or in some public personage, to whom it belongs to inflict penalties'.

robust public authority could be justified given our conception of ourselves as free and equal moral persons.

The next three chapters deepen and explore this connection in three essential directions: jurisdiction, policing and criminal procedure.

Petter Asp[7] contends that jurisdictional limits are best understood not as reflecting the boundaries of a polity's legitimate concern with harm and wrongdoing, but as reflecting what are, in a certain sense, secondary concerns about the political appropriateness and practical feasibility of exercising governmental functions beyond territorial borders. This approach explains why, as modes of governance become increasingly supranational and fragmented, the jurisdictional reach of state criminal justice systems is in constant flux.

Anthony Bottoms and Justice Tankebe[8] address legitimate policing through the lenses provided by the theorisation of Bernard Williams (the 'Basic Legitimation Demand')[9] and Amartya Sen (the 'impartial spectator').[10] If we accept that what Thorburn calls 'robust public authority' exists to resolve the problem of order—to preserve conditions in which humans have a sense of ontological security and are able to pursue their various projects cooperatively—then, given the pivotal role of public police in maintaining that order, a crucial question becomes how to ensure that police remain 'part of the solution' and do not become 'part of the problem'. What is of crucial importance here, Bottoms and Tankebe argue, is how police officers themselves see their task in their interactions with members of the public. Police practice built on accepting that every member of the public with whom police interact can legitimately expect an answer to the question 'why do you exert power over me' will exercise power dialogically and avoid sapping citizens' goodwill. 'Robust public authority' is only defensibly exercised when those who claim to exercise it accept that 'power itself does not justify'[11] and accordingly offer different grounds of legitimation.

Lucia Zedner[12] similarly argues that the legitimacy of criminal law depends, also, on a criminal procedure that appropriately binds law enforcement to the requirements of the rule of law. Focusing on recent developments in UK criminal justice that restrict or deny due process rights in the name of security, she explores how far the criminal process can travel from its ideal type before it erodes the legitimacy of the law it is set up to enforce.

[7] P Asp, 'Extraterritorial Ambit and Extraterritorial Jurisdiction', ch 2 in this collection.
[8] AE Bottoms and J Tankebe, 'Police Legitimacy and the Authority of the State', ch 3 in this collection.
[9] B Williams, *In the Beginning was the Deed: Realism and Moralism in Political Argument*, edited by G Hawthorn (Princeton NJ, Princeton University Press, 2005).
[10] A Sen, *The Idea of Justice* (London, Allen Lane, 2009).
[11] Williams, above n 9 at 5.
[12] L Zedner, 'Security Against Arbitrary Government in Criminal Justice', ch 4 in this collection.

For public lawyers, legitimacy is created by, and hinges (though perhaps not exclusively so) on the legislative process—and reflecting on this process is one way of bringing the distinctive perspectives of public law to bear on questions of criminalisation that have animated criminal law scholars for some time. Iain Cameron's chapter[13] addresses the effectiveness of such (from the perspective of criminal law) 'external' limits on criminalisation. He argues, and demonstrates, that legal cultural practices of public deliberation and legislative oversight can impose sensible restrictions on the reach of criminal law.

The chapter by Anat Scolnicov[14] addresses a particularly problematic instance of criminalisation: the offence of treason, which appears equally troubling from a distinctly public law and a distinctly criminal law perspective. For the criminal lawyer, it is concerning that the connection to harm to persons is contingent (and often not strong enough to justify the sanctions threatened, and imposed). For the public lawyer, the offence raises fundamental questions about the relationship between the state and the legal subject. Does the offence presuppose that legal subjects owe the state loyalty—and is this an obligation that could be coercively enforced? The offence of treason puts our understanding of what a legitimate authority may demand squarely on the table.

Normative constraints on the exercise of state authority can also arise for systemic reasons. Systemic coherence is widely recognised as important for the realisation of rule of law values: it contributes to making the application of the law predictable; it avoids placing legal subjects in impossible positions (where one law demands what another law prohibits, or where negative legal consequences follow from compliance with the law). A reasonable degree of systemic coherence is thus essential for the law's ability to guide people's conduct, and (in assuring fair warning) for the legitimacy of the coercive enforcement of its commands.

Cameron's description of the Swedish legislative process brings out the attention given to legal certainty and concerns of systemic coherence by those who scrutinise proposed legislation.[15] Erik Svensson's chapter[16] explores the contribution 'legal dogmatics' makes to this task. 'Legal dogmatics'—the term used by Neil MacCormick and Ruth Adler for the German word *Rechtsdogmatik*[17]—is concerned with the rational reconstruction and systematisation of a body of legal materials such that this material forms a

[13] I Cameron, 'A Constitutional Perspective on the Criminalisation Process in Sweden', ch 5 in this collection.

[14] A Scolnicov, 'Against the State', ch 6 in this collection.

[15] Cameron, above n 13.

[16] E Svensson, 'Legal Dogmatics, Theory and the Limits of Criminal Law', ch 7 in this collection.

[17] In their translation of R Alexy, *A Theory of Legal Argumentation* (Oxford, Oxford University Press, 1989).

coherent and structured whole. Svensson addresses the role that this method plays in achieving (internal) coherence. Whereas philosophical theory as such cannot generate legally relevant restrictions for a court tasked with the application of criminal law, a position developed through 'dogmatic reconstruction' of the criminal laws of a specific legal system can do so. Legal dogmatics is thus essential to setting limits to criminal law.

Matthew Dyson's chapter[18] turns to another—and extremely important—area where coherence must be achieved: in relation to the state's obligation to provide appropriate remedial mechanisms across crime and tort. All Western legal systems have evolved a distinction between tort and crime, and the distinction is perceived as essential for a proper understanding of the remit and aims of criminal justice practices. But pitfalls abound in the interaction of the remedial regimes offered by tort law and criminal law. Dyson's chapter explores these with a view to helping states identify appropriate structural arrangements and mechanisms to regulate the interface between tort and crime.

The remaining chapters look at aspects of the imposition of penal sanctions by the state. Antje du Bois-Pedain[19] puts forward a conceptualisation of the sentencing judgment as setting the terms of future relationship with an offender. Drawing on the writings of Johann Gottlieb Fichte, she develops a reintegrative conception of state punishment and argues that a constitutionally legitimate proportionality assessment must be 'bifocal'—focused not just on the seriousness of the offending behaviour but also on what undergoing the punishment will mean for and do to the offender. The final chapter by Alon Harel[20] takes up a 2005 decision by the Israeli Supreme Court that detention in a private prison would, as such, violate the prisoners' dignity, to develop an argument that state punishment is denatured, and invariably delegitimised, when it is carried out by private agents (even if supposedly on behalf of the state).

II. ACKNOWLEDGEMENTS

We are grateful to all participants at the exploratory workshop held in Cambridge in the summer of 2013 and generously supported by a Cambridge Humanities Research Grant. We also acknowledge the financial support of Uppsala University's fund for the criminal law chair.

[18] M Dyson, 'The State's Obligation to Provide a Coherent System of Remedies Across Crime and Tort', ch 8 in this collection.

[19] A du Bois-Pedain, 'Punishment as an Inclusionary Practice: Sentencing in a Liberal Constitutional State', ch 9 in this collection.

[20] A Harel, 'Why Privatisation Matters', ch 10 in this collection.

1

Punishment and Public Authority

MALCOLM THORBURN*

OVER THE PAST 30 years or so, criminal law theory has lost sight of the important role of criminal justice in the business of government. Legal moralism, the school of criminal law theory that has dominated the debate over the past three decades, is an attempt to justify the state's coercive criminal justice powers as mere tools for doing to moral wrongdoers what morality requires. Proceeding in this way allows moralists to avoid dealing with the intricacies of state institutions but it places enormous weight on one's moral intuitions. For in order for the moralist position to succeed, we must first accept that moral wrongdoers actually deserve to suffer something like the hardship that criminal justice administers simply in virtue of the fact that they have committed moral wrongs. And this is not an intuition that many people share. As HLA Hart famously put the point, it 'seems to rest on a strange amalgam of ideas. … [It] is uncomfortably close to human sacrifice as an expression of religious worship'.[1] TM Scanlon concludes that 'the idea that when a person has done something that is morally wrong it is morally better that he or she should suffer some loss in consequence … [is] morally indefensible'.[2]

With the perceived failure of legal moralism to provide a plausible moral justification of the institutions of criminal justice, many scholars nowadays are turning back to an old idea: the thought that the moral justification of criminal justice turns on its role in a larger story about the morally important role of government. One way to tell this story is to focus on the role of

* This chapter is a distant relative of the draft presented at the Uppsala workshop. I am grateful to Anthony Bottoms, Matt Dyson, Alon Harel, and Lucia Zedner for insightful comments on that earlier draft. Thanks also to my University of Toronto colleagues Vincent Chiao, David Dyzenhaus, Larissa Katz, Arthur Ripstein and Hamish Stewart for extremely helpful comments and discussion on a later draft. I owe special thanks to Antje du Bois-Pedain for much helpful criticism, discussion and patience.

[1] HLA Hart, *Law, Liberty, and Morality* (Palo Alto CA, Stanford University Press, 1962) 65.

[2] TM Scanlon, *What we Owe to Each Other* (Cambridge MA, Harvard University Press, 1998) 274.

government in setting standards of conduct and ensuring general compliance with them, all for the sake of the general welfare. Two centuries ago, Jeremy Bentham suggested that criminal justice should be understood as part of the state's legitimate role in securing general compliance with morally valuable legal rules. '[A]ll punishment is mischief: all punishment in itself is evil',[3] Bentham wrote, but it could be morally redeemed if we could show that it serves to prevent even greater harm (by inducing compliance with morally valuable legal rules). On this account, crimes are just whatever forms of conduct the law prohibits and punishments are just whatever threats the state deems appropriate to deter such undesirable conduct. So long as the good we do indirectly (by inducing greater compliance with the law) is greater than the harm we do directly (by punishment and other coercive measures) and perhaps so long as those harms and benefits are fairly distributed among persons, it seems that the operations of criminal justice are morally justified.

Like the legal moralist account of criminal justice, the instrumentalist account is very attractive in its simplicity. It seems plausible on first inspection that we might be able to redeem the terrible coerciveness of criminal justice institutions by showing them to be essential means to producing the great benefit of general compliance with morally valuable legal rules. But this vision of well-placed incentives seems to fit more easily with what are often called regulatory offences than it does with criminal punishment.[4] For when we are required to pay a late fee at the public library or for overstaying at a parking meter or for being in possession of undersized lobsters,[5] it might seem that there is nothing more to it than the fact that the state needs some way to induce compliance with its rules and these fines are effective tools for inducing compliance. But what is sometimes referred to as 'true criminal law'—where crimes call for subjective mens rea,[6] and where

[3] 'An Introduction to the Principles of Morals and Legislation' in J Bentham, *A Fragment of Government with an Introduction to the Principles of Morals and Legislation* edited by W Harrison (Oxford, Basil Blackwell, 1960) 281.

[4] On the nature of regulatory offences (also called public welfare offences), see FB Sayre, 'Public Welfare Offenses' (1933) 33 *Columbia Law Review* 55; RM Perkins, 'The Civil Offense' (1952) 100 *University of Pennsylvania Law Review* 832.

[5] The best-known Canadian case concerning regulatory offences is *R v Pierce Fisheries* [1971] SCR 5 in which the accused was found to be in possession of 26 undersized lobsters, contrary to the Lobster Fishery Regulations made pursuant to the Fisheries Act RSC 1952 C 119.

[6] *R v Sault Sainte Marie* [1978] 2 SCR 1299 per Dickson J at 1309–10: 'Where the offence is criminal, the Crown must establish a mental element, namely that the accused who committed the prohibited act did so intentionally or recklessly, with knowledge of the facts constituting the offence or with wilful blindness toward them. Mere negligence is excluded from the concept of the mental element required for conviction'. Jerome Hall is the best-known scholarly advocate for the centrality of subjective mens rea to 'true criminal law'. See J Hall, *General Principles of Criminal Law* (Indianapolis, Bobbs-Merill, 1960) 146ff.

conviction involves formal state condemnation and a criminal record as well as the imposition of a penalty—seems to involve a good deal more than just this.

In this chapter, I argue that the moral justification of 'true criminal law' is indeed wrapped up with the business of government, but it is concerned with something even more basic to the project of government than the enforcement of specific legal rules. The central focus of 'true criminal law' is the very authority of the state itself as the sole lawmaker for the jurisdiction. When the state makes laws for its people, it does not just set out some rules and then try to do what it can to ensure general compliance with them; it does so *as* the public authority—the entity that has the sole authority to determine the basic rules according to which people shall organise their shared lives together in the jurisdiction. So when the state makes a law, say, prohibiting assault, it purports to decide authoritatively that people *shall not* assault one another within the jurisdiction. When one of the state's subjects intentionally assaults another in violation of the legal prohibition, he thereby arrogates to himself the mantle of law-maker, imposing his own favourite terms of interaction on the rest of us in place of the rules set down by the state. The offender does not merely fail to conform to the legal rule, he usurps the state's role in setting the terms under which he may interact with others, thereby challenging the state's claim to be the sole authority on the matter. In this way, the offender challenges the most basic promise of the rule of law: that we will never be subject to the arbitrary will of others, but only to the general laws that are the product of the legitimate public authority. If the offender's claim were allowed to stand, it would show the state's claim of sole authority on the matter to be a sham.

It is for this reason that any state that claims the authority to make the law over its jurisdiction must claim those powers necessary to ensure that its authority is supreme within the jurisdiction. It is usually sufficient to induce compliance ex ante with deterrent threats and the use of pre-emptive force by the police. But where someone disregards deterrent threats and evades the pre-emptive force of the police, the state must have some other means of reasserting its sole law-making authority over the jurisdiction. The institution of criminal punishment is that means. For when the state threatens criminal offenders with a deterrent sanction, it claims not only the power to impose costs on those who would violate its laws. It also claims the last word over the normative position of the offender. The offender tried to take on decision-making authority over how he shall relate to others (by acting on his own view of the matter rather than according to the state's law). If he were to evade punishment, then his decision would in fact be the last word on his normative relations with others. But where he is subject to criminal punishment, the state reasserts its authority over him (and everyone else in the jurisdiction). His act can then be seen as just another factual precondition to the operation of the state's laws: those who violate the laws shall be subject to the punishments prescribed by law. The institution of punishment allows the state's authority to expand to cover even those cases where it appears that individuals have been able to evade it. Seen in this way, the institution of criminal punishment is the ultimate vindication of the rule of law.

This chapter proceeds in four parts. In part one, I review some of the better known versions of legal moralism and of the instrumentalist account of punishment as a deterrent sanction. I do not purport to provide anything like a conclusive rebuttal of their positions; my purpose is simply to contrast their positions on some of the basic issues of criminal law theory with the view I espouse in this chapter. In part two, I provide an account of what I call here the state's 'robust public authority'—the claim that it and it alone is in charge of making the law in the jurisdiction. I consider the place of criminal justice, and especially criminal punishment, in an account of the state's robust public authority. In part three, I explore a number of arguments one might propose for why the state's robust public authority should be so important to our moral life. In part four, I present some conclusions, qualifications and clarifications of the view set out in this chapter.

I. CRIMINAL JUSTICE WITHOUT PUBLIC AUTHORITY

Punishment is morally problematic in a way that many other activities are not. It is not just that punishment involves the imposition of hardship on the punished person. Many worthwhile activities impose hardship on someone. We generally take this (within limits) to be morally acceptable. What makes punishment so particularly difficult to justify is that the imposition of hardship in this context is not merely a side-effect of our pursuit of some good; it is in some sense the whole point of the exercise. If we could pursue most of our ends without imposing any costs on others, we would take this to be an unmitigated good. But if we were to try to impose punishment in a way that imposed no hardship on anyone, this would simply constitute a failure to punish.[7]

In recent years, criminal law theorists have pursued two quite different strategies to justify the practice of criminal punishment. The first strategy—legal moralism—aims to show that it is a basic fact about the structure of

[7] This distinction between direct and oblique intention has its roots in the Catholic doctrine of double effect. In the years since Philippa Foot's celebrated article on the topic first appeared in 1967, this distinction between what we set out to do and what we merely foresee as a side-effect of our actions has taken centre-stage in moral theory. See 'The Problem of Abortion and the Doctrine of Double Effect', reprinted in P Foot, *Virtues and Vices* (Berkeley CA, University of California Press, 1978).

interpersonal morality that the punishment of wrongdoers is required, or at least permissible. The second strategy—instrumentalism—aims to show that the punishment of wrongdoers is acceptable as an essential part of a larger instrument for the pursuit of our collective welfare. Although these two justificatory strategies differ in many of their most fundamental aspects, they share one crucial feature: they both try to make sense of criminal justice without reference to the idea of the state's public authority. The justification of punishment, they assume, can be understood simply as a function of the morality of inter-personal relationships.

A. Legal Moralism

In recent years, legal moralism of one sort or another has come to dominate criminal law theory in the English-speaking world. The dominant strain of moralism (in the United States, at least) is what we may call 'moral retributivism'.[8] Moral retributivists insist that it is simply a moral fact that wrongdoers deserve to suffer in virtue of their wrongdoing. Although they might disagree about whether the suffering of wrongdoers is a requirement of justice[9] or whether it is even a good to be pursued,[10] they agree that interpersonal morality endorses the suffering of moral wrongdoers simply in virtue of their wrongdoing. Now if this is true, then there is no great puzzle at all about the moral justification of criminal punishment: the state is simply doing what interpersonal morality endorses or even requires. The trouble here is to explain why it is that interpersonal morality could ever demand or even permit that individuals should suffer hard treatment simply because of their past wrongdoing.

Michael Moore has tried to defend retributivism as a basic feature of interpersonal morality by means of a thought experiment. He invites us to imagine that someone (oneself or another person) has committed an unspeakably awful crime and then asks: 'Should you or the other offender be punished, even though no other social good will thereby be achieved?'

[8] Alan Brudner uses this term to distinguish this school of thought from what he calls 'legal retributivists' (A Brudner, *Punishment and Freedom* (Oxford, Oxford University Press, 2009) 19ff.). The latter category includes Brudner's own view as well as the position I espouse in this chapter.

[9] Michael Moore endorses this view in M Moore, 'The Moral Worth of Retribution' in FD Schoeman (ed), *Responsibility, Character, and the Emotions* (Cambridge, Cambridge University Press, 1987) 179 at 182: 'Retributivism … is truly a theory of justice such that, if it is true, we have an obligation to set up institutions so that retribution is achieved'.

[10] Michael Moore argues in M Moore, 'Justifying Retributivism' (1993) 27 *Israel Law Review* 15 at 19 that, 'what is distinctively retributivist is the view that the guilty receiving their just deserts is an intrinsic good'.

He replies: 'The retributivist's "yes" runs deep for most people'.[11] Although we might hesitate to punish others where no good will come of it, Moore suggests, most of us feel that offenders still ought to suffer punishment for their moral wrongs. Our responses to these sorts of thought-experiments, Moore asserts, are reliable guides to the structure of inter-personal morality. But, as Hart, Scanlon and many others have pointed out, these intuitions are not nearly so widely shared as Moore would like us to believe.

Antony Duff's communicative account of criminal punishment takes a different approach to the legal moralist intuition: he tries to turn it into a justified system for the communication of moral censure.[12] Duff writes: '[W]hatever puzzles there might be about the general idea that crimes "deserve" punishment ... there is surely nothing puzzling about the idea that wrongdoing deserves censure'.[13] So, Duff argues, there is nothing morally troubling about criminal punishment if we think of it as just a highly formalised and especially emphatic mechanism through which the state communicates the political community's moral censure of offenders for their wrongdoing. The trouble is that Duff's argument cannot explain why the state should be entitled to communicate its message of moral censure *through the means of hard treatment*.[14] For there is something quite distinctive about criminal punishment that is not captured in Duff's account, in at least two ways. First, we might all be entitled to criticise others for their moral failings as we see fit, but it would be a crime for any of us to take it upon ourselves to fine, to imprison or to impose any of the other standard forms of criminal punishment on another person. Second, it is acceptable for someone to receive moral criticism from any number of sources for a single wrong; but it would not be acceptable for him to be *punished* multiple times for the same wrong. The puzzle is not how one could have the standing to communicate moral criticism; it is how anyone could have the standing to *punish*—to deprive someone of his basic legal rights on the grounds that he deserves it in virtue of his criminal conduct.

The problems with legal moralism do not end there. For not only does the legal moralist account seem unable to justify the *punishment* of moral wrongdoers, he also seems unable to provide a plausible account of what

[11] M Moore, *Placing Blame* (Oxford, Oxford University Press, 2010) 163.

[12] Duff is building on Joel Feinberg's claim that punishment is essentially expressive in 'The Expressive Theory of Punishment' in J Feinberg, *Doing and Deserving: Essays in the Theory of Responsibility* (Princeton, Princeton University Press, 1970).

[13] RA Duff, 'Punishment, Communication and Community' in M Matravers, *Punishment and Political Theory* (Oxford, Hart Publishing, 1998) 48 at 50.

[14] As Scanlon famously put the point: 'Insofar as expression is our aim, we could just as well "say it with flowers" or, perhaps more appropriately, with weeds.': TM Scanlon, 'The Significance of Choice' in S McMurrin (ed), *The Tanner Lectures* Vol 7 (Salt Lake City, University of Utah Press, 1986) 149 at 214.

constitutes a criminal *wrong*. According to legal moralists, criminal offenders deserve moral censure and perhaps punishment because their conduct constitutes a freestanding *moral* wrong. Of course, they insist, what constitutes a moral wrong depends on the factual context. Most importantly, Duff points out, it is morally wrong to disregard the safety and convenience of others. This, he argues, renders it morally wrong to drive on the left-hand side of the road where all others drive on the right-hand side (because there are regulations in place requiring that one drive on the right-hand side).[15] The question of whether something constitutes a crime thus depends on our moral evaluation of the conduct in light of all the facts (among which are the relevant legal regulations in place within the jurisdiction). This argument allows the moralists to expand the scope of moral wrongs considerably, but it still fails to track anything like the actual scope of criminal wrongs as found in the positive law of most jurisdictions. Section 126 of the Criminal Code of Canada makes clear this basic structure of 'true crimes' in the following words: 'Every one who, without lawful excuse, contravenes an Act of Parliament by wilfully doing anything that it forbids or by wilfully omitting to do anything that it requires to be done is … guilty of an indictable offence'.[16] That is, we suffer criminal condemnation and punishment for contravening the demands of the positive law with mens rea, whether or not the law in question identifies a form of conduct that is morally wrongful. Legal moralists, who insist on turning the criminal law into a proxy for the enforcement of interpersonal morality, are simply unable to account for this basic feature of the law.

B. Instrumentalism and Distributive Justice

For those who find legal moralism to be a non-starter, there is a second strategy available for consideration. HLA Hart's account is the standard-bearer for those who have tried to turn criminal punishment into a generic instrument of state policy.[17] Hart takes it as given that, as Jeremy Bentham puts it, 'all punishment is mischief: all punishment in itself is evil'.[18] So if it

[15] RA Duff, *Answering for Crime* (Oxford, Hart Publishing, 2007) 92.

[16] Criminal Code of Canada s 126(1). S 127 of the Criminal Code is also relevant to this point. This makes it a crime to 'disobey a lawful order made by a court of justice or by a person or body of persons authorized by any Act to make or give the order'.

[17] I discuss Hart's account in greater detail in M Thorburn, 'The Radical Orthodoxy of Hart's *Punishment and Responsibility*' in MD Dubber (ed), *Foundational Texts in Modern Criminal Law* (Oxford, Oxford University Press, 2014).

[18] Bentham, above n 3 at 281.

is to be justified at all, this cannot be as something valuable in itself, but only as a means to some end beyond itself. Hart suggests that we should think of punishment in the same way as the harmful side-effects of our collective pursuit of valuable policy goals. For example, if we are able to dispose of waste in a way that serves the public good, individuals should be willing to accept some costs (in smells, noise, even some risks to their personal safety) that are necessary parts of the system that is required to secure that public good.[19] Indeed, one could even build into the system distributional constraints to ensure that no particular individual would have to bear more than his fair share of the burden of our collective pursuit of a valuable end. The same, Hart argues, should be said of criminal punishment. The system of punishment, like the system of waste disposal, is a policy instrument designed to secure some collective good (in this case, the reduction of anti-social behaviour). Since the imposition of deterrent sanctions is a necessary part of the system, we should think of the costs it imposes on offenders as just the unavoidable side-effects of our collective pursuit of a valuable aim. So long as the benefits of the system outweigh its costs, Hart argues, and so long as the costs are distributed fairly,[20] we should think of the system of hard treatment as a morally justified 'form of social hygiene'.[21]

A number of recent accounts have sought to render the basic Hartian insight more palatable to contemporary tastes by replacing his choice principle of distribution with some other principle (such as one or other form of egalitarianism: luck, opportunity or outcome; Pettit-style republicanism; etc) or by expanding the scope of the theory's concern to include not only the allocation of punishment but also the allocation of security and other goods.[22] Notwithstanding these differences, however, the basic structure of such accounts is the same as Hart's: we are concerned with the minimisation of harm and with the fair distribution of the benefits and burdens within a community. Old-fashioned talk of punishment as deserved in virtue of the offender's wrongdoing has no place in such instrumentalist accounts.

The trouble is that these instrumentalist arguments succeed in justifying something that looks more like regulatory offences rather than 'true

[19] I take this example from TM Scanlon in his discussion of the logic of what he calls 'substantive responsibility' in Scanlon, above n 2 at 256ff.

[20] Like most contemporary instrumentalists, Hart insists that there are side-constraints on the pursuit of our aims. He chose a principle of fair choice, but one might choose any number of other principles depending on what one takes to be the relevant conception of distributive justice in this context.

[21] HLA Hart, *Punishment and Responsibility: Essays in the Philosophy of Law* 2nd edn edited by J Gardner (Oxford, Oxford University Press, 2008) 6.

[22] The instrumentalist style includes a great many self-described 'political' theories of criminal punishment including the explicitly policy-oriented approach set out in V Chiao, 'What is the Criminal Law For?' (2016) 35 *Law and Philosophy* 137.

criminal law'. For on the instrumentalist account, there is nothing more to criminal punishment than the imposition of an effective deterrent sanction: for the instrumentalist, the positive rationale for punishing offenders (what Hart calls the 'General Justifying Aim' of the practice) is that this will deter undesirable conduct. But something much weightier seems to be at work in the punishment of 'true crimes'. Common law courts presume a subjective mens rea element for all 'true crimes'—something that (as Hart himself points out)[23] is beside the point when it comes to the fair distribution of deterrent sanctions. And when they impose criminal punishment (rather than mere regulatory penalties), they claim that this is deserved punishment for the offender's wrongdoing. On the instrumentalist account, criminal offenders may be seen as ordinary citizens shouldering their part of the collective burden in society's pursuit of some valuable collective end (as we might think of ourselves as we go down to the library to pay our overdue fines). But when it comes to the punishment of 'true crimes', it seems that, as John Gardner put the point, 'punishment must, by its nature, be imposed *by reason of* actual or supposed wrongdoing'.[24] As I shall argue below, the nature of the wrong involved in 'true crimes' is of a very particular kind—a wrong against the state's claim of legitimate law-making authority—but it is a wrong all the same. Any account of 'true crimes' that does away with this aspect of criminal law fails to account for one of its most basic features.

Recognising the weaknesses of both Hart's instrumentalist strategy and Duff's communicative account, Andrew Ashworth and Andrew von Hirsch have suggested that we should combine the two models into a sort of hybrid with the benefits of both.[25] That is, they side with Duff that the central role of criminal punishment must be to communicate moral censure for wrongdoing, but they also recognise that punishment necessarily involves hard treatment. So, they argue, criminal punishment should be thought of as a hybrid of two distinct elements: the communication of censure for moral wrongdoing coupled with hard treatment imposed as a deterrent sanction. In this way, von Hirsch and Ashworth suggest, we can provide a neat justification for both aspects of criminal punishment. Attractive though this hybrid might at first appear, however, it still does not provide the right sort of justification for criminal punishment. For the point, of course, is not simply that the hard treatment of criminal punishment can *accompany* the

[23] Hart, above n 21 at 113ff.

[24] J Gardner, 'Introduction' in Hart, *Punishment and Responsibility*, above n 21 at xxv–xxvi (emphasis added).

[25] A Ashworth and A von Hirsch, *Proportionate Sentencing: Exploring the Principles* (Oxford, Oxford University Press, 2005) at 21ff. TM Scanlon makes a similar sort of suggestion in Scanlon, above n 2 at 267.

communication of moral censure, but that it is *itself* imposed by reason of wrongdoing. We are still no further ahead.

C. The Inconveniences of the State of Nature

There is something missing from both the legal moralist and the instrumentalist strategies for the moral justification of criminal punishment. And yet each approach seems to have something important to recommend it. The moralist strategy, although it fails to provide a compelling moral justification for punishment, works with a plausible understanding of what punishment is: the very nature of punishment requires that it be imposed as a matter of justice in response to the offender's wrongdoing. The instrumentalist strategy, although it fails to justify the imposition of hard treatment as punishment for wrongdoing, makes clear that deterrence must play a central role in the justification of criminal punishment, for it is only by connecting punishment to this positive objective that we are able to show that it is capable of performing a morally valuable task. The trouble is that neither account has the tools necessary to draw together these two aspects of criminal punishment into a single, plausible account. In the next two sections of this chapter, I argue that the element that is missing from both the moralist and the instrumentalist strategies—the element that can connect the role of punishment as a deterrent to its place as the deserved response to wrongdoing within a legal order—is a robust account of the authority of the state over the punished wrongdoer.

II. PUBLIC AUTHORITY AND THE FORM OF PUNISHMENT

The criminal law theory debate of the past century or so has made one thing abundantly clear: despite enormous ingenuity and creativity, no one has come up with a compelling account of how we can square our basic assumptions about the structure of morality with the right of one person to punish another for his wrongdoing. It is not difficult to show (with Duff) that we have good reason to communicate moral censure of others for their moral wrongdoing. And we might even be able to show (with Hart) that we can set up incentives for others to deter them from violating legal rules. But it is quite another thing to be able to show that we are entitled to impose hard treatment on criminal offenders *as* a deserved punishment for their wrongdoing. This, it still seems, is 'morally indefensible'.[26]

[26] Scanlon, above n 2 at 274.

In this section of the chapter, I argue that the many proposals that have littered criminal law theory over the past century have failed because they have tried to make sense of it as a practice that exists between individuals taken simply as natural persons, none answerable to any other. And this is something that simply cannot be done. For, as Thomas Aquinas pointed out many centuries ago, 'this coercive power is vested in the whole people or in some public personage, to whom it belongs to inflict penalties'.[27] That is, we cannot make sense of the institution of criminal punishment simply as a feature of the relations between individuals as moral equals; it is an institution that has its place only within a relationship of robust public authority. Now, if that is true, then the moral justification of punishment will have to proceed rather more indirectly than was contemplated by either of the strategies we have considered so far. That is, to justify the institution of criminal punishment, we must first make clear how it fits into the relationship of robust public authority; once this step is in place, we can then consider how such a relationship of robust public authority could be justified given our conception of ourselves as free and equal moral persons.

In this part of the chapter, I sketch out a conception of robust public authority, indicating how criminal law and punishment are essential parts of it. I leave until the next section the question of how we might justify the existence of a public authority of the sort sketched out here. In one way, then, we might think of this section as the part where we engage in punishment theory properly speaking. In the next section of this chapter (where I consider various ways in which one might justify this conception of public authority) we depart the field of punishment theory properly speaking and enter into political theory more broadly. By distinguishing these two moments of the argument, I mean not only to show how political philosophy and criminal law theory are distinct from one another, but also to show how they are importantly related, as well.

A. Parental Authority

Criminal punishment is in many ways a unique institution: unique in its harshness, unique in the demandingness of its procedural requirements,[28] and unique in the role it plays in defining a society's values.[29] Nevertheless,

[27] St Thomas Aquinas *Summa Theologica* I–II Q 90 a 3 ad 2 in *Introduction to St Thomas Aquinas* edited by A Pegis (New York, Modern Library, 1948) 614.

[28] Although many of these procedural protections are now on the wane. See: A Ashworth, 'Is the Criminal Law a Lost Cause?' (2000) 116 *Law Quarterly Review* 225.

[29] Winston Churchill (Hansard 20 July 1910 col 1354): 'The mood and temper of the public in regard to the treatment of crime and criminals is one of the most unfailing tests of civilisation of any country'.

it may be helpful as a way of understanding the institution of criminal punishment and its place within a larger system of public authority to consider a somewhat less procedurally complex and less harshly punitive institution: parenthood.[30] The relationship between parents and their minor children is apposite because it is one of the few relationships of robust authority other than the one between state and subject. Although it is generally agreed that children are bearers of the same basic rights (to life, liberty, security and the rest) as all other human beings,[31] they are nevertheless incapable of exercising meaningful choices on their own behalf in a wide array of areas. The moral relationship between parents and children is one that is designed to square the status of children as beings of the same moral worth as adults with the fact of their inability to make meaningful decisions for themselves over certain matters.

Parents have a robust form of authority over their minor children. By this I mean that it is up to them—and *not* up to their children—to decide how their children may behave in a great many respects (which of course diminish in number as a child's capacity grows). This is a very familiar claim but it is also a very unusual one for it appears to run counter to our understanding of all persons as free and equal. How could one person be in charge of the most basic decisions relating to another person's life: where he shall live, what he shall eat, how he shall be educated, and so on? Although parents are not free to decide these matters in any way they would like, of course (for they must always make such decisions 'in the best interests of the child'),[32] it remains the case that it is up to the parents (and *not* up to the children themselves) to decide all these matters. We shall return to the question of whether such a relationship of robust authority between two human beings is ever morally justifiable in the next part of this chapter. For the time being, we can simply note that we quite easily recognise this sort of relationship in the parental context. We can now move on to explore its implications for the justification of punishment.

The story so far about the rights of parents to make decisions for their minor children is quite familiar. What is slightly less obvious is what is

[30] I have drawn this comparison before. See: M Thorburn, 'Justifications, Powers, and Authority' (2008) 117 *Yale Law Journal* 1070.

[31] But see M Moore, *Law and Psychiatry: Rethinking the Relationship* (Cambridge, Cambridge University Press, 1984) 91: '[B]uilt into the concept of a right is an image of its holder as one who *chooses*. The idea of a choice, in turn, implicates rights holders as beings who act for reasons in exercising the choice of whether to enforce their rights. … [R]ights are meaningfully ascribed only to those who reason practically and are thus capable of choice'.

[32] This has long been part of our understanding of the parent's relationship to his children. *Young v Young* [1993] 4 SCR 3 at 38 per L'Heureux-Dubé J: 'It has long been recognised that the custodial parent has a duty to ensure, protect and promote the best interests of the child'.

required for parents actually to maintain their decision-making authority over their children. For children might be the objects of parents' decision-making authority, but they are also human beings with wills of their own, and this adds a very important complication into the picture. For, as any parent knows all too well, it is a very real possibility that a child will not act as his parent has decided that he should. What, then, is required for parents to maintain decision-making authority over their (sometimes recalcitrant) children? There are three related mechanisms that are required. The first is the one we have already considered: parents may engage with their children as agents who are capable at least on some level of recognising and responding to reasons. In doing so, they set down directives for their children to follow: 'don't eat those sweets', 'don't cross the street on a red light', 'go to bed', etc. In at least some cases, the children might simply comply with these authoritative directives from their parents. And when they do, the parents will have thereby actualised their decision-making authority over their children.

But children will not always obey their parents: they might choose to disobey or to ignore their parents, they might not hear or (particularly with very young children) they might simply not understand what the directive requires. In order for parents to be able to actualise their decision-making authority over their children in these more complex situations, they must act toward their children in another way, by using pre-emptive coercive force over them. In order for parents actually to have the power to decide how their children shall live, it must be possible for them to take sweets out of their child's hand, to carry their recalcitrant child to bed, to restrain their child from crossing the road on a red light, etc. When asked why it is that the parent uses pre-emptive coercive force against her child, one might be tempted to say that the use of force is justified merely as a *means* to induce compliance with the parent's directive. But this would not be quite right. Of course, the point of pre-emptive force is to bring about a certain result, but the relationship between the use of coercion and the directive it is meant to enforce is not just one of a means to a distinct end. This is so for the same reason that we also deny that the parent's communicating of the rule to her child is merely a means to inducing compliance with her decisions.[33] It would be more accurate to say that both the communication of rules and their pre-emptive enforcement are partly *constitutive* of the parent's robust authority over her child: if she could not act in these ways, we could not properly say that she had such authority at all.

[33] Joseph Raz suggests that the point of the rule of law virtues of clarity, prospectivity, etc is just this—as a means to ensuring greater compliance with the law's directives. See: 'The Rule of Law and its Virtue' in J Raz, *The Authority of Law: Essays on Law and Morality* (Oxford, Oxford University Press, 1979).

In order for parents actually to maintain a position of decision-making authority over their children, however, they must be capable of acting toward them in yet a third way. For there will be occasions when children will not only disobey their parents, they will also evade their parents' pre-emptive coercion. So, if parents had no other mechanisms through which to vindicate their authority than the issuing of directives and the use of pre-emptive force to ensure compliance, their authority over their children would quite regularly fail. When parents threaten to punish their children for disobedience of their directives, this opens up a way for them to vindicate their authority over their children, even when those children have in fact disobeyed them. This third way of relating to one's children is even more complex in its structure than the first two, however. Indeed, it seems rather mysterious how threatening and carrying out punishment for disobedience could be aspects of the parental decision-making power at all. Surely, one might object, if a parent decides that her child shall do one thing and in fact he does another, this shows that she does *not*, in fact, have decision-making authority over the child. Tempting though that conclusion might be, it is mistaken. For this would be to confuse the question of whether parents can actually ensure compliance with each and every directive with the question of whether they remain in the position of robust authority over their children at all times.

It is important to recall what we mean by the claim of robust authority: it is the claim that parents (and *not* their children) are in charge of their children's lives (with respect to certain matters). Now, if we believe that it is morally significant that parents and children should stand in this sort of 'in charge of' relationship of robust authority, then we will think that there is good reason to try to vindicate it—to ensure that this form of relationship *always* governs relations between the parties—even in the face of conduct that is inconsistent with its terms. It is for this reason that we will look to remedies whose aim it is to restore the parent's robust authority in the face of conduct that attempts to challenge it. Remedies aimed primarily at restoring a certain form of relationship between the parties are most clearly in evidence in private law.[34] If I own a new car and you steal it from me, then you must give it back to me. This is necessary to vindicate my sole authority to decide whether or not you may have it in the face of your conduct that attempted to undermine that authority. If you scratch my new car, you must pay me the amount of money necessary to restore it to the status quo ante. This is necessary to vindicate my sole authority to decide what happens to

[34] At least, on one reading of private law. For the most thorough recent treatment of this way of thinking, see A Ripstein, *Private Wrongs* (Cambridge MA, Harvard University Press, 2016).

my car; anything you do to it[35] must either be undone or endorsed by me so that only my decisions affect what happens to my car. And so on.

If we mean to vindicate the parent's claim of robust authority over her child even in the face of conduct that is inconsistent with that claim, things are somewhat more complex, for the nature of the challenge is somewhat deeper. If we are only concerned with possession or a loss that is inconsistent with claims of right (as in many private law cases), then the remedy simply requires us to adjust factual possession or loss to accord with the allocation of rights. But when we are concerned with a direct attack on a claim of robust authority itself (as in the case of parental authority), it is not quite as obvious how we might bring the situation back into alignment with rightful relations. The solution lies in an extension of the parent's authority into the future—into a situation that the child's disobedience cannot disturb. When the parent threatens punishment for disobedience, she extends her claim of authority in just this way. Without the threat of punishment, the parent has nothing more to say in response to the child's disobedience. It appears that it is the child, rather than the parent, who determines how things shall stand between them. Once we include the threat of punishment, however, the parent has a further outlet for her claim of robust authority over her child. For now the child's disobedience is set in a very different light. Once the parent renders judgment and administers punishment, the child's wrongdoing can be seen as merely a factual precondition to the effectuation of the parent's ultimate authority. Although the child's disobedience remains regrettable—indeed, we should properly see it as a genuine moral wrong against the parent's authority—it is no longer a genuine threat to the parent's claim of robust authority over the child.

B. Interlude: Two Kinds of Authority

It is important to distinguish the robust sort of authority parents hold over their children from the sort of authority set out by Joseph Raz and that has become the common currency of much contemporary legal philosophy. For Raz seems to deny the core of the idea of robust authority I am concerned with here: that sometimes it is *not* up to each of us to decide how we should act. On Raz's account, it must always be up to each person to decide how

[35] In this case, what I *do* to something is not the same as the consequences of my actions on a thing. Where I use my own body or property legitimately, this might have certain (negative) consequences for others, but they are not things that I do *to* others in the technical sense I am invoking here. A full account of this distinction would involve a discussion of the terms of equal freedom to use one's body and property as one would like—a topic which is well beyond the scope of the present chapter.

he should act—to suggest otherwise would seem to be almost an absurdity. So the account of authority he proposes must turn on some other idea. That other idea is a sort of instrumental rationality. According to Raz,

> the normal way to establish that a person has authority over another person involves showing that the alleged subject is likely better to comply with reasons which apply to him ... if he accepts the directives of the alleged authority as authoritatively binding and tries to follow [its directives], rather than by trying to follow the reasons which apply to him directly.[36]

That is, to say that A is an authority for B is not to insist that it is up to A to decide how B should act. Rather, it is simply that B has good instrumental reasons to do as A says—for it is most likely to guide B to do as he already has reason to do.

As a result of this difference, a claim of robust authority of the sort I am concerned with here and a claim of Razian practical authority have a number of significantly different implications. As Raz himself notes, the Normal Justification Thesis

> invites a piecemeal approach to the question of the authority of governments, which yields the conclusion that the extent of governmental authority varies from individual to individual, and is more limited than the authority most governments claim for themselves in the case of most people.[37]

This follows from the fact that authority is a matter of the instrumental value to the subject of following the putative authority's directives. Where this is of instrumental value in complying with reasons that apply to us, we have reason to follow the putative authority's directives. But where they are not, there is no broader reason for us to defer to them whatsoever. By contrast, on the account of robust authority I am concerned with here, the concern is not with the instrumental value to the subject of following any particular directive from the authority. It is, rather, the justification of the relationship of robust authority as such. Once we have established that parents have robust authority over their children, the conclusion of that argument is that certain decisions about their children's lives are simply up to them. Now, of course, it remains to be seen whether it is possible to justify such a relationship of robust authority—but this is a task for part three of this chapter.

[36] J Raz, *The Morality of Freedom* (Oxford, Oxford University Press, 1986) 53.
[37] Ibid at 80.

C. The King's Peace and the Authority of the State

It is perhaps easy to concede that parents have robust authority over their minor children in at least some aspects of their lives: young children are simply not capable of making sensible decisions about many aspects of their lives, so it is incumbent upon their parents to make those decisions for them. Those decisions are properly up to the parents to make and not to the children. But it is not nearly so easy to see how competent adults could be subject to a similar sort of robust authority from the state of which they are subjects. We do not conceive of competent adults as incapable of exercising meaningful choice on their own behalf. How, then, can we reconcile our self-conception as free moral agents with the thought that it is the state (and not us) who has the standing to make certain decisions about how we should live *our* lives?

In this context, the very thin picture of authority painted by Raz and his followers might seem more plausible. On the Razian picture, all that we mean when we say that the state has authority over us is that we have good reason simply to follow the state's directives rather than trying to figure out how to act from first principles. This is not because these decisions are the state's (and not ours) to make; rather, it is simply that as we make our own decisions about our lives, we will tend to make better decisions if we acted *as though* these decisions were up to the state to make. On this picture, we do not suggest that decision-making authority has passed from individuals to the state over any particular matter; it is just that we will exercise our own decision-making authority better if we acted *as though* this were the case.

In this section of the chapter, I do not present a substantive argument for why we should recognise the robust public authority of the state. I take up that question in part three. For now, my focus is on what criminal law and punishment would look like when seen in the context of such a commitment. I take the idea of the king's peace as an organising idea as the clearest example of how we might think of the state's powers to make laws, to prevent wrongdoing with the use of pre-emptive force, and to punish those who violate its laws as parts of a single idea: the state's robust public authority over its subjects. The Roman Empire claimed not merely the power to extract taxes over its subject lands and peoples; it claimed—and simultaneously promised—to impose its peace, the *pax romana*, over those lands and peoples.[38] Similarly, in England, from the time of Henry II, the king claimed

[38] TB Lambert and D Rollason (eds), *Peace and Protection in the Middle Ages* (Toronto, Pontifical Institute for Medieval Studies, 2009).

and simultaneously promised to impose his peace: 'the king's peace'.[39] The possessive form is significant. That is, the king did not merely promise to provide peace for his subjects; he promised to provide *his* peace—that is, peace under his terms. By imposing his peace on his subjects, the king would tell them what they could and could not do—but they could also be sure of the terms under which they would live with one another. That is, to be under the king's peace was to be simultaneously under the *authority* of the king and under his *protection*—all according to terms set by the king.

We see this idea of the king's peace at work in a variety of ways in the early English criminal law. Acts committed in war that would otherwise be crimes were deemed not to be crimes because they were not committed under the king's peace. That is, the reason why killing in war was not subject to criminal punishment was simply because it was not committed in violation of the king's laws—for the king's jurisdiction did not extend to acts committed in war.[40] Similarly, the status of 'outlaw' was for many years a recognised status in English law: to be an outlaw was to be someone who was not under the king's peace.[41] Although it is always morally wrong to assault or to rob or to murder a person, such offences would not be punishable if committed against an outlaw. The reason, once again, was bound up with the idea of the king's peace: if the victim was not subject to the king's peace, then the king did not claim jurisdiction over any offences committed against that person.

On this understanding of sovereign authority, we treat the power to legislate, the power to use pre-emptive force to ensure compliance and the power to threaten and carry out punishment of those who disregard the king's directives as three incidents of a single normative position of robust public authority akin to the position of parents over their children.[42] As we saw in

[39] According to GO Sayles, *The Medieval Foundations of England* (London, Methuen, 1948) 170–72, 'the king's peace' had earlier been used to refer to a special privilege granted to those favoured by the king. It was under Henry II that this took on a broader meaning of a form of protection for all.

[40] J Fitzjames Stephen, *A History of the Criminal Law of England* Vol 2 (Cambridge, Cambridge University Press, 2014) at 62: 'The older definitions of murder expressly say that it is the killing of a person "within the King's peace", but an open enemy is not within the King's peace'.

[41] Henry de Bracton, *On the Laws and Customs of England* Vol 2, edited by GE Woodbine, translated with revisions and notes by SE Thorne (Cambridge, Cambridge University Press, 1968) 357: After people are declared outlaws, 'they bear the wolf's head and in consequence perish without judicial inquiry; they carry their judgment with them and they deservedly perish without law who have refused to live according to the law'.

[42] As Martin Loughlin (citing FW Maitland) points out, Parliament 'came into existence as an emanation of royal power'. That is, it is quite plausible to see the legislative power as part of the king's public authority. See M Loughlin, 'The State, the Crown and the Law' in M Sunkin and S Payne (eds), *The Nature of the Crown* (Oxford, Oxford University Press, 1999) 33 at 47.

the case of parents and their children, there are three powers implicit in the position of robust authority. First, the king shall communicate his decisions to his subjects so that they may conform their own conduct to those directives. Second, the king must also have the power to use pre-emptive force to ensure his subjects' compliance with his directives where necessary. Thus, the king's officials must have the power to use coercive force to prevent individuals from committing criminal offences.[43] And third, the king must have the power to threaten and to carry out punishment for disobedience of his directives.

D. Wrongs and Crimes

I return to these early roots of the criminal law in England because I believe this illustrates an important aspect of criminal punishment that has been lost in contemporary criminal law theory. This is that the idea of criminal punishment is tied up with a larger notion of the king's (or, in modern times, the state's) exclusive authority over a certain subject matter. Take theft. Where one person takes the property of another, this might be a matter of moral significance—within a reasonably just system of property, there are good reasons of interpersonal morality not to take the property of another without her consent. But the fact that theft is morally wrong is (as we have seen at some length in part one, above) not sufficient grounds for anyone to punish the thief. The crucial question for criminal law theory is not what makes theft morally wrong, but what makes it properly the object of criminal punishment by the state. And this is a question of robust authority. If the king claims the exclusive right to decide what property belongs to whom within the jurisdiction, then anyone who takes it upon himself to upset that arrangement by stealing the property of another has violated the king's authority over the allocation of property. And in order to vindicate the king's claim of robust authority over the matter, punishment—making good on the king's threat—is required.

On this account, then, the relationship that is of crucial significance to the criminal law is not the one between victim (where there is a victim) and perpetrator; rather, it is the one that obtains between state and citizen. Returning once more to the parental analogy, it is the parent who is entitled to punish her child for wronging another child because punishment is

[43] As Sir Frederick Pollock points out in F Pollock, 'The King's Peace in the Middle Ages' (1899) 13 *Harvard Law Review* 177 at 186, the king in medieval England did not in fact make good on this promise in any serious way. Instead, the king simply assumed the power to supervise the enforcement of his laws by local authorities. It was not until the nineteenth century that the state in the common law world attempted to control crime directly through public policing.

an aspect of the parent's robust authority over her child. The wrong done to the other child, from the point of view of punishment, is of significance insofar as it constitutes an attack on the parent's claim of robust authority. The victim, from the point of view of punishment, is neither here nor there. A child may disobey his parent by wronging a specific victim (say, by hitting his sister) but he might just as easily do so by committing a victimless wrong (such as eating sweets when forbidden to do so). Similarly, the fact that the offender has committed a moral wrong against a particular victim is not in itself significant to criminal law and punishment. It is significant only insofar as the state has prohibited that form of conduct and attached the threat of punishment to anyone who chooses to violate that prohibition.

III. JUSTIFYING ROBUST PUBLIC AUTHORITY

It is a commonplace in much of the history of political thought that private persons cannot legitimately punish one another for wrongdoing, for this is something that only a robust public authority can do to its subject.[44] We can now see why. As we saw in the first part of this chapter, criminal law theorists have been unable to come up with a good moral justification for criminal punishment without recourse to the idea of robust public authority. But as we saw in the second part of this chapter, the idea of punishment can be understood as one aspect (along with the ideas of setting norms of conduct and of enforcing them with pre-emptive coercion) of a larger idea of robust authority. The question that remains, then, is whether there is a plausible moral justification for such a relationship of robust authority between the state and its subjects. If such an argument can be found, it will provide what has hitherto proven elusive in the philosophy of punishment: an argument for why it is morally justifiable for the state to punish criminal offenders. In what follows, I do not pretend to provide anything like an exhaustive

[44] Eg, Aquinas, above n 27: 'this coercive power is vested in the whole people or in some public personage, to whom it belongs to inflict penalties'; Thomas Hobbes, *Leviathan* edited by JCA Gaskin (Oxford, Oxford University Press, 1996) 205: 'A punishment is an evil inflicted *by a public authority*, on him that hath done, or omitted that which is judged by the same authority to be a transgression of the law; to the end that the will of men may thereby the better be disposed to obedience' (emphasis added); Immanuel Kant, *Metaphysics of Morals* Ak 6:331 in I Kant, *Practical Philosophy* translated and edited by MJ Gregor (Cambridge, Cambridge University Press, 1996) 472: 'The right to punish is *the right a ruler has* against a subject to inflict pain on him because of his having committed a crime' (emphasis added); John Locke, 'A Letter Concerning Toleration' in J Locke, *A Letter Concerning Toleration and Other Writings* edited by M Goldie (Indianapolis, Liberty Fund, 2010) 14: 'Every man is entitled to admonish, exhort, and convince another of error, and lead him by reasoning to accept his own opinions. But it is the magistrate's province to give orders by decree and compel with the sword'.

treatment of these issues. My aim is simply to show that there are a number of efforts in this regard in the history of political philosophy that offer very promising beginnings for a theory of justified criminal punishment.

A. Parenthood Again

As we saw in part two, parents claim robust authority over their children in a great many areas of life: where they may live, how they shall be educated, how they shall eat, and how they shall behave more generally. These questions concerning the most basic aspects of children's lives are up to their parents to decide, and not up to the children themselves. In many cases, of course, it seems that almost any account of authority would recognise that this is as it should be. Even on Raz's instrumentalist account of authority, children ought generally to defer to their parents' directives rather than trying to conform to the reasons that apply to them on their own. But on Raz's account, this is just because they would be more likely actually to conform to those underlying reasons if they deferred to their parents than if they tried to do so on their own.

The account of robust authority, however, provides considerably more assistance to us as we try to make sense of state authority in matters of criminal law. In the case of parents and children, the account of robust authority does not merely insist that children generally have good instrumental reasons to defer to their parents' directives. Rather, it insists that many decisions are simply not up to the children to make in the first place. In the case of minor children, this is because they are simply not equipped to make such decisions—they are incapable of exercising the kind of judgement that is required for us to be able to say that they are exercising their basic rights. Whether it is because their decisions are irrational, unintelligible, too radically uninformed or for some other reason,[45] we recognise that minor children are simply not in a position to make responsible decisions over certain matters. So although they are, in principle, holders of the same rights as competent adults, they are not capable of exercising meaningful choice about the exercise of those rights.

So the problem that gives rise to robust parental authority is this: children are bearers of certain rights but they are incapable of exercising responsible agency in the enjoyment of those rights. The role of parents, then, is not to provide useful guidance to the perplexed child, allowing him to make wiser decisions than he otherwise would. It is to take over the role

[45] Moore, above n 31 explores several of the grounds for denying that a particular agent is capable of responsible agency.

of decision-maker altogether in certain matters.[46] Minor children are not merely in need of *guidance* as they exercise rational agency in certain matters; they are in need of someone to completely take over their decision-making authority. But in order for parental decision-making over matters concerning their children's lives to be consistent with the children's claim of autonomy, we insist that parents must exercise that decision-making authority in the best interests of their child. That is, we must think of parents (and they must think of themselves) as making decisions not as dispassionate experts but as defenders of the child's interests, acting in the child's name.

The rationale for robust authority in the case of parents, then, is not an instrumentalist one—assisting children in the exercise of their agency. It is, rather, an argument about the necessary conditions for the possibility of children enjoying rights in any way at all. If parents were not available to exercise decision-making authority over their children, their claim of individual rights would be meaningless. Parental authority, therefore, need not be justified as an infringement on children's rights, but as a necessary condition for their very existence. This leaves only the question of why it should be *parents* rather than any other competent adult who should make such decisions. The most plausible answer is that parents must take on this responsibility insofar as they are the cause of the child's predicament in the first place. It is through the parents' choice that the child was brought into the world in a situation where he is unable to exercise decision-making authority over his rights, so it is the parents who must bear the duty to make decisions on behalf of their children and in their best interests.

B. State Instrumentalism

In earlier times, the authority of the king over his subjects was often derived from the authority of God over all his children, and often explained in terms of the authority of a father over his children.[47] But that sort of argument has not had any real purchase for many years. The beginning of any plausible moral justification of the state's authority to decide how we may live and interact with others today must be a recognition of the status of all persons as free and equal in our moral standing. Whether it is Raz's instrumentalist

[46] I do not mean to ignore the educative role of parents. But this is an obligation parents bear in addition to their obligation to make decisions for their children.

[47] The best-known example of such an argument is R Filmer, *Patriarcha* edited by J Somerville (Cambridge, Cambridge University Press, 1991), to which Locke's Two Treatises are said to be a response. Another interesting example is the treatise penned by James I of England (James VI of Scotland) arguing that the normative basis of his right to rule lay in the Christian doctrine of the apostolic succession. See 'The True Law of Free Monarchies' in *The Political Works of James I* edited by CH McIlwain (Cambridge MA, Harvard University Press, 1918).

account of authority or the account of robust authority contemplated here, any plausible modern account of authority must take the claim of all persons to equal freedom as a starting point.[48] The division among accounts, then, will turn on differences among them in their understanding of precisely what a claim of individual freedom entails, how claims of individual freedom and equality might relate to one another, etc.

Arguments for the state's robust public authority turn on a claim of necessity of some kind. In one version, the necessity is practical. John Locke is usually understood to argue that a state is necessary in order to allow people to escape the 'inconveniences' of the state of nature.[49] That is, given certain predictable facts about human beings, conditions of life will be miserable unless we are able to live together under a central authority with the jurisdiction to set laws of general application and to settle disputes under that law, to enforce laws with pre-emptive coercive force and to punish ex post facto those who choose to disobey the law. This is because when people take it upon themselves to interpret the demands of morality, they will tend to disagree; when people take it upon themselves to prevent violations of morality's demands, they will tend to overreact; and so on. On this account, the price we pay in a loss of autonomy is well worth paying for the benefit we receive in securing the stability, predictability and even-handedness of state action in all these areas.

An instrumentalist argument for robust public authority of this sort, based on the costs and benefits of granting the state robust public authority over us, is liable to a number of trenchant critiques. Most importantly, it is unclear whether the cost–benefit justification of state authority can ever succeed in accomplishing its aim. For if, as seems clear from part one of this chapter, individuals do not have the authority to impose laws on one another and punish those who violate such laws (or to do many of the other things that states usually do: collecting taxes, adjudicating disputes, waging war and much else), then they could not grant such a power to the state even if they wanted to. If the state is nothing more than a tool we have created together to deal with a number of inconveniences in the state of nature, it could not have any powers beyond those we each possess as individuals.

This critique is especially important today. For we should keep in mind that none of the accounts we considered in part one of this chapter were concerned with private punishment of wrongdoers. Both the direct strategy of Moore, Duff, et al and the indirect strategy of Hart and his many

[48] To be explicit: the class of justifications I am concerned with are broadly liberal ones. In this, however, I do not diverge from the main currents of criminal law theory today.

[49] J Locke, *Second Treatise of Government* in *Two Treatises of Government* edited by P Laslett (Cambridge, Cambridge University Press, 1960) 326–27: 'For where-ever any two men are, who have no standing rule, and common Judge to Appeal to on Earth ... they are still in the state of Nature, and under all the inconveniences of it'.

contemporary followers were self-consciously set out as accounts of *state* punishment. The trouble that all these accounts shared was that they could not explain how the state could have a power to set norms of conduct for its subjects and to enforce them with coercive force in a way that private individuals did not already have. So if we were to follow an instrumentalist account of state authority of the sort Locke proposes, we should not be able to provide a plausible basis for the sort of robust public authority that is required to solve the problem of justified punishment.

C. Equal Freedom

The instrumentalist intuition—that life without a stable state to secure civil peace would be unbearable—is a powerful one, but it is incapable of providing the sort of normative justification for state authority that our account of criminal punishment requires. For even if we are willing to make a trade-off of individual liberty for security, we will find that the deal does not provide what we need—as the state that results from this account cannot possess any powers beyond those that each of us already possessed ex ante. We need an account of robust state authority in order to explain how it could do what no individual has the right to do: to impose laws of general application and to enforce them with pre-emptive force and ex post facto punishment. No account based on a transfer of individual powers to the state can do that.

Instead, we may look to an argument for the moral necessity of robust state authority on quite different grounds. In much of the natural law tradition, the argument for robust state authority is based on the recognition that the state is necessary precisely because we require it to do things that no private person is morally entitled to do. On one reading of that account, a public authority is morally necessary in order to make it possible for persons to live together under the rule of law. The central problem with private punishment and private law-making is that it presumes that one person has the authority to make and to enforce a set of norms over another person. So if one person assumes that role over another, this undermines the equal status of each. But if we try to do without anyone setting and enforcing norms of conduct, then everyone is vulnerable to the unilateral norm-setting of others at all times. Where there are no coercively enforced norms in place, the stronger (or the more cunning or the more reckless) will be able to impose the terms of interaction of his choosing on others, without any answer. The role of punishment in a regime of robust authority, as we have seen, is to reassert the continued authority of the legitimate authority in the face of an attempt by wrongdoers to usurp that role. Punishment is not designed to undo the harm caused by the wrong (this, if anything, is to be accomplished by damage awards in private law); its purpose is to carry through on the authoritative ex ante threat of punishment, showing that exercise of authority to be determinative of the relations between the authority and the offender.

IV. CONCLUSIONS, QUALIFICATIONS AND CLARIFICATIONS

The two main strategies for justifying the workings of criminal justice simply as a matter of interpersonal morality—either as matter of giving moral wrongdoers their due or as a scheme for encouraging people to conform to morally valuable legal rules—have generally failed to convince. My central aim in this chapter has been to revive a way of thinking about criminal justice that once dominated the debate. From Aquinas through to Hobbes, Rousseau, Kant and many others, it was generally assumed that criminal justice was not something we could justify in terms of interpersonal morality; it was something that only a robust public authority could undertake—and the form of moral justification appropriate to this enterprise was one that reflected the moral powers, obligations and limits of such an entity. These writers recognised that there are many things that individuals are morally justified in doing to one another—communicating censure, offering incentives and much else—but these activities are importantly distinct from the practices of criminal justice. Although we might be tempted to do away with criminal justice as traditionally understood and replace it with something that can fit into our favourite moral accounts, we might benefit from broadening our moral horizons to recognise other forms of moral justification that might be better suited to making sense of criminal justice as we know it.

The strategy outlined here is only the beginning of a larger research programme. For once we have identified the connection between robust public authority and the operations of criminal justice, there are still at least two major tasks ahead. The first is to sketch out an account of the legitimacy conditions for a robust public authority: what sorts of matter are properly within the public authority's jurisdiction and what modes of deliberation ought to constrain the public authority as it addresses these matters? This first task is a matter of constitutional theory, broadly understood.[50] The second is to contribute to the substantive political debate about how the public authority ought to exercise its legitimate powers in the operation of criminal justice institutions today. This task is a matter of substantive moral theorising: an attempt to provide our own favoured answer to the moral questions relevant to the institutions of robust public authority.

[50] To be more specific: it is not a matter of how to interpret a particular constitution document. Rather, it is a matter of working out what the very idea of a constitution means and what limits it might impose on robust public authority.

2

Extraterritorial Ambit and Extraterritorial Jurisdiction

PETTER ASP

I. INTRODUCTION

AT THE COLLOQUIUM initiating this project, Antony Duff, in passing and as an example of a relevant question, asked what kind of an idea of the state, and what kind of an idea of the relation between the state and its citizens, we need in order to justify extraterritorial jurisdiction. He also discussed the relation between defining a wrong through a criminal prohibition and establishing jurisdiction. Despite my admittedly hazy recollection of the precise terms in which they were put by Duff, these questions have been my starting point in writing this chapter.[1]

The chapter focuses on the question of extraterritorial jurisdiction in general. Thus, I do not confine myself to cases, or situations, where the offence is committed extraterritorially by a citizen of the state that exercises jurisdiction, but also consider cases where the offence is committed by someone else. In what follows, I will refer to the state wishing to exercise jurisdiction as $\text{STATE}_{\text{JUR}}$ and to the state where the offence is committed as $\text{STATE}_{\text{ACT}}$. My main thesis is that there are at least two questions in play when discussing extraterritorial application of the criminal law: one that concerns the area of application of the substantive criminal law norms (the *ambit* of the criminal law provisions of $\text{STATE}_{\text{JUR}}$), and one that concerns the competence of courts to try a certain case (the *jurisdiction* of courts and authorities of $\text{STATE}_{\text{JUR}}$). I also argue that the reasons for defining the ambit of an offence to cover acts committed abroad are different from those that are relevant when deciding upon the question of extraterritorial jurisdiction.

Throughout the chapter, my point of departure is that we are discussing core criminal law offences, such as murder, rape, aggravated assault,

[1] The ideas presented in this chapter are also expounded in P Asp, *The Procedural Criminal Law Cooperation of the EU* (Skrifter utgivna av Juridiska fakulteten vid Stockholms universitet no 84), see especially ch 6.III.

robbery etc. Thus, I take it for granted that qualifications would be needed were we to consider administrative or regulatory offences, whether or not they formally belong to the criminal law (compare below in section III.B). By concentrating on the core of the criminal law, we can see things that might otherwise be hard to observe.

The argument I set out in this chapter still has gaps and needs to be developed further. My objective in this chapter is to address the general question of principle, leaving the elaboration of detail for another occasion.

II. ON THE CONCEPT OF JURISDICTION: SUBSTANTIVE AMBIT VERSUS PROCEDURAL COURT COMPETENCE

If by 'jurisdiction' we mean something like 'the competence of the courts of a certain state to adjudicate a certain case', then it concerns the *exercise* of the criminal law's authority. Jurisdiction in this sense is clearly a procedural notion. It is about enforcing the law in a specific case. Jurisdiction in this procedural sense presupposes, however, that someone (usually the prosecutor) has arrived at the conclusion, or at least claims, that the act in question falls under the criminal law of the state in question, ie, it presupposes that the prohibitions and offence definitions contained in the criminal law of $\text{STATE}_{\text{JUR}}$ are, as such, applicable to the case at hand. One might perhaps say that this shows that the question of (extraterritorial) jurisdiction has both a substantive and a procedural side. The substantive side concerns the question whether the substantive criminal law norm (the offence description) in $\text{STATE}_{\text{JUR}}$ covers, or concerns itself with, the case in question. It is a question about the *ambit of the substantive criminal law*. Can, for example, the offence of murder under the law of $\text{STATE}_{\text{JUR}}$ at all be applied in relation to acts committed outside the realm of $\text{STATE}_{\text{JUR}}$? The procedural side involves the question whether the prosecutors and courts of $\text{STATE}_{\text{JUR}}$ can concern themselves with the case in question, whether they should put the substantive law into action in a particular case.

In some jurisdictions the two questions are not (always) thought of as separate, or at least not treated as separate. Under such an understanding, the ambit of the law coincides with the jurisdiction of the courts to apply the law. In other states a clear distinction is drawn between the ambit of offences, on the one hand, and the procedural competence of the national courts, on the other.[2] In yet other states the questions are considered separate, but the rules on jurisdiction are thought of as having a double nature,

[2] This is the case in eg Denmark and Sweden. See K Cornils and V Greve, 'Denmark' and 'Sweden' respectively, in T Elholm and B Feldtmann (eds), *Criminal Jurisdiction. A Nordic Perspective* (Copenhagen, DJØF Publishing, 2014) 14 and 128.

ie, the rules are regarded as regulating both the procedural competence of the courts and the ambit of the substantive offences.[3]

To my mind, there are strong reasons against the view that the rules on jurisdiction have such a substantive function, that is, regulate the ambit of the offences of a certain jurisdiction. The most important of these reasons is that a state can—according to the laws of many states—acquire jurisdiction (in the procedural sense) *after* the act in question, ie, a state can obtain jurisdiction in relation to a certain act on the basis of factors which arose after the offence in question was committed. For instance, $\text{STATE}_{\text{JUR}}$ can acquire jurisdiction in relation to an act (merely) due to the fact that the perpetrator, after having committed the offence, travels to the territory of $\text{STATE}_{\text{JUR}}$.[4] The resulting jurisdiction is, in such a situation, difficult to explain if one does not separate the issue of ambit from the issue of jurisdiction. Unless one separates these issues, one would have to take the position that there was, at the time of the act, no offence under the law of $\text{STATE}_{\text{JUR}}$, but that an offence *came into being* when the perpetrator entered the territory of $\text{STATE}_{\text{JUR}}$. It seems clear that such an understanding is artificial. This way of dealing with questions of ambit and jurisdiction actually means that you will: (i) *at the time of, or rather, right before, the offence*, provide presumptive perpetrators with the following message: 'if you perform this act you will commit no offence under our law, since our law is not applicable', but (ii) *at the same time*, be prepared to regard the act as an offence and be willing to exercise jurisdiction over the offence should the perpetrator (later and after having committed the 'offence') travel to $\text{STATE}_{\text{JUR}}$ or acquire domicile or citizenship in $\text{STATE}_{\text{JUR}}$.

[3] This is the case in, eg, Germany. See Asp, above n 1 at 125ff for further discussion on the structure of thinking in this area.

[4] See, eg, § 7(2) of the German Criminal Code (*Strafgesetzbuch*): '(2) German criminal law shall apply to other offences committed abroad if the act is a criminal offence at the locality of its commission or if that locality is not subject to any criminal law jurisdiction, and if the offender:

1. was German at the time of the offence or became German after the commission; or
2. was a foreigner at the time of the offence, is discovered in Germany and, although the Extradition Act would permit extradition for such an offence, is not extradited because a request for extradition within a reasonable period of time is not made, is rejected, or the extradition is not feasible.'

See also Ch 2 s 2 of the Swedish Criminal Code: 'Crimes committed outside the Realm shall be adjudged according to Swedish law and by a Swedish court where the crime has been committed:

1. by a Swedish citizen or an alien domiciled in Sweden,
2. by an alien not domiciled in Sweden who, after having committed the crime, has become a Swedish citizen or has acquired domicile in the Realm or who is a Danish, Finnish, Icelandic, or Norwegian citizen and is present in the Realm, or
3. by any other alien, who is present in the Realm, and the crime under Swedish Law can result in imprisonment for more than six months.'

Thus, in my view, the very structure and function of the rules on jurisdiction presuppose that there is something—an object if you will—to which the rules relate and which is decided upon independently of the question of (procedural) jurisdiction.

If one accepts that there are at least two questions in play—ambit and jurisdiction—it becomes clear both (i) that we have to start with the question of ambit (it precedes the question of procedural jurisdiction) and (ii) that it may be possible to give different answers regarding extraterritoriality in light of the difference between (substantive) ambit and (procedural) jurisdiction.[5] Thus, the question whether a state may justifiably exercise extraterritorial jurisdiction in relation to a certain act, cannot be answered unless we first answer the question whether the state in question may legitimately criminalise the act in question. This adds a flavour of substance to an issue that might seem to be mainly procedural in character, and, importantly, implies that we should start by focusing on the substance (substantive criminal law) rather than on procedure (criminal procedure).

III. ON CRIME CONCEPTIONS AS A BASIS FOR A DEFAULT POSITION REGARDING AMBIT

As indicated at the start of this chapter, relations may be of importance when discussing questions of legitimate or justifiable jurisdiction. For example, we may be interested (i) in the relation between $\text{STATE}_{\text{JUR}}$ and the accused (*cf* the active personality principle), (ii) in the relation between $\text{STATE}_{\text{JUR}}$ and the holder of the protected interest in question (*cf* the passive personality principle and the protective principle) and (iii) in the relation between $\text{STATE}_{\text{JUR}}$ and other states. I think that (reasons that build upon) such relations matter, but I will argue in this section that they are *secondary rather than primary*. What I will argue is, in short, that, before we can address the question whether we should concern ourselves with a certain act committed in a certain place, we must address the more general question why we are at all concerned about wrongdoing. What is wrong with committing an offence? What are we doing (or what are we saying) when we criminalise something? Why do we bother in the first place?

[5] Though the question of ambit can be seen as primary in relation to the question of jurisdiction, the former question is often, or at least at times, finally answered at the stage when a court actually exercises jurisdiction. This is due to the simple fact that rules on jurisdiction build upon preliminary assumptions (which are decided in court ex post). When the prosecutor indicts someone for an offence, he or she takes the position that the act falls within the ambit of the law of the state in question. Nothing prevents, however, the court from finding that this position is wrong, which means that it has based its jurisdiction to try the case on an assumption that, at the end, turned out to be false.

A. Jareborg's Crime Conceptions

In order to explain and develop my position, I will draw on Nils Jareborg's writings on crime ideologies or crime conceptions.[6] A crime ideology explains, according to Jareborg, what it is that is wrong with committing an offence, ie, 'what makes a crime reprehensible'.[7] Thus, a crime ideology does not answer the central 'why' question (why are we criminalising this act?), but rather the question what it is that is wrong with committing an offence (once it exists).

Jareborg sketches three different crime conceptions and claims that which crime conception is held by a state affects (or, at least, should affect) the way that state deals with certain central questions within the criminal law. For example, the crime conception held by a given state should affect how it deals with 'impossible' attempts, with prior convictions, with extraterritorial jurisdiction, etc.[8] I agree with Jareborg that the crime ideology held by a state should affect the way it thinks about central criminal law questions. I also think that he is correct regarding most of the implications of accepting a certain crime ideology. When it comes to the exercise of extraterritorial jurisdiction, however, I do not share his preliminary conclusions about what the choice of a certain crime ideology implies in every detail.

Jareborg provides us with three different crime conceptions:

(a) the primitive conception (according to which the wrongfulness of an offence lies, at least partly, in the fact the offender disobeys the ruler, '[t]he offence was[9] seen as directed against an individual in a position of power or authority'[10]);

(b) the collective crime conception (according to which the wrongfulness of an offence lies, at least partly, in the fact that the offender disregards or shows indifference in relation to the authority, not of the ruler, but of the law, 'the offender is no longer disturbing someone's peace; he is disturbing the law's peace'[11]); and

(c) the radical crime conception (according to which the wrongfulness of an offence lies in the fact that the offender by committing the offence harms (endangers etc) the protected interest in question; 'that what is wrong with a crime is *solely what makes it worthy of criminalization*, ie, an invasion of or a threat to a value or interest worthy of protection by criminal law'[12]).

[6] See N Jareborg, *Scraps of Penal Theory* (Uppsala, Iustus Förlag, 2002) ch V.

[7] Ibid at 74.

[8] Ibid at 83–87.

[9] The past tense is used simply because Jareborg connects the primitive crime conception with the past.

[10] Jareborg, n 6 at 75.

[11] Ibid at 77.

[12] Ibid at 79.

One distinctive difference between the radical crime conception and the two other crime conceptions is that the latter does not presuppose any specific attitude on the part of the perpetrator. It is not about disobedience or indifference in relation to authority; it is all about the harm caused or threatened.

As regards the implications of a particular crime conception for the the rules on jurisdiction, Jareborg writes as follows:

> Under the primitive conception there is little reason to claim jurisdiction over acts committed outside the realm of the ruler, or over acts committed by foreigners against other foreigners. Under the radical conception there is, in principle, reason to take jurisdiction over all acts that invade or threaten interests or values that are protected by criminal law. For example, a murder should be the concern of any country, irrespective of the place of commission or the citizenship of the offender and the victim. Under the collectivistic conception, legitimate jurisdiction over foreign acts seems to depend on whether the norm orders involved largely share the same values.[13]

I am not convinced by Jareborg's conclusions about the implications of (a) the primitive and (b) the collectivistic crime conceptions. To me, it seems clear that the primitive and the collective crime conceptions imply that criminal law is, at least partly, based on the relation between the norm-provider and the norm-addressee. That this relation matters does not, however, mean that it is the sole factor of relevance. Even if one accepts, for example, the idea that citizens have to obey the ruler, it is necessary to decide when, or under what conditions, citizens have to do so, and it is, of course, possible to decide that the ruler has to be obeyed only within a certain territory. It is, however, also possible to decide that citizens have to obey the ruler all over the world. Conversely, there might be reasons to require non-citizens to obey the rules to some extent, perhaps depending upon where the act in question takes place. Thus, while I accept that relations may, under ideologies (a) and (b), be relevant to the questions of ambit and/or jurisdiction, I do not think that this necessarily gives clear answers about jurisdiction. Whether or not the primitive crime conception implies that $\text{STATE}_{\text{JUR}}$ should take jurisdiction over crimes committed abroad will depend on how one constructs the obligation to obey the ruler; whether or not the collective crime conception implies that $\text{STATE}_{\text{JUR}}$ should take jurisdiction over acts committed abroad will depend on how the authority of the law is understood, and so on.

This minor objection is, however, not very important for our purposes, since I will take my point of departure in (c) the radical crime conception, the essence of which is that the wrongfulness of a crime lies in the invasion of, or the threat to, the protected interest in question.

[13] Ibid at 85–86.

I will not justify this point of departure properly. That is the topic of another article; here I will consider the question of extraterritorial jurisdiction on the assumption that there is reason to adhere to the radical crime conception. I do, however, think that it can be taken for granted in a modern criminal law system built on the protection of interests, on *Rechtsgüterschutz*,[14] that the wrongfulness of offending does not lie in the relation to the ruler or to the law, but in the way the act interferes with the protected interests in question.[15] This is reflected, inter alia, in the fact that we find it so essential to ensure that criminalisation is legitimate in view of the harm done to the protected interest.[16] If we thought that disobedience to the ruler or the breach of the authority of the law was seriously wrong in itself there would be little reason to put such emphasis on developing theories of harm etc as a basis for criminalisation. This interest in harm as a basis for criminalisation shows that we consider it necessary to justify the imposition of punishment independently of factors such as disobedience or breach of authority.

B. Ambit Under the Radical Crime Conception

Under the radical crime conception (c), it seems to be an open question whether the relation between the norm-provider and the norm-addressee matters (at all). If the wrongfulness of the offence depends on the harm (or danger) caused, we have to ask whether it really matters who is responsible for the harm, who is harmed and where the harm is caused.

Jareborg suggests that the radical crime conception supports assuming worldwide jurisdiction over acts that infringe upon interests or values protected by criminal law. Under this conception there is, according to Jareborg, 'in principle, reason to take jurisdiction over all acts that invade or threaten interests or values that are protected by criminal law'.[17]

I think that Jareborg is right, in principle, but only insofar as his suggestion is limited to the question of the ambit of the criminal law, ie, the

[14] See, eg, C Roxin, *Strafrecht: Allgemeiner Teil* vol I, 4th edn (Munich, CH Beck, 2006) ch 2.

[15] Acceptance of the radical crime conception is not at odds with the fact that criminalisation is primarily a state business and depends on the interests of the state. Nor is it at odds with the idea that the individual may, at times, have the authority of the law as his or her only reason for not committing an offence (namely in situations where the individual cannot see what is wrong with a certain act that is criminalised). See Jareborg, above n 6, at 88 (this provides a short answer to A Duff, 'Conceptions of Crime' and J Zila, 'Två iakttagelser rörande brottsideologier', both in P Asp et al (eds), *Flores Juris et legum: Festskrift till Nils Jareborg* (Uppsala, Iustus Förlag, 2002) 183 and 743).

[16] Here, general reference could be made to the vast literature dealing with the harm principle, the *Rechtsgutstheorie* etc. See, eg, R Hefendehl, A von Hirsch and W Wohlers (eds), *Die Rechtsgutstheorie* (Baden-Baden, Nomos, 2003).

[17] Jareborg, above n 6, at 85.

question whether the conduct norm of the offence description as such should cover cases where the offence is committed abroad, where the perpetrator is a foreigner, etc.

As regards ambit it could be argued that the default position must be that harm is harm. This position seems to get support from the fact that we live in a world that, at least formally and legally, is built on the idea that 'all humans are born free and equal in dignity and rights'.[18] If it is considered seriously wrong to kill, does it really matter whether the perpetrator is Swedish or British, whether the victim is Swedish or British or whether the offence is committed in Sweden or in the UK? I suggest that it does not matter, and that the default position must be that offences should be applicable worldwide, unless we find reasons for taking a different position in relation to a specific offence. Although some might consider this to be an extreme position, I do not think that is the case.

Consider the example of the rape of a child. This is a realistic example for our purposes as such offences are committed abroad and states do, to a certain extent, in fact exercise extraterritorial jurisdiction in relation to such offences.

Let us first consider an offence committed by a citizen of $\text{STATE}_{\text{JUR}}$. I don't think anyone would say that jurisdictional rules, which provide $\text{STATE}_{\text{JUR}}$ with extraterritorial jurisdiction over serious offences committed by its citizens, reflect an extreme position. On the contrary. Where $\text{CITIZEN}_{\text{JUR}}$ (a citizen of $\text{STATE}_{\text{JUR}}$) has raped a child in $\text{STATE}_{\text{ACT}}$ it seems, already as a starting point, quite plausible to say that $\text{STATE}_{\text{JUR}}$ has prima facie normative reasons to be concerned about the offence in question.

Indeed, under international agreements, $\text{STATE}_{\text{JUR}}$ may be obliged to have rules that make it possible to exercise jurisdiction in such cases.[19] This fact, ie, the possibility of an obligation on $\text{STATE}_{\text{JUR}}$, indicates, I would say, a basic acceptance of the idea that an act committed abroad by a citizen of $\text{STATE}_{\text{JUR}}$ may cause harm to interests in a manner that is relevant to the criminal law of $\text{STATE}_{\text{JUR}}$. It may be an open question whether this competence will actually be exercised, but it seems clear that this depends not on factors concerning the wrongfulness of the behaviour, but rather on factors of a practical nature (whether or not $\text{STATE}_{\text{ACT}}$ exercises its jurisdiction based on territoriality, whether $\text{CITIZEN}_{\text{JUR}}$ is in $\text{STATE}_{\text{ACT}}$ or in $\text{STATE}_{\text{JUR}}$, etc).

Let us now, as a second step, assume that there is not one, but two offences committed in $\text{STATE}_{\text{ACT}}$: first $\text{CITIZEN}_{\text{JUR}}$ rapes the child, and thereafter the same child is raped also by $\text{CITIZEN}_{\text{X}}$. It would seem strange, indeed, if $\text{STATE}_{\text{JUR}}$ would consider the first act to constitute a serious offence and the second one to be a 'criminal law-nothing'. $\text{STATE}_{\text{JUR}}$ could perhaps say that

[18] See Art 1 of the Universal Declaration of Human Rights.

[19] See, eg, Art 25 of the Council of Europe Convention on the Protection of Children against Sexual Exploitation and Sexual Abuse.

it should not (or even cannot) exercise jurisdiction as regards the offence committed by CITIZEN$_X$ (just as there might be impediments to exercising jurisdiction over the offence committed by CITIZEN$_{JUR}$), but it seems hard to maintain that the two acts are *substantively* different in the sense that the first, but not the second, harms a protected interest.

In support of my conclusion one could say that the act of criminalising something is an act that expresses a normative statement about an abstract class of behaviour, and that such an act is, by default and by nature, general in character, that is, deviations from this starting point have to be justified. I therefore do not deny that there might be reasons for restricting the ambit of an offence so that it can be committed only on the territory of STATE$_{JUR}$ or only against the authorities of STATE$_{JUR}$. The term 'default position' is intended to acknowledge that there might be reason to limit the ambit of the offence where the protected interest is clearly local in character or where it is directly connected to the state in question. To take one obvious example, there seems to be good reason to apply offences that concern less serious disturbances of the public peace only when committed within the state in question. The main rationale behind such limitations is, arguably, that it is from the start clear that the proscribing state will not take action against breach of the rules unless the offence is committed on its territory. That is, the limitation is justified mainly on pragmatic grounds. Or perhaps one could also say that such offences are merely regulatory in character, ie, they do not primarily aim at expressing normative statements about the act proscribed, but rather at being a tool for retaining order.

All of this indicates that what is extreme is not the default position itself, but rather a combination of (i) the default position and (ii) a complete absence of limitations regarding the exercise of jurisdiction. That is: the default position regarding ambit is extreme only if it is assumed that jurisdiction will be exercised without limits. But no one—I take it—defends such a position.[20]

As indicated indirectly by the example, the default position is at least arguably reflected in the fact that we tend to uphold a very broad or even an unlimited jurisdiction in relation to offences that are such that we all agree on their wrongfulness. According to several international agreements states are required to criminalise certain behaviour and, in addition, are

[20] Arguably, Massimo Renzo comes close to such a view when he asserts that all acts that violate basic human integrity rights, thereby denying their victims the status of a human being, should be classified as crimes against humanity and consequently be subject to universal jurisdiction. Renzo's range of proposed crimes against humanity extends to many acts normally simply viewed as core crimes (such as rape and murder). Renzo builds up his argument from a consideration that such acts are pre-institutionally and pre-legally wrongs, and that for wrongs of this kind we are accountable to all other human beings even through the institutions of the criminal law. See M Renzo, 'Crimes Against Humanity and the Limits of International Criminal Law' (2012) 31 *Law and Philosophy* 443 at 458 ff.

often required to assume jurisdiction, at least in relation to acts committed by citizens and by people having their habitual residence in the state in question. When there is even more agreement and a common understanding, we talk about *universal crimes*. Thus, where we agree upon wrongfulness, and the need to fight the wrong in question everywhere, extraterritorial jurisdiction seems to be the rule rather than the exception.

In an earlier world where borders made a real difference, the default position could perhaps have been considered extreme. However, the infrastructure of the modern world (the existence of internet, the increased possibilities to travel etc) literally makes state boundaries much less important than they used to be and the world much smaller. In the modern world, where companies can easily move parts of the production that are especially harmful to the environment to another state, paedophiles can take a holiday and abuse children in another state etc, it is simply artificial to draw a sharp substantive difference between acts depending on where they are committed.

IV. ON POSSIBLE LIMITATIONS

If we accept the thesis that there are—in principle and given endorsement of the radical crime conception—reasons to sanction offences without regard to where or by whom they were committed, we could ask ourselves why the jurisdiction of states is (generally speaking) limited in accordance with the 'full-jurisdiction-over-the-territory-plus-limited-extraterritorial-exceptions-principle'. Here there are, at least, three plausible answers.

First, there are reasons relating to costs and to the practicality of investigating offences committed abroad. All states have limited resources and some states have much more limited resources than others. Consequently, it is quite natural that states focus on the investigation and prosecution of offences to which they have a strong link. Given the way the world is organised, there are, normally, no, or only weak, reasons for a state to invest resources in the investigation and prosecution of an offence committed abroad.

The possibilities for investigating offences committed abroad are—generally speaking—limited: it is costly and it is practically difficult as state functionaries cannot exercise public authority on foreign soil. The latter problem is enhanced if the act in question does not even constitute an offence in $\text{S}{\small\text{TATE}}_{\text{ACT}}$ (since this will normally mean that $\text{S}{\small\text{TATE}}_{\text{ACT}}$ will be more reluctant when it comes to assisting $\text{S}{\small\text{TATE}}_{\text{JUR}}$ with different kinds of investigative measures). Thus, the fact that a state does not prosecute certain offences (eg, offences committed abroad by foreigners against foreigners), does not mean that it considers that the behaviour in question does not harm the protected interests in a relevant way. Neither does it exclude that it counts the behaviour—in principle—as an offence against its criminal code. To a large extent it is merely a concession to reality.

Second, there are reasons that concern relations to other states. Giving offences extraterritorial ambit and exercising extraterritorial jurisdiction may, of course, intervene in the affairs of other states.[21] If $\text{STATE}_{\text{JUR}}$ applies its criminal law also to acts committed in $\text{STATE}_{\text{ACT}}$, it will, at least indirectly, affect the possibilities for $\text{STATE}_{\text{ACT}}$ to decide what one is permitted and what one is not permitted to do in $\text{STATE}_{\text{ACT}}$. This may be objected to as a matter of principle—it affects on an abstract level the possibilities to self-determination of $\text{STATE}_{\text{ACT}}$—but it may also have direct practical consequences both for the individual concerned and for $\text{STATE}_{\text{ACT}}$. For example, the extraterritorial application of offences involving speech and expression to acts committed in $\text{STATE}_{\text{ACT}}$ may affect the political dynamics of the $\text{STATE}_{\text{ACT}}$, and the extraterritorial application of prohibitions concerning economic activities may affect the economy of the $\text{STATE}_{\text{ACT}}$. Thus, the principle of non-intervention in the internal affairs of other states provides us with reasons against the extraterritorial application of criminal law proscriptions.

There is also a, not unimportant, reciprocity argument, which can be derived from the non-intervention principle. If $\text{STATE}_{\text{JUR}}$ were allowed without limitation to prosecute acts committed in $\text{STATE}_{\text{ACT}}$, what then would stop $\text{STATE}_{\text{ACT}}$ (which would then be $\text{STATE}_{\text{JUR}}$) from prosecuting other types of acts committed in $\text{STATE}_{\text{JUR}}$ (which, in such a situation would be the $\text{STATE}_{\text{ACT}}$)? Let us say that, as has been suggested by several Swedish politicians, Sweden should take jurisdiction over all cases involving Swedish citizens buying sexual services abroad. It is hard to argue that the buying of sexual services is less wrong merely because engaged in abroad; if one considers the buying of sexual services to be seriously wrong, why would it be less wrong if the offence is committed in the UK? However, Sweden may, nevertheless, have strong pragmatic reasons (based on the idea of reciprocity) against establishing such a broad jurisdiction. Sweden would not, eg, be keen to accept the conviction of a person with a Swedish domicile in another state for having had sex with a person of the same sex on Swedish soil.

One could say that in a world which consists of a fairly large number of nation states, the ability of each state to decide upon right and wrong in its own territory presupposes that other states do not allow themselves to intervene, or at least that they allow themselves to intervene only within fairly strict limits when it comes to acts committed on the territory of other states.

The intervention caused by extraterritorial application of criminal law offences can, of course, be mitigated by application of the principle of

[21] See, eg, P O Träskman, 'Should we take the Condition of Double Criminality Seriously?' (1989) *Nordisk Tidsskrift for Kriminalvidenskab* 147. Träskman is discussing the double criminality requirement as a condition for extraterritorial jurisdiction, but reasons for a double criminality requirement amount to reasons against unlimited extraterritorial jurisdiction.

double criminality. The principle of non-intervention is one of the main reasons for upholding the double criminality requirement when it comes to the exercise of extraterritorial jurisdiction. The principle of double criminality does not, however, take account of differences in prosecutorial practices. As an offence may exist in $\text{STATE}_{\text{ACT}}$ without being prosecuted at all, this principle does not always prevent 'intervention' in the internal affairs of $\text{STATE}_{\text{ACT}}$ through extraterritorial application of criminal law. Consequently, even when a state applies the principle of double criminality, there is reason to practice restraint when exercising extraterritorial jurisdiction.

The reasons for non-intervention can be supported by ideas about relativism and 'ethical uncertainty'. One does not have to be committed to ethical subjectivism to accept the proposition that there exists a grey area where it is an open question whether something is wrongful or not. In addition, the wrongfulness of an act is, at least to some extent, context dependent: not only may the meaning of an act be different in different contexts, but also the evaluation of acts may be affected by the context. Thus, the fact that $\text{STATE}_{\text{JUR}}$ has criminalised a certain act does not necessarily mean that it wants to export that prohibition to the whole world. If one adds the purely criminal law questions (is the act such that it is proper to criminalise it?)—and notes that this assessment may be dependent also on views about the function and proper use of criminal law—the case for restraint becomes even stronger.

Third, we have reasons that build upon the relation between $\text{STATE}_{\text{JUR}}$ and the individual concerned (or presumptively concerned). If $\text{STATE}_{\text{JUR}}$ were to exercise jurisdiction over offences committed abroad without restraint, this would lead to a situation in which it would be very hard for the individual to foresee before which court he or she would (or could be) prosecuted.

This is, in itself, perhaps not a problem. It is an open question to what extent the principle of legality (and the rationale behind it) applies to the question of court competence as such: could anyone reasonably argue that he or she has a claim to know—in advance—which court will adjudicate a certain offence? Would anyone abstain from committing an offence for the reason that it might be adjudicated by a certain court? Perhaps not. However, the question of jurisdiction is not only a question about the competence of courts, but also a question about the applicable law. Since criminal courts (at least in principle) only apply national law, the choice of the competent court does, in practice, involve also the choice of applicable law. If the courts of STATE_{X} are competent to deal with a certain case this means that the criminal law of STATE_{X} will be applied to the case (provided that the competence is actually exercised). And if the choice of jurisdiction affects the choice of applicable law, it can clearly affect the foreseeability of substantive questions, such as the question whether a certain act, ACT_{X}, is criminalised at all. ACT_{X} may, eg, be criminalised in STATE_{X} but not in STATE_{Y} and if there are no reasons for the acting person in question to think that the act will be adjudicated in STATE_{X}, then it may not at all be foreseeable to the agent that ACT_x is criminalised—and this would arguably not be in line with the general rationale behind the principle of legality.[22]

It could perhaps also be argued that STATE_{JUR} would not show full respect for the individual unless the individual were allowed—at least to some extent—to follow the rules of the place where he or she is (at present). It seems clear that the full extraterritorial application of offences could put individuals in quite awkward situations. There may be tensions between the rules of different states and ultimately the rules of different states may also be in direct conflict with each other: this could mean that the individual under the law of STATE_{ACT} could be required to perform an act that is criminalised under the law of STATE_{JUR}.

The purpose of all this has been to show that there is nothing unreasonable in looking upon the rules on jurisdiction as mainly procedural in character, and nothing unreasonable in arguing that definitions of criminal offences should as a default position be regarded as having an extraterritorial ambit. This will mean that the normative ambit of criminal proscriptions will, generally speaking, be broader than their practical reach. Jessberger rejects this position on the ground that it would mean that the function of the rules of jurisdiction would be to decide to what extent 'das Strafgesetz nicht Weltgesetz sei'.[23] However, this is obviously something of a caricature. A better way of describing the function of the rules of jurisdiction would be to say that the rules decide to what extent 'das Strafgesetz' can be enforced in a given case.

The position defended above is not a new one. For example, Schröder adopted a similar position when he concluded that the idea that a state such as Germany could have jurisdiction over complicity also when the main offence is committed abroad,

> presupposes that for German criminal law there is no place in the world where what is done is outwith its normative concern; to the contrary, German law takes a position in relation to every act performed in the world, and when particular foreign acts are left unpunished, merely abstains from exercising its competence to punish, not from assessing under its norms whether the act is a culpable wrong.[24]

[22] See, eg, Träskman, ibid, at 148 ff.

[23] F Jessberger, *Der transnationale Geltungsbereich des deutschen Strafrechts* (Tübingen, Mohr Siebeck, 2011) 122. A rough translation of the quoted phrase is: to what extent 'the criminal law fails to be a universal law'.

[24] H Schröder, 'Die Teilnahme im internationalen Strafrecht. Zugleich ein Beitrag zur Lehre vom Geltungsbereich des deutschen Strafrechts' (1942) 61 *Zeitschrift für die gesamte Strafrechtswissenschaft* 57 at 94: [The idea that a state could have jurisdiction over complicity also when the main offence is committed abroad] 'setzt also voraus, daß es für das deutsche Strafrecht keinen wertfreien Raum gibt, in dem geschehen mag, was will, ohne daß das deutsche Recht ein Interesse daran nähme; vielmehr wird jede menschliche Handlung der Welt von der deutschen Rechtsordnung als Wert oder Unwert normiert und sie verzichtet, wenn sie bestimmte ausländische Handlungen straflos läßt, lediglich auf die Strafkompetenz, auf das ius puniendi, nicht aber auf die Bewertung der Tat als im Sinne der deutschen Normen "schuldhaft begangenes Unrecht"' (references in the quotation have been omitted).

V. CONCLUSION

The main thesis of this chapter has been that discussions of extraterritorial jurisdiction should focus (a) *less* on the basic normative reasons for being concerned about extraterritorial acts, and (b) *more* on the mostly practical and contingent factors that provide us with reasons not to exercise the competence that it would otherwise be reasonable to exercise.

To avoid misunderstanding, it should perhaps be emphasised that I am not saying that 'relation', 'standing' or 'link' should not matter. What I am saying is that such reasons are secondary: the absence of 'relation', 'standing' or 'link' are reasons *not to do* what we could otherwise have done justifiably and legitimately.

If an alien from outer space were to ask us why we care about MURDER_X but not about MURDER_Y, we would not—that is my thesis—answer the question by saying that there are relevant differences between the two acts or that our concern about the act (as such) depends upon where it has been committed. We would rather say that we are, in principle, concerned about both acts and then—by reference to the way the world is organised—explain why we nevertheless limit our exercise of criminal law jurisdiction.

The reader may perhaps, at this point, ask him- or herself where the basic thought that jurisdiction requires a *(genuine) link* to the act in question comes into play. I would argue that this requirement is not itself a reason for taking or not taking jurisdiction over a certain case, but rather a way of dealing with the (partly colliding) interests identified above. If we consider a genuine link to be a precondition for the exercise of jurisdiction, this limits the problems concerning the relation between states as well as the problems connected to the relation between state and individual; as a rule of thumb it is a good starting point for any discussion on the legitimate exercise of jurisdiction.

In conclusion, it should be noted that the reasons regarding the proper exercise of extraterritorial jurisdiction do not necessarily have much to do with the relation between state and citizen. In my view, this is simply not the right place to start. The exercise of criminal jurisdiction does not presuppose a special link between state and perpetrator, but rather that the exercise of jurisdiction can be justified in relation to other states as well as in relation to the individual (having regard to the individual's interest in foreseeability and freedom). This is reflected in the fact that states exercise jurisdiction on the basis of territoriality and on the basis of the protective principle. When an offence is committed in or directed against STATE_{JUR} we do not care about the relation between STATE_{JUR} and the perpetrator. In these cases we assume that the link to the offence established by the place of commission or by the protected interest is enough to justify jurisdiction. Thus, what needs to be justified is the interest of a state in prosecuting a particular act, and a specific relation to the perpetrator is only one way of doing that.

3

Police Legitimacy and the Authority of the State

ANTHONY E BOTTOMS AND JUSTICE TANKEBE

Leslie Green begins his book on the authority of the state with the following observations:

> All modern states claim authority over their citizens, and that is one thing which distinguishes them from bands of robbers. … [T]he state's authority … also claims to be supreme … It claims to regulate [people's] most vital interests, and to do so with supremacy over all other mechanisms of social control. Sometimes these grandiose claims are hollow. In a society undergoing upheaval they cannot be made effective and quickly become legal fictions. Even when they are effective they may be unjustified, for legitimacy is not among the existence conditions for a state. However—and here is the real importance of Weber's celebrated argument—a belief in its legitimacy tends to increase its stability and effectiveness. It is therefore a crucial question in what circumstances, if any, such beliefs are justified.[1]

In this paragraph may be found three key propositions, each of which is of importance for this chapter. They are as follows.

First, Green claims that all modern states claim *authority*, and that this makes them different from 'bands of robbers' or (let us say to simplify matters) from hostage takers. Hostage takers have power over their captives, but that power is exercised only by force or threat of force; they do not claim more than this. The point of the comparison that Green makes is, precisely, that modern states do claim something more than this naked power; they claim (note the normative language) the *right* to rule. Accordingly, in the famous distinction drawn by Herbert Hart between the state and a gunman, those held in thrall by a gunman/hostage taker feel *obliged* to obey him, whereas the state's claim to exercise authority, if substantiated, results in citizens feeling a sense of *obligation* to obey those in power.[2]

[1] L Green, *The Authority of the State* (Oxford, Clarendon Press, 1990) 1.
[2] HLA Hart, *The Concept of Law* 3rd edn edited by L Green (Oxford, Oxford University Press, 2012) 82ff.

Second, Green claims that even a state that has claimed authority over its citizens, and is maintaining effective government, is not necessarily legitimate, because effectiveness does not in itself guarantee legitimacy. Rather, the state will only be legitimate if its claim to authority is *justified*. This raises, of course, the question of what is meant by 'justification' in this context; and that is a point to which we must return.

Third, Green draws attention to Max Weber's argument that if citizens believe that a state is legitimate, this will increase the state's 'stability and effectiveness'.[3] Green endorses Weber's view, but Weber's argument has subsequently been criticised as inadequate by David Beetham,[4] in a discussion in which the concept of justification plays a pivotal role. This point will also require further consideration.

We shall pursue some of these theoretical issues about legitimacy and justification before turning, in the second section of this chapter, to our main empirical focus, namely the public police. The third and fourth sections then examine aspects of police legitimacy through the lenses provided by the theorisation of Bernard Williams (the 'Basic Legitimation Demand')[5] and Amartya Sen (the 'impartial spectator').[6] In the final section, we turn to a consideration of how the police might best respond to the public's 'Basic Legitimation Demand'.

I. LEGITIMACY AND JUSTIFICATION

To develop some of the issues raised in the introduction, two questions are tackled in this section. First, is the justification provided by legitimacy empirical or normative? Second, if legitimacy is (or to the extent that it is) empirical, is the test of legitimacy adequately captured by Weber's claim about 'beliefs in legitimacy'?

A. Empirical or Normative Justification?

As regards the first question, the definitions provided by Wilfried Hinsch have been influential. According to Hinsch, in empirical conceptions of legitimacy, 'a norm or an institutional arrangement is legitimate if, as a matter of fact, it finds the approval of those who are supposed to live in

[3] M Weber, *Economy and Society: An Outline of Interpretive Sociology* 2 Vols, edited by G Roth and C Wittich (Berkeley, University of California Press, 1978).

[4] D Beetham, *The Legitimation of Power* (London, Macmillan, 1991).

[5] B Williams, *In the Beginning was the Deed: Realism and Moralism in Political Argument*, edited by G Hawthorn (Princeton NJ, Princeton University Press, 2005).

[6] A Sen, *The Idea of Justice* (London, Allen Lane, 2009).

this group'.[7] By contrast, in the normative conception, a norm or an institutional arrangement is legitimate if it meets 'objective [normative] criteria of legitimacy'.[8] Which of these conceptions is to be preferred?

The empirical justification is vulnerable to some obvious criticisms. Suppose that those in power in a given state ('Dystopia') propose, in Hinsch's language, an 'institutional arrangement' whereby members of an unpopular ethnic minority group (comprising only 0.01 per cent of the whole population) will all be compulsorily deported, against their will, to a barren uninhabited island owned by Dystopia, simply because the minority group is disliked. Suppose also that this proposed policy is overwhelmingly approved in a referendum. On the empirical conception of legitimacy, the policy must be considered legitimate, since it has secured, in Hinsch's just-quoted formulation, 'the approval of those who are supposed to live in this group'. On the other hand, the policy is clearly wrong, and indeed offensive, to anyone who takes the concept of equal human rights seriously. Accordingly, on what Hinsch in the quotation above calls 'objective [normative] criteria of legitimacy' it is illegitimate because it is morally unjustifiable.

This line of thought provides a very real objection to an *exclusively* empirical conception of legitimacy. However, the objection should not lead us too quickly to dismiss the relevance of empirical issues when analysing the legitimacy of state power. To see why this is so, it will be helpful to turn to Bernard Williams' analysis of legitimacy.

According to Williams, 'the first political question' for any society is essentially Hobbesian; it concerns how that society can establish and maintain 'order, protection, safety, trust, and the conditions of cooperation'.[9] Williams considers this to be the *first* question because an adequate response to it is a necessary 'condition for solving, indeed, posing others'.[10] That is to say, if there is no order, safety, trust or co-operation in a given society (or a part of that society), it will not be possible properly to consider issues such as the promotion of the health and education of members of its population. Moreover, this first question is, in Williams' view, a perennial question; in specific situations, threats to 'order, safety, trust' and so on can and do arise, often unexpectedly. Thus, in any given society there is no once and for all solution to the first question; it needs to be solved '*all the time*'.[11]

These thoughts can be developed by reference to Dennis Wrong's analysis of social order, in which he postulates that social order always requires both

[7] W Hinsch, 'Justice, Legitimacy, and Constitutional Rights' (2010) 13 *Critical Review of International Social and Political Philosophy* 39 at 40.
[8] Ibid at 41.
[9] Williams, above n 5 at 3.
[10] Ibid.
[11] Ibid.

regularity and *rule.*[12] When someone speaks of order (not specifically social order), she or he '*means* regularity, predictability and system as opposed to randomness, chance and chaos'; accordingly, in the social world, order requires the development of 'regular and recurrent patterns of [social] interaction'.[13] Such patterns in turn generate a significant level of predictability in social life, and thus of stable expectations among citizens. Stable expectations are very important both for the establishment of trust and for the well-being of individuals; the social-scientific evidence is clear that a degree of regularity or routine (leading to expectations of 'how things will be tomorrow') is vital to what Anthony Giddens has termed humans' sense of 'ontological security'.[14]

To create this sense of stability in groups of any size, it is necessary that certain people should have greater power than others to shape how the group or society will function. This is what Wrong refers to as *rule.*[15] Williams is blunt in his analysis of one basic feature of 'rule'; it means, he says, that 'one lot of people' has power over 'another lot of people'.[16] Since 'might does not imply right' (or, more technically, 'power itself does not justify'), this in turn entails that some justification for holding power needs to be provided. If power is not justified, then the result will be, according to Williams, terror, not a truly *political* solution; moreover, the power-holders will become part of the problem, instead of the solution to the problem. To avoid power-holders becoming part of the problem, they accordingly need to develop narratives of legitimation: '*something* has to be said to explain (to the less empowered, to concerned bystanders, to children being educated in this structure, etc) what the difference is between the solution and the problem'.[17]

As will be clear from the preceding paragraph, Williams places himself firmly within what is sometimes called the 'realist' camp of political philosophy; indeed, he argues for 'concepts and explanations which are rooted in our more local practices, our culture, and our history',[18] and therefore 'ring true in the historical context in which they are made'.[19] He contrasts

[12] D Wrong, *The Problem of Order: What Unites and Divides Society* (Cambridge MA, Harvard University Press, 1994) ch 3.

[13] Ibid at 37, 5.

[14] A Giddens, *The Constitution of Society* (Cambridge, Polity Press, 1984) 50–64.

[15] In the memorable language of the American jurist Karl Llewellyn, the question of 'rule' involves asking who has 'The Say' in a given society, where 'The Say' is defined as 'the allocation of authority and the arrangement of procedures which legitimize action as being authoritative': K Llewellyn, 'The Normative, the Legal and the Law-Jobs: The Problem of Juristic Method' (1940) 49 *Yale Law Journal* 1355 at 1373 and 1383–87.

[16] Williams, above n 5 at 5.

[17] Ibid.

[18] B Williams, *Philosophy as a Humanistic Discipline*, edited by AW Moore (Oxford, Oxford University Press, 2006) 186–87.

[19] E Hall, 'Bernard Williams and the Basic Legitimation Demand: A Defence' (2015) 63 *Political Studies* 466 at 468. Hall's article contains a useful summary of, and responses

realism with what he calls 'political moralism', defined as 'views that make the moral prior to the political'.[20] Williams argues that among the deficiencies of political moralism is a 'universalistic tendency which encourages it to inform past societies about their failings', although such judgements are 'useless'.[21] By contrast, the notion of political legitimacy can sensibly be applied to past societies, taking into account the socio-political character of those societies:

> It is a human universal that some people coerce or try to coerce others, and nearly a universal that some people live under an order in which some of the coercion is intelligible and acceptable. [It can therefore] be an illuminating question … to ask how far, and in what respects, a given society of the past is an example of the human capacity for intelligible order, or of the human tendency to unmediated coercion.[22]

In contemporary societies, the judgement of legitimacy must be equally contextual.

> What we acknowledge as legitimate, here and now, is what, here and now, makes sense as a legitimation of power as authority; and discussions about whether it does make sense will be engaged, first-order discussions using our moral, social, interpretive and other concepts.[23]

It will be noted that 'moral concepts' are included within this process; this emphasises that Williams' rejection of political moralism is a rejection only of the *priority* of the moral in political discussion, and 'does not deny that there can be local applications of moral ideas in politics'.[24]

Taking Williams' analysis together with the identified weakness of the purely empirical version of legitimacy (see above), it is possible to advocate the adoption of a primarily empirical approach to legitimacy that will nevertheless work on a bedrock of inalienable normative (or moral) commitments. A model of this kind will allow us to avoid describing as 'legitimate' situations (such as the imagined proposal in Dystopia, above) where the majority empirical view is morally abhorrent. We shall develop this point later in the chapter.

to, various criticisms of Williams' approach that have appeared in the political science literature.

[20] Williams, above n 5 at 2. According to Williams, political moralism includes both utilitarianism and Kantianism, and therefore also much recent political philosophy, including that of John Rawls in his classic *A Theory of Justice* (Oxford, Oxford University Press, 1972) and *Political Liberalism* (New York, Columbia University Press, 1993).

[21] Williams, above n 5 at 10.

[22] Ibid.

[23] Ibid at 11. In this quotation, we have spelled out in full Williams' abbreviations of 'LEG' (legitimacy) and 'MS' (make sense).

[24] Ibid at 8.

B. 'Belief in Legitimacy' or 'Justified by Moral Beliefs'?

In the early 1990s, the political sociologist David Beetham developed what has now become a classic conceptualisation of legitimacy.[25] As a sociologist, Beetham insists that legitimacy must be understood '*in given social contexts* rather than independent of any particular context'.[26] However, he is critical of Max Weber's view that when, sociologically, one observes a 'reliable basis for a given domination', this is normally supported by a 'belief in [the] legitimacy' of the domination.[27] Beetham has two principal objections to Weber's view. First, he claims that by emphasising beliefs, Weber has ignored certain elements of legitimacy that 'are not really to do with beliefs at all', such as actions that *confer* legitimacy (ie contribute to making power legitimate), regardless of the beliefs of the actor; Beetham gives the examples of swearing an oath of allegiance, or voting in an election.[28] This aspect of legitimacy can sometimes cause real dilemmas for those who oppose a given political regime: for example, within an authoritarian state, if a civil rights organisation decides to try to challenge a particular law, it knows that the very act of using the courts of the state could be read as conferring legitimacy upon it.

Second, Beetham argues that Weber 'misrepresents the relationship between beliefs and legitimacy'. That is because, according to Beetham, 'a given power relationship is not legitimate because people believe in its legitimacy, but because it can be *justified in terms of* their beliefs'.[29] He agrees that this 'may seem a fine distinction', but he regards it as fundamental because only the latter formulation properly captures the fact that legitimacy, as seen by citizens, is '*an assessment of the degree of congruence, or lack of it, between a given system of power and the beliefs, values and expectations that provide its justification*'.[30] These are subtle points, which are perhaps better understood when we realise that the two authors are writing from different standpoints. As we shall show more fully later, Weber's main concern is whether a given power-holder can secure obedience from his/her subjects; and from that point of view, as Leslie Green put it in his comment on Weber quoted at the beginning of this chapter, it is true that 'belief in [the state's] legitimacy tends to increase its stability and effectiveness'.[31] However, within such a framework, there might be little interest in exploring the content of the beliefs in question. By contrast, Beetham

[25] Beetham, above n 4. See also D Beetham, 'Revisiting Legitimacy, Twenty Years On', in J Tankebe and A Liebling (eds), *Legitimacy and Criminal Justice: An International Exploration* (Oxford, Oxford University Press, 2013).

[26] Beetham, above n 4 at 6.

[27] Weber, above n 3 at 213.

[28] Beetham, above n 4 at 12.

[29] Ibid at 11.

[30] Ibid (emphasis added).

[31] Green, above n 1 at 1.

is more substantively concerned with the 'beliefs, values and expectations' of the subjects of a given state, and how these relate to the justification of authority offered by power-holders. A main virtue of his approach is therefore that it focuses research attention on the justifications offered by power-holders, and how these justifications are responded to by citizens; hence, it can address more directly the question 'why people acknowledge the legitimacy of power at one time or place and not another'.[32] As we shall argue more fully later in this chapter, to understand such matters will normally require close attention to the history and cultural context of a given society.

Within this theoretical framework, Beetham goes on to propose that there are three components of legitimacy that are universal in form, but which vary in their specific content in different societies. These are, first, the *legality* of the actions of power-holders; second, the justifiability of the actions of power-holders in terms of the *shared values* within that society; and third, expressions of *consent* by citizens (that is, actions conferring legitimacy).[33] This threefold conceptualisation has proved very influential in criminal justice-related discussions of legitimacy.

II. POLICING AND THE ENFORCEMENT OF STATE AUTHORITY

Max Weber famously defined the state as a ruling political organisation that, within a given territorial area, 'successfully upholds the claim to the *monopoly* of the *legitimate* use of physical force in the enforcement of its order'.[34] Others have claimed that the state arose historically as a solution to 'the problem of order' (which is Bernard Williams' 'first question'—see above).

Both of these claims have considerable relevance for contemporary police services. In modern societies, the public police are the principal non-military group authorised to use force, and they also play a fundamental role in helping to resolve Williams' 'first question' (which, it will be recalled, is also a perennial question). For example, if a situation of violent disorder develops in a city centre, it is the police who will be called upon to deal with it, using force if necessary. This is why it has been claimed that the police are 'the state made flesh … [T]hey are the most direct representatives of the state for citizens given their visible, uniformed, 24-hour presence on the streets and their crucial involvement in social intervention and law enforcement'.[35] It

[32] Beetham, above n 4 at 10.

[33] Ibid at 20.

[34] Weber, above n 3 at 54; see also N MacCormick, *Institutions of Law* (Oxford, Oxford University Press, 2007) 39–40.

[35] M Punch, 'Police Corruption and Its Prevention' (2000) 8 *European Journal of Criminal Policy and Research* 301 at 322. There is a known danger in overstating claims of this kind. This danger has been described by Newburn and Reiner as 'police fetishism', founded on 'the

follows that the role of the public police must be an important topic in any serious discussion of the authority of the state.

We need to note, however, that the police, while themselves part of the state, can be and often are held to account by other elected or appointed bodies (for example, a parliamentary committee, or a national or regional government). This can, importantly, include being held accountable for their *failure* to provide, for a particular group, an adequate solution to Williams' 'first question', namely the establishment of conditions of 'protection, safety [and] trust'.[36] An example of such a failure, and subsequent calling to account, can be seen in the report of an independent inquiry into widespread child sex abuse in Rotherham, England. The Inquiry Report, in its Executive Summary, commented that 'it is hard to describe the appalling nature of the abuse that child victims suffered'; these sufferings included some victims being 'raped by multiple perpetrators, trafficked to other towns and cities … [and being] abducted, beaten and intimidated'.[37] The police for the area were among those criticised for a very inadequate official response:

> At an operational level, the Police gave no priority to [child sexual abuse], regarding many child victims with contempt and failing to act on their abuse as a crime … [S]tark evidence came in 2002, 2003 and 2006 with three reports known to the Police and the Council which could not have been clearer in their description of the situation in Rotherham. The first of these reports was effectively suppressed … The other two reports … were ignored and no action was taken to deal with the issues that were identified in them.[38]

The importance of policing in relation to issues of public order and public protection is both physical and symbolic. One traditional way of assessing the relevance of the police's physical presence has been by researching the relationship between crime rates and the numbers of police working in an area. However, a high-profile academic review body in the United States (the Committee to Review Research on Police Policy and Practices) concluded that, despite some evidence from econometric studies that supported the existence of such a relationship, in general it is 'difficult to draw strong

ideological assumption that the police are a functional prerequisite of social order, the thin blue line defending against chaos'. The case against such fetishism, these authors argue, is that many societies have existed without a formal police service, and that many contemporary societies are experiencing a 'pluralization of policing', with a multiplicity of actors involved in the provision of aspects of security and protection: T Newburn and R Reiner, 'Policing and the Police' in M Maguire, R Morgan and R Reiner (eds), *Oxford Handbook of Criminology* 4th edn (Oxford, Oxford University Press, 2007) at 912. We do not deny that 'police fetishism' exists, but Punch's quotation does not exemplify it; the public police are indeed, in contemporary states, the principal non-military institutional guarantors of social order, and therefore, as Punch claimed, in a real sense 'the state made flesh'.

36 Williams, above n 5 at 3.

37 A Jay, *Independent Report into Child Sexual Abuse in Rotherham, 1997–2013* (Rotherham, Rotherham Metropolitan Borough Council, 2014) 1.

38 Ibid.

policy conclusions' from this type of research, given the number of potentially confounding variables in play.[39] Of course, also, mere numbers are a crude criterion, because much depends on what the employed police are doing with their time. Thus, the real evidence for the effectiveness of police activity lies elsewhere: the same US committee concluded that where the police applied *a diverse array of approaches* (not simply law enforcement) in *a focused way*, the research showed moderate to strong evidence of effectiveness in crime reduction.[40]

Turning to the symbolic effects of policing within social order, a leading British police scholar, Martin Innes, has pointed out that in much of the criminological literature on the effects of police actions, 'the extent to which [the intervention] ... depends upon and pivots around communication has been neglected'.[41] As an illustration of this point, he describes events in two areas where homicides had recently been committed, and the local police had followed the standard operating procedure in such circumstances, namely to increase the levels of uniformed patrols. There were contrasting citizen reactions (respectively positive and negative) in the two areas, and the explanation of the difference was straightforward. In the first site, the police had 'explained to local residents what was happening, and why they would see more police patrolling'. By contrast, in the second area there was no explicit communication with residents, and they reached the conclusion that with all these police about 'there must be something [bad] going on'—a perception that created anxiety precisely because it seemed to be a signal that the regular normative order was under threat.[42] Thus, the same policy had unintentionally generated different normative messages in the two areas, with contrasting outcomes; and the contrast well illustrates the important symbolic effect that the actions of a police service can have on social order and social confidence.[43]

In liberal democracies, members of the public know that an important function of public police is to protect them; and even in residential areas with active criminal subcultures, citizens' preference is often for more rather

[39] WG Skogan and K Fryall (eds), *Fairness and Effectiveness in Policing: The Evidence* (Washington DC, National Academies Press, 2004) 225.

[40] Ibid ch 6, especially Fig 6.1. Of the more focused strategies, 'problem-oriented policing' was found to be moderately effective, and 'problem solving in crime hot spots' strongly effective. On the latter, see also AA Braga and DL Weisburd, *Policing Problem Places: Crime Hot Spots and Effective Prevention* (New York, Oxford University Press, 2010).

[41] M Innes, *Signal Crimes: Social Reactions to Crime, Disorder and Control* (Oxford, Oxford University Press, 2014) 129.

[42] Ibid at 135.

[43] Innes describes an act of symbolic communication that helps to sustain social order as a 'control signal'. For an argument, supported by small-scale empirical research, that there are important links between civil renewal, control signals and neighbourhood safety, see AE Bottoms and A Wilson, 'Civil Renewal, Control Signals and Neighbourhood Safety', in T Brannan, P John and G Stoker (eds), *Re-Energizing Citizenship: Strategies for Civil Renewal* (Basingstoke, Palgrave Macmillan, 2007).

than less police presence.[44] Yet in order to protect, the police must on occasion act coercively against certain individuals, and in some circumstances this can raise genuine questions about their legitimacy. Take, for example, the police practice of stopping and searching individuals suspected of possible involvement in crime. It has been said that 'no form of direct government control comes close to these stops in sheer numbers, frequency, proportion of the population affected, and, in many instances, the degree of coercive intrusion'.[45] Research shows that if such stops are conducted in very large numbers, and/or disproportionately against a particular minority group, and/or in a very aggressive manner, then issues about the legitimacy of the police are raised.[46] Such practices, carried out by a front-line state authority, therefore communicate 'powerful messages', positive or negative, concerning whether the state truly values the 'citizenship and equality' of those who live under its protection.[47]

In the context of strategic thinking about policing, at least in Britain, issues of this kind have led to the widespread use by police leaders of the phrase 'policing by consent'. Although this phrase has its difficulties (see later discussion), it is intended to capture the correct insight that the police can, in the last resort, only retain full authority and effectiveness with the consent of the general population. That is to say, they claim *the right to exercise state power*, but that claim requires the consent of those whom they police if it is not to appear, in Leslie Green's apt word, 'hollow'[48] (see the introduction to this chapter).

III. 'POLICING BY CONSENT' AND THE BASIC LEGITIMATION DEMAND

We can usefully pursue the important question of 'policing by consent' by returning to the theorisation of Bernard Williams. In his view, as in that of Leslie Green, a state is only legitimate if the claimed authority of the power-holders has been justified. For Williams, what distinguishes a legitimate from an illegitimate state is that the former meets what he calls the

[44] For example, in a high-crime public housing development in Sheffield, where there was an active although not organised criminal subculture in one part of the area, over 60 per cent of survey respondents thought there were not enough police patrols in the area, and only 3 per cent thought there were too many: AE Bottoms, RI Mawby and P Xanthos, 'A Tale of Two Estates' in D Downes (ed), *Crime and the City: Essays in Memory of John Barron Mays* (Basingstoke, Macmillan, 1989) Table 6.

[45] CR Epp, S Maynard-Moody and DP Haider-Markel, *Pulled Over: How Police Stops Define Race and Citizenship* (Chicago, University of Chicago Press, 2014) 2.

[46] For a famous British example of this, see the report by a senior judge into the 1981 riots in Brixton, London: Lord Scarman, *The Brixton Disorders 10–12 April 1981,* Cmnd 8427 (London, Her Majesty's Stationery Office, 1981).

[47] Epp et al, above n 45 at 2.

[48] Green, above n 1 at 1.

'Basic Legitimation Demand'.[49] This concept connects directly to his earlier analysis of 'the first political question' (see above), as Geoffrey Hawthorn explains:

> The first question is always with us, and fundamental to all politics. In principle, and, if there are no scruples, in practice also, putting a stop to disorder is not difficult. It requires the effective use of state power. But if there are no scruples, the solution will become the problem. Those subject to state power will lose their freedom, and worse. They will ask what the nature of state's protection and its price are to be, and they will want a reasonable reply. They will make what Williams calls a 'Basic Legitimation Demand'.[50]

The terminology is significant here. As we have commented elsewhere, there is a distinction between *legitimation*, which occurs when 'a ruler seeks to make, enhance or cultivate his/her claim to have the right to rule' and *legitimacy*, which is 'an attribution conferred on a power-holder by his or her audience(s), acknowledging that he/she [has] … the right to rule'.[51] The basic legitimation demand is therefore a demand by subjects that the power-holder should provide adequate justification of his/her claim to rule.

We should note also that, as Williams describes it, the basic legitimation demand is a *normative* demand by subjects, but he insists that this does not make it a version of 'political morality'. Political morality claims the priority of the moral over the political, but the basic legitimation demand does not; rather, it 'comes from a conception of what could count as answering a demand for justification of coercive power'. Such a demand is 'implicit in the very idea of a legitimate state, and so is inherent in any politics'.[52]

A. A Legitimation for Every Citizen?

Williams develops his argument about the basic legitimation demand in the following way. Suppose that

> A coerces B and claims that B would be wrong to fight back … By doing this, A claims that his actions transcend the conditions of warfare, and this gives rise to a demand [by B] for justification of what A does. When A is the state, these claims constitute its claim of authority over B. So we have a sense in which the [basic legitimation demand] itself requires a legitimation to be given to every subject.[53]

[49] Williams, above n 5 at 4.

[50] G Hawthorn, 'Introduction' in Williams, above n 5 at xii. This collection of essays by Williams was published posthumously, with Hawthorn as the editor of the volume.

[51] AE Bottoms and J Tankebe, 'A Voice Within: Power-Holders' Perspectives on Authority and Legitimacy' in Tankebe and Liebling, above n 25 at 64.

[52] Williams, above n 5 at 8.

[53] Ibid at 6.

As noted above, Williams also claims that what political subjects 'acknowledge as legitimate' is what 'makes sense [to them] as a legitimation of power as authority'.[54] These are very interesting arguments, which we need to examine with some care.

What Williams is addressing in the first part of the above quotation is the question of *political authority*—an issue which, as Margaret Gilbert has noted, has received far less attention from political philosophers than has that of political obligation.[55] But authority is not a trivial question, and indeed for front-line police officers their authority is something that can be (and is) regularly put to the test on their working shifts.[56]

Margaret Gilbert's suggested account of political authority, or the 'basic case of one person's standing to issue commands, as opposed to mere imperatives, to another' is as follows:

> X has the standing to command Y, subject to conditions C, if and only if X and Y are subject to a joint commitment such that, in order to conform to it, Y must do what X says, subject to conditions C. For in that case Y owes it to X to do what X says, and *it is not clear that there is any other way of bringing that situation about*.[57]

Within this formulation, two concepts are of special interest. The first is that of 'command', which carries with it the implication that the person giving the command has appropriate standing within a system of normatively-generated authority. As Gilbert notes, this makes the concept of a 'command' philosophically interesting, whereas 'there is little that needs [philosophical] explanation about uttering imperatives, yelling at someone … and so on'.[58] The second crucial concept is that of a 'joint commitment', which according to Gilbert is based on an understanding of the dynamics of social groups:

> A social group is founded on one or more *joint commitments* of the parties. That gives the social group a substantial kind of unity, a unity perceived by its members, without whose appropriate understandings it cannot be. This particular species of perceived unity provides a basis for a range of phenomena that have been associated with an individual's identification with a group … It thus accords with much that has been thought about social groups … by social theorists and political philosophers.[59]

[54] Ibid at 11.

[55] M Gilbert, *A Theory of Political Obligation* (Oxford, Clarendon Press, 2006) 46: 'the "problem of political obligation" is a standard phrase, whereas the "problem of political authority" is not'.

[56] WK Muir, Jr, *Police: Streetcorner Politicians* (Chicago, University of Chicago Press, 1977), discussed in Bottoms and Tankebe, above n 51 at 74–76.

[57] Gilbert, above n 55 at 248–49.

[58] Ibid at 246.

[59] Ibid at 91. To the researchers mentioned by Gilbert, one could add also 'empirical social psychologists'. For a classic text on 'normative social similarities and differences between people in their perceptions, cognitions, feelings and actions' within group settings, see JC Turner, *Social Influence* (Milton Keynes, Open University Press, 1991) 2.

As Gilbert makes clear, a 'joint commitment' does not have to involve an actual contract. On that basis, it is reasonable to assume that, at least in most contemporary states, there is an implicit 'joint commitment' to the effect, roughly, that in order to maintain order the community needs a functioning police service. Moreover, in most states, while many people are aware of the imperfections of their police service, they do not think it is so dreadful that they owe no commitment to it.[60]

In light of Gilbert's analysis, we can usefully return to Williams' 'A and B' example (above), and flesh it out with some imaginary narrative details. In a large English city, Alan and Brenda went to school together, and had a brief teenage romance before they went to separate universities and lost touch. A decade later, Alan is a police officer and Brenda, who was always interested in politics, has become a prominent young elected member of the city council. Late one winter evening, when Alan is on vehicle patrol, he notices a car veering substantially over the white line in the middle of the road before returning to the correct side. He signals the car to stop, explains to the driver why he has stopped her, and orders her to take a breathalyser test, only then realising that it is Brenda. He has therefore issued what Gilbert calls a 'command' to Brenda, and he would claim, if asked, that (in Williams' words) 'it would be wrong for B to fight back'.[61] Brenda, who has immediately recognised Alan, experiences considerable personal discomfort at being given an order by a former boyfriend. However, as a councillor she accepts the legitimacy of the police service, and she recognises that Alan has given a reasoned justification for ordering a breathalyser test.[62] She realises, therefore, that she cannot reasonably refuse to obey Alan's order. This is because Alan, as a police officer, has the *standing* and the *authority* to give this order, and this public normative context transcends their personal relationship. The case therefore fulfils Gilbert's requirement (see above): 'X has the standing to command Y, subject to conditions C, if and only if X and Y are subject to a joint commitment such that, in order to conform to

[60] There are exceptions: for example, in the divided society of Northern Ireland at the beginning of the 'peace process', a high-profile independent review body reported that in 'meetings in strongly Catholic/Nationalist areas ... participants expressed strong criticism of the RUC [Royal Ulster Constabulary] and demanded a new police service', and in a survey 'less than 5% of Catholics said they had a lot of confidence in the police'. Even here, however, across Northern Ireland as a whole, 43 per cent of Catholics surveyed expressed 'overall satisfaction' with the police at that time: *A New Beginning: Policing in Northern Ireland*, Report of the Independent Commission on Policing for Northern Ireland (chairman: Rt Hon Christopher Patten) (London, The Stationery Office, 1999) 15.

[61] Williams, above n 5 at 6.

[62] In contrast to some other common law jurisdictions, in England and Wales the police do not have power to order breathalyser tests on a random basis. Under s 6 of the Road Traffic Act 1988, such a test can only be required where a constable 'reasonably suspects' that a driver has either committed a moving traffic offence, or has consumed alcohol or drugs. Evidence of erratic driving constitutes a sufficient ground for reasonable suspicion.

it, Y must do what X says, subject to conditions C'.[63] Williams' analysis is crucial, however, in insisting that one of the 'conditions C' must always be that the power-holder is able to respond adequately (as Alan could in this case) to a citizen's 'Basic Legitimation Demand'—that is, a demand by her that the power-holder should offer normatively appropriate reasons why the citizen must obey the command.

A further important point arises from this discussion. The inclusion within Williams' analysis of the need for a legitimation to be offered to *every subject* seems to go at least some way towards defusing the standard critique of empirical conceptions of legitimacy previously discussed. (Namely, that if a majority is content with the legitimacy of the power-holder, then the power-holder's legitimacy is assured, even if the power-holder is systematically mistreating a minority.) This is because, if legitimation has to be offered by the state to every subject, then in places like Dystopia (see above), where the state wishes to deport a minority en masse, this policy will need to be expressly argued for in normative terms to all members of the minority group. Moreover, in a contested decision of this kind, it will be a requirement of offering a legitimation to every subject that representatives of the state should be willing to listen carefully to the (almost certainly opposing) views of those over whom it is planning to exercise coercive control. Since, as everyday experience attests, it is easier to make a decision that is unfavourable to a given individual if one does not have to discuss that decision with him/her on a face-to-face basis, it follows that Williams' 'meeting the basic legitimation demand' principle constitutes, in Hinsch's terms,[64] a partial normative brake within a basically empirical conception of legitimacy. However, it is not a complete brake, because the state would still be able to take coercive action against the minority (ie, deport them) after it has listened carefully to their representations; and on an exclusively empirical conception of legitimacy, it could call this action legitimate if it is democratically approved.[65]

We began this discussion by referring to the doctrine of 'policing by consent', so we now need to note that there is a subtle yet crucial difference between the state 'giving a legitimation to every subject' and every subject needing to consent to the state's use of power. We can illustrate the difference by reference to some events in an English high security prison in the early 1990s. This prison contained within it a small and dedicated 'Special Security Unit' (SSU), which was reserved for prisoners deemed to require

[63] Gilbert, above n 55 at 248.

[64] Hinsch, above n 7.

[65] This analysis necessarily raises the question: 'who counts as a subject in discussions of this kind?' To consider this question fully would require a separate essay, but, in brief, Williams' answer is: 'anyone who is in [the state's] power, whom by its own lights it can rightfully coerce under its laws and institutions' (Williams, above n 5 at 4).

the very highest levels of security. Prisoners in this unit objected, on grounds of privacy, to prison staff patrolling the small exercise yard attached to the SSU, and requested them to stop doing so. According to an official report, staff acceded to this request, because 'they had not felt welcome' in the yard.[66] They relied on CCTV instead, but there was a known deficiency in the CCTV's coverage of the yard, and this became highly relevant in a subsequent high-profile escape. Clearly, the prisoners had not consented to officers patrolling the yard, but could such patrolling have been more robustly defended as legitimate? There is little doubt that it could have been, provided that the patrolling was being carried out in accordance with normal professional standards (and there was no suggestion to the contrary). The prison staff could offer a reasonable legitimation to each prisoner as to why, on security and control grounds, it is necessary to patrol prison exercise yards,[67] and a legitimation along these lines would have fallen squarely within the mainstream of shared values in British society.[68]

This analysis helps us to see that 'policing by consent' is in some ways an unfortunate phrase—the police do not, for example, need the 'consent' of organised crime groups when they are policing these groups' activities. What the phrase is trying to convey is, of course, the notion of *legitimate* policing. In line with Beetham's helpful formulation (see previous discussion), the concept of legitimate policing can be rephrased as policing where there is *congruence between the system and the practices of policing,* on the one hand, *and the societal beliefs, values and expectations that provide its justification,* on the other.[69] Williams' concept of the basic legitimation demand then helps us to sharpen that formulation by insisting that the police must always be willing to offer justifications for their actions ('the system and the practices of policing') to each citizen with whom they interact. It is a tough requirement, but a necessary one.

B. Williams and Weber

An instructive contrast can be drawn between the approaches to legitimacy of Williams and of Weber. Like Williams, Weber claims that all politically-constituted states seek legitimation, but while for Williams this is a necessary

[66] J Woodcock, *Report of the Enquiry into the Escape of Six Prisoners from the Special Security Unit at Whitemoor Prison, Cambridgeshire, on Friday 9th September 1994*, Cmnd 2741 (London, Her Majesty's Stationery Office, 1994) 56.

[67] Since exercise yards are normally outdoor facilities, they are in principle easier to escape from than cellblocks, and so require appropriate staff vigilance. Additionally, a staff presence can help to prevent physical conflicts between prisoners.

[68] For a fuller discussion of this example, see R Sparks, AE Bottoms and W Hay, *Prisons and the Problem of Order* (Oxford, Clarendon Press, 1996) 329–36.

[69] Adapted from Beetham, above n 4 at 11.

condition of politics as opposed to terror (see above), for Weber it is an empirical observation. ('Experience shows that in no instance does domination voluntarily limit itself to the appeal to [citizens'] material or affectual or ideal motives as a basis for its continuance. In addition, every such system attempts to establish and to cultivate the belief in its legitimacy.'[70]) Yet despite this similarity, the two authors differ crucially in what can be described as the 'standpoint' of their respective analyses. Williams insists that, precisely because it is seeking to exercise justified power, the state needs to offer a legitimation justification to each citizen; accordingly, within his analysis the standpoint of each citizen is central. By contrast, Weber approaches legitimacy primarily from the standpoint of power-holders, and their concern with securing assent to their rule. Accordingly, Weber defines legitimacy as 'the probability that to a relevant degree the appropriate attitudes [ie, acceptance of the validity of the power-holder's claim to be a valid authority] will exist, and the corresponding practical conduct [ie, obedience] ensues'.[71] He elaborates the point by making clear that these 'attitudes' and the corresponding 'conduct' can be motivated by many reasons:

> Loyalty may be hypocritically simulated … on purely opportunistic grounds, or carried out in practice for reasons of material self-interest. *Or people may submit from individual weakness and helplessness because there is no acceptable alternative.* But these considerations are not decisive … What is important is that in a given case the particular claim to legitimacy is to a significant degree … treated as 'valid' [and] that this fact confirms the position of the persons claiming authority.[72]

As the italicised sentence shows, Weber's approach allows for the possibility of a stable domination, described as 'legitimate', in which the demands of power-holders are obeyed simply because the citizens realise that they are powerless and there is no alternative—that is, for what sociologists have described as 'fatalistic' reasons.[73]

We have argued elsewhere that Weber's approach is unsatisfactory, 'because it leaves the social scientist without any adequate means of distinguishing between obeyed legality ['fatalism'] and truly normative [empirical] legitimacy'.[74] In the context of policing, the difference between his

[70] Weber, above n 3 at 213.

[71] Ibid at 214. See further P Lassman, 'The Rule of Man over Man: Politics, Power and Legitimation' in S Turner (ed), *The Cambridge Companion to Weber* (Cambridge, Cambridge University Press, 2000).

[72] Weber, above n 3 at 214 (emphasis added).

[73] As David Lockwood has observed, in social conditions of entrenched social inequality it is not the case that 'widespread agreement on the ultimate values legitimating institutions is a prerequisite of social stability'; rather, in such contexts, a 'sufficient condition of order is simply that the structure of power, wealth and status is believed to be inevitable': see D Lockwood, *Solidarity and Schism* (Oxford, Clarendon Press, 1992) 43.

[74] AE Bottoms and J Tankebe, 'Beyond Procedural Justice: A Dialogic Approach to Legitimacy in Criminal Justice' (2012) 102 *Journal of Criminal Law and Criminology* 119 at 130.

conception and that of Williams can be vital. Imagine an oppressed ethnic minority who regularly receive aggressive, coercive and disrespectful policing, and who resent this. However, they do not protest much, or fight back, because of what they perceive to be their powerless position. (Sadly, this scenario is not very difficult to imagine.) According to Weber's definition, this is legitimate domination, but for Williams it is not because the basic legitimation demand is not met. Does this matter in practice (as opposed to in academic articles)? In brief, it does, for two main reasons. First, such an ethnic group will not readily provide information to the police, whereas if the policing were more in line with the basic legitimation demand, more information would probably be supplied. Second, there will probably be a significant attitudinal difference between members of a Weber-influenced and a Williams-influenced police service. The former will consider themselves legitimate as long as they are obeyed, and not concern themselves too much with how citizens regard their policing style. The latter, by contrast, will always recognise that they are 'one lot of people' who hold significant power over 'another lot of people'; that reasons always need to be given as to why their power is justified; and that citizens have reason to make some 'basic legitimation demands' about how members of their police service should justify their authority (and therefore how they should behave). Accordingly, a Williams- influenced police service will be more likely to generate a managerial strategy that takes seriously the interests of the policed; and is easy to see that this is likely to result in better local policing.

Although Williams' approach is to be preferred to that of Weber, it is nevertheless a weakness of his analysis that he does not mention fatalism. Serious consideration of fatalism makes one recognise the falsity of Williams' view (see above) that if power is not justified the result is always terror; another possible result of unjustified power can be a coercive social order breeding fatalism. But in conditions of fatalism, other aspects of Williams' analysis still hold. For example, in fatalism overweening policing can very easily become part of the problem of order, not part of the solution.[75] Moreover, conditions of fatalism are a good example of the general point made by Williams that an answer to the first political question is a necessary, but not necessarily a sufficient, condition for a state to achieve legitimacy.[76]

[75] Sparks et al, above n 68 ch 6, in their study of high security prisons, describe conditions in a 'Vulnerable Prisoner Unit' (VPU) reserved for prisoners (such as sex offenders) who would face hostilities and perhaps injury from other prisoners if they were located on a main prison wing. Naturally, such prisoners felt themselves to be in a weak position, and they therefore fatalistically accepted the prison regime. Prison staff, on being transferred to the VPU from the main prison, sometimes acted improperly, as one prison staff member explained: 'they've had years and years working up on the main wings, and they get down here and think …"I don't believe this … I shouted at him and he never shouted back" … then one thing develops into another, and … the power can go to your head easy' (at 214).

[76] Williams, above n 5 at 3.

IV. SUPPLEMENTING THE BASIC LEGITIMATION DEMAND: THE ROLE OF THE IMPARTIAL SPECTATOR

Throughout his chapter on legitimacy, Williams shows a degree of preoccupation with the relationship between legitimacy and liberalism. This is an illuminating discussion, but it also reveals a need to supplement the analysis concentrated on the basic legitimation demand.

A. The Basic Legitimation Demand and Liberalism

Williams summarises his conclusions on liberalism and the basic legitimation demand by saying (in the form of an equation) that, 'very roughly speaking', 'Legitimacy + Modernity = Liberalism'.[77]

What does he mean by this? His thesis is that in contemporary societies, the historical conditions that we find ourselves in, together with the concept of the basic legitimation demand, 'permit only a liberal solution; other forms of answer are unacceptable'. He argues that, at least in part, this is because in a post-Enlightenment era 'other supposed legitimations are seen to be false and in particular ideological'.[78] Williams does not specify what these 'other supposed justifications' are, but they would certainly include, for example, the claim that kings have a divine right to rule—a concept which those supporting 'modernity' spent considerable time and effort in contesting in the seventeenth and eighteenth centuries. Williams insists, however, that the 'unacceptability' of non-liberal solutions arises only from contemporary *political* conditions, and not because 'some liberal conception of the person, which delivers the morality of liberalism, is or ought to be seen as correct'.[79]

In making these comments, Williams is of course aware that not all contemporary states fully endorse the principles of liberal democracy. Hence, we find him asking how we should assess a society where there is, apparently, widespread acceptance of a theocratic regime, and/or of laws promoting a subordinate role for women. It is reasonable, he thinks, in such a context to ask whether 'the acceptance of these ideas can … be plausibly understood as an expression of the power relations that are in question'—that is, whether the dominant group has deliberately inculcated a belief system in order to sustain its own domination.[80] He accepts, however, that this might not be

[77] Ibid at 10.
[78] Ibid at 8.
[79] Ibid.
[80] Ibid at 27. Williams says that this might sound 'improbably extreme'; but he could have cited evidence from some religious cults, where this kind of ideological manipulation has sometimes been shown to have taken place.

the case, and therefore that the widespread acceptance of non-liberal ideas in a given society might indeed be genuine. Although he does not make this further point, the implication of this argument must be that in principle, and despite the current ideological dominance of liberal-democratic ideas, a contemporary non-liberal state could be regarded as fulfilling Beetham's three sociological criteria for legitimate government, namely lawfulness, shared beliefs and expressions of consent.[81]

Ultimately, therefore, Williams leaves us with a degree of unresolved tension in relation to these issues. This tension can also be directly mirrored in the world of policing. For example, it is certainly the case that—to an increasing extent—police services throughout the world are being expected to take account of human rights declarations and conventions, in line with Williams' contention that 'Legitimacy + Modernity = Liberalism'. Yet police practices that do not conform with human rights standards continue to be regularly applied in many states, sometimes with explicit or tacit official approval.[82] We have ourselves encountered senior police officers in a particular jurisdiction who were open in their espousal of torture as an appropriate tool within police interrogations, and who believed that this practice was supported by the population in their state (and was therefore empirically legitimate, on Hinsch's definition).[83]

The tension described in the previous paragraph undoubtedly raises some very difficult issues. We believe, however, that some further understanding of these issues can be obtained by examining Amartya Sen's approach to the concept of justice.[84]

B. The Test of the Impartial Spectator

In July 2009, 13 women, all wearing trousers, were arrested in a Sudanese restaurant for the offence of 'disturbing the public order by dressing indecently' under the Sudanese criminal code, which is based on Islamic Sharia law. Most of the arrestees pleaded guilty, and were promptly flogged, each receiving 10 lashes. However one woman, a Sudanese journalist called Lubna Ahmed al-Hussein, was told that she would not be prosecuted because she was working for the United Nations, in a post that carried diplomatic immunity. She then deliberately resigned her UN post in order to be able to stand

[81] Beetham, above n 4 at 20.

[82] See for example, R Wahl, 'Justice, Context, and Violence: Law Enforcement Officers on Why They Torture' (2014) 48 *Law and Society Review* 807; B Jauregui, 'Law and Order: Police Encounter Killings and Routinized Political Violence' in I Clark-Decès (ed), *A Companion to the Anthropology of India* (Chichester, Wiley-Blackwell, 2011); J Belur, *Permission to Shoot? Police Use of Deadly Force in Democracies* (London, Springer, 2010).

[83] Hinsch, above n 7.

[84] Sen, above n 6.

trial, and she told the BBC that she wanted 'a public flogging to make a point about the treatment of women in Sudan'; she also sent out 500 invitations to various people to come and witness her lashing. However, when she was eventually tried, she was sentenced not to a flogging but to a fine. She refused to pay the fine on the grounds that this would legitimate the conviction, and so she was sent to prison. However, the fine was very soon paid on her behalf (but against her wishes) by an association of journalists, and she was freed.[85]

In this case, there was an explicit contestation of the legitimacy of the police and prosecutors' interpretation of the Sudanese indecency law. In this contest, two views of justice were invoked. The first was rooted in Sharia law, which claims the allegiance of all Muslims. However, Lubna Ahmed Al-Hussein, herself a Muslim, rejected the view that women wearing trousers has anything to do with either indecency or Islamic religion, and made it clear that in her view the prosecution was motivated by a worldview that inappropriately espoused the discriminatory treatment of women. This view, of course, was much closer to liberal assumptions than was the view of the Sudanese prosecuting authorities. Not surprisingly, the case quickly generated international interest, and a flurry of statements supporting Lubna's cause emerged from a variety of liberal-oriented organisations. Rather similar sequences of events have occurred in subsequent dress-related prosecutions of women in Sudan, and in the press reports of these cases the previous experience of Lubna Ahmed Al-Hussein is regularly cited.[86]

We have told this story as an illustration of the way in which contestations of legitimacy frequently develop. A state has one set of practices; these are challenged as unjust and illegitimate; people within the state, and sometimes outside it, take positions one way or the other; the issue is revisited in subsequent cases of a similar nature; citizens' views often change as the debates develop; sometimes, but by no means always, the law (or a given set of institutional practices) is modified.

Amartya Sen's theory of justice is rooted in this kind of empirical reality. He makes clear at the beginning of his book that his main aim is 'to address questions of enhancing justice and removing injustice', and that this makes his theory different in significant respects from other 'pre-eminent theories of justice in contemporary moral and political philosophy',[87] notably that of John Rawls.[88] Two of these differences are of special interest in the present

[85] AH Fadlalla, 'State of Vulnerability and Humanitarian Visibility on the Verge of Sudan's Secession: Lubna's Pants and the Transnational Politics of Rights and Dissent' (2011) 37 *Signs* 159. For the quotation to the BBC, see LW Sherman, 'Defiance, Compliance and Consilience: A General Theory of Criminology' in E McLaughlin and T Newburn (eds), *The Sage Handbook of Criminological Theory* (London, Sage Publications 2012) 361 at 362.

[86] See for example Zeinab Mohammed Salih, 'Outrage as Nine Sudanese Women Face 40 Lashes for Wearing Trousers' *Guardian Africa Network* (14 July 2014).

[87] Sen, above n 6 at ix.

[88] Rawls, above n 20.

context. First, Sen's focus is on the 'actual lives ... that people are able to lead', as well as on the social institutions designed to promote justice.[89] Second, Sen has no interest in searching for the characteristics of perfectly just societies. Instead, his method is comparative. He advocates a reasoned comparison of the qualities of justice contained in two or three approaches to policy, or to a particular decision. Arising out of this comparison, there is then a choice of the option that is the most just in all the circumstances.[90]

Clearly, Sen's is a 'realist' perspective, and in that respect it has much in common with the approach of Bernard Williams previously described. (Their substantive foci are different—respectively justice and legitimacy—but the intellectual approach is similar.) That commonality has led us to be interested in the possibility that Sen's theorisation might be utilised to complement Williams' approach to the study of legitimacy.

Of particular interest in this regard is Sen's approach to the process of comparing policy options—a process in which he places much emphasis on both the importance and the complexity of reasoned argument. His discussion is too rich to be easily summarised here, but we want to focus on one topic in particular, that of impartiality in decision-making. Here, Sen calls in aid the work of Adam Smith in his *Theory of Moral Sentiments*:

> We can never survey our own sentiments and motives, we can never form any judgment concerning them; unless we remove ourselves, as it were, from our own natural station, and endeavour to view them at a certain distance from us. But we can do this in no other way than by endeavouring to view them with the eyes of other people, or as other people are likely to view them.[91]

This is Smith's concept of the 'impartial spectator'; and Sen claims that in developing his theory of justice he is drawing upon and 'extending' Smith's concept.[92] He then draws an instructive contrast between this methodological

[89] Sen, above n 6 at xi. This focus led Sen to develop the so-called 'Capabilities Approach', now sometimes called the Human Development Approach: ibid at chs 11–13; also MC Nussbaum, *Creating Capabilities: The Human Development Approach* (Cambridge MA, Harvard University Press, 2011).

[90] A crucial feature of Sen's preference for a comparative approach is his 'rejection of the belief that questions of value can have only one right answer': ibid at 12n. He illustrates this point (ibid at 12–15) with an engaging tale of three children quarrelling over which of them should possess a flute, given that A, who is poor, has many fewer things to play with than B and C; B has made the flute; and C is the only one who currently knows how to play it.

[91] A Smith, *The Theory of Moral Sentiments* (Oxford, Clarendon Press, 1976) 110; cited in Sen, above n 6 at 125.

[92] Sen, above n 6 at 134. There is a significant literature that is critical of Sen's understanding of Adam Smith. This literature is fully referenced by Bréban et al, who helpfully point out that Smith's conceptualisation 'is concerned with *individual deliberation*, whereas Sen is concerned with *collective deliberation*'. (L Bréban, M Gilardone and B Walraevens, *A Missing Touch of Adam Smith in Amartya Sen's Public Reasoning: The Man Within for the Man Without* (Paris, Laboratoire d'Économie Dionysien Université Paris 8, Working Paper No 55, 2014) 11). In this chapter, we work simply with the concept of the impartial spectator as presented by Sen.

device and that used by John Rawls, in which, famously, people decide the ideal principles of justice for a hypothetical society when they are behind a 'veil of ignorance' which prevents them from knowing whether, in that society, they will be rich or poor, male or female, healthy or disabled, etc.[93] The veil of ignorance is, of course, a methodological strategy that encourages impartial judgements; but, as Sen points out, those judgements are made by people who will be part of the society once it is established ('closed impartiality'). By contrast, Sen's concept of the impartial spectator explicitly allows the views of persons from other societies and cultures to be considered and weighed as part of the reasoning process ('open impartiality').[94]

It is this feature of Sen's methodological approach that makes it valuable in the context of the debate initiated by Bernard Williams, and exemplified in the case of Lubna Ahmed Al-Hussein, concerning the relationship between legitimacy and liberalism. It seems clear that there are some contemporary states, and some contemporary police services, which have successfully legitimated themselves while adhering to values other than those of mainstream liberal-democratic political theory. In that sense, Williams' equation ('Legitimacy + Modernity = Liberalism') is incorrect as a universal statement. But, as the case of Lubna Al-Hussein vividly demonstrates, there remains an important truth in Williams' formulation, which is that, in contemporary societies, *liberal values are always available as a powerful conceptual tool that can be deployed in debates and contestations about legitimacy in any society.*

We would also argue that the concept of the impartial spectator has a wider relevance to the themes of this chapter, beyond the debate about liberalism, modernity and legitimacy. We highlight two further possible applications of the concept, one relating to the macro level, and one to the micro. The first of these is of particular importance to our overall argument.

To discuss the macro-level issue, let us return to a problem previously identified, namely the difficulties that can arise from adopting an exclusively empirical approach to the study of legitimacy. At the end of our discussion of this topic (see section I.A above), we advocated the adoption of a primarily empirical approach to legitimacy, but we also argued that—to avoid the 'Dystopia' problem—this approach should be located within a set of inalienable normative commitments. We did not then discuss how this could be achieved, but an obvious model is to be found in the entrenchment of the Bill of Rights within the constitution of the United States, and of the European Convention of Human Rights within the national laws of most European countries. A provision of this kind would back up, and give additional substance to, the partial 'normative brake' that we identified above, arising

93 Rawls, above n 20 at 12, 136–42.

94 Sen, above n 6 ch 6 (on 'Closed and Open Impartiality').

from Williams' identification of the need for the state to provide a justified legitimation of its uses of power to every citizen. It would provide what we described at the end of section I.A (above) as a 'bedrock of inalienable normative commitments' on which more empirical analyses of legitimacy could be built.

But suppose there is a state where there is currently no entrenched 'Bill of Rights'-style commitment, yet its legislature has been persuaded that it should adopt a model of this type. How should it go about creating the content of the entrenched provisions? Here, the concept of the impartial spectator seems to have much merit as a methodological device—not least because this concept explicitly requires its users to look outside their own cultural framework. That is not to say, of course, that it will be sensible for any given state or cultural group to disregard the accumulated wisdom available within that community.[95] Such sources of wisdom should certainly be drawn upon, yet they should also be appropriately tested by considering insights from elsewhere, in a reasoned process of 'open impartiality', as advocated by Sen.

At a more theoretical level, the complementary insights of Williams' basic legitimation demand and Sen's impartial spectator can be characterised in terms of subjectivity and objectivity. Williams insists that 'the [basic legitimation demand] … requires a legitimation to be given [by the state] to every subject',[96] which implies that each citizen can formulate a basic legitimation demand. This inevitably introduces an element of subjectivity and empirical difference into the dialogues relating to the basic legitimation demand, although, as we have seen, an adequate legitimation can be offered without requiring the consent of each individual or group. In consequence, Williams' theorisation of the basic legitimation demand is ultimately, in Hinsch's terms, empirical,[97] and to be fully adequate it requires some objective normative buttressing. Sen's impartial spectator strategy seems a good way of providing that normative buttressing.

Turning now from the macro to the micro level, the concept of the impartial spectator has, we believe, some practical relevance in relation to the (rather too frequent) ethical failures of police leaders. In an important psychological study, Terry Price has argued that the ethical failures of societal leaders are very often not *volitional* but *cognitive*.[98] 'Volitional' ethical

[95] One might think this is improbable, but see Brian Tamanaha's description of how, as an American expatriate working as a young lawyer in Micronesia, he discovered that Micronesian 'customs and values could hardly have been more different from the legal system and its norms', because Micronesian law had been 'transplanted in its entirety from the United States': BZ Tamanaha, *A General Jurisprudence of Law and Society* (Oxford, Oxford University Press, 2001) xi.

[96] Williams, above n 5 at 6.

[97] Hinsch, above n 7.

[98] T Price, *Understanding Ethical Failures in Leadership* (Cambridge, Cambridge University Press, 2006).

failures, in Price's conceptualisation, occur when someone wilfully chooses to act wrongly, usually for reasons of self-interest or personal gain; he or she is fully aware that the act is wrong. 'Cognitive' ethical failures, by contrast, occur when people persuade themselves that the rules do not apply to them, or that they are exempt from them, perhaps because they perceive themselves to be a 'special person' without whom the organisation would struggle, or because they think the particular situation requires them to 'bend the procedural rules' a little, in order to achieve an obviously desirable outcome. A recent exploratory research study, carried out for the College of Policing in England and Wales, has found that among very senior police officers investigated for ethical failures, 'cognitive failures' very significantly outnumbered 'volitional failures'.[99] By definition, a 'cognitive failure' should be open to correction by a process of reasoning; and an 'impartial spectator' should be able to provide that reasoning. Accordingly, it would seem that putting in place consultation procedures that could mimic the concept of the impartial spectator should reduce ethical failures among senior police officers—and therefore, probably, improve police legitimacy.

From the above discussion, we can reasonably conclude that, in both its micro and its macro applications, the concept of the impartial spectator is a useful methodological device for state authorities and police services to utilise when they think seriously about police legitimacy.

V. RESPONDING JUSTIFIABLY TO THE BASIC LEGITIMATION DEMAND

The principal remaining task of this chapter is to attempt to suggest some content for justifiable police responses to the basic legitimation demands of those who are policed. We have seen that, according to Williams, citizens are entitled to 'ask what the nature of state's protection and its price are to be, and they will want a reasonable reply'.[100] The challenge is to provide an analysis of the kinds of response that will normally satisfy citizens as being a justifiable legitimation, while also recognising that such responses might well vary in different cultural and political conditions.

Aspects of this topic have been of interest to researchers and theorists in criminology for the last quarter of a century, albeit not in the context of Williams' theorisation. Given this, we shall first sketch, in broad-brush terms, two different theoretical contributions within this literature, as a prelude to a more specific consideration of the possible content of justifiable responses to the basic legitimation demand in relation to policing.

[99] G Hales, T May, J Belur and M Hough, *Chief Officer Misconduct in Policing: An Exploratory Study* (Ryton-on-Dunsmore, College of Policing, 2015).

[100] Hawthorn, above n 50.

Criminological scholars came late to the serious study of criminal justice legitimacy, and the first major text on this subject was Tom Tyler's seminal *Why People Obey the Law,* published in 1990.[101] This has been followed by many other empirical studies and theoretical analyses in the same tradition, both by Tyler and by others. Together, these studies have generated a very impressive, and mostly consistent, body of knowledge, usually referred to as 'procedural justice theory'.[102]

Tyler's initial main interest was in the topic of legal compliance, as the title of his 1990 book makes clear. At a time when 'much traditional social [science was] built on the assumption that behavior is motivated by rewards and punishments in the external environment',[103] Tyler produced strong evidence from survey data of the relevance to compliance of normative factors, especially 'procedural justice', which—it was shown—generated attributions of legitimacy, leading to compliance. In later analyses, procedural justice was perceived to have two distinct but interconnected strands.[104] The first, akin to the well-developed administrative law concept of 'natural justice',[105] is concerned with issues such as whether, within a contentious incident, a citizen is allowed by a power-holder to express his/her point of view, whether the decision-maker acts in a professional manner and appears competent to deal with the issues involved, and so on. This strand is termed *the quality of decision-making*. The second strand, by contrast, is more personal, and embraces a set of issues focused upon whether the individual dealt with by the authority figure has been treated with appropriate dignity and recognition as a person. This strand is called *the quality of treatment*. Studies show that both strands need to be in place if full procedural justice is to be delivered.

A further important insight developed by procedural justice theory has been the concept of the 'teachable moment'. In his original study, Tyler commented that when people encounter legal authorities, 'more is at stake' than the specifics of that particular encounter, because 'the procedures experienced are viewed as information about the group that the authority represents'.[106] In other words, if a driver is stopped by

[101] TR Tyler, *Why People Obey the Law* (New Haven, Yale University Press, 1990); reissued with a new Afterword by Princeton University Press, 2006. Page numbers of the main text are the same in both editions.

[102] Some of the main contributions are: TR Tyler and YJ Huo, *Trust in the Law* (New York, Russell Sage Foundation, 2002); J Sunshine and TR Tyler, 'The Role of Procedural Justice and Legitimacy in Shaping Public Support for Policing' (2003) 37 *Law and Society Review* 513; J Jackson, B Bradford, E Stanko and K Hohl, *Just Authority? Trust in the Police in England and Wales* (London, Routledge, 2012).

[103] Tyler, above n 101 at 20.

[104] See for example TR Tyler, 'Procedural Justice, Legitimacy, and the Effective Rule of Law' (2003) 30 *Crime and Justice: A Review of Research* 283.

[105] W Wade and CF Forsyth, *Administrative Law* 11th edn (Oxford, Oxford University Press, 2014) 373–474.

[106] Tyler, above n 101 at 175.

Constable Smith, in her mind she did not simply encounter Constable Smith; she encountered *a police officer,* and she will tend to treat the behaviour of Constable Smith as providing information about the police service as a whole. Hence, in a later work, Tyler advised that 'every encounter that the public have with the police ... should be treated as a socialising experience that builds or undermines legitimacy. Each contact is a "teachable moment" in which people learn about the law and legal authorities'.[107] This insight can be linked with Margaret Gilbert's analysis of authority and 'standing', as previously described. For Gilbert, it will be recalled, 'X has the standing to command Y, subject to conditions C, if and only if X and Y are subject to a joint commitment'.[108] However, if X's colleagues, P and R, last week treated Y very disrespectfully when they stopped and searched him, then Y will probably be less inclined to believe in any 'joint commitment' with the local police service—and so X's standing (or political authority) in his encounter with Y will have been damaged by the behaviour of P and R. There is indeed empirical evidence confirming that citizens often interpret their encounters with the police in light of previous experiences with police officers—sometimes including experiences in other countries.[109]

Although it has been dominant, procedural justice research and theory has not been the only strand within the study of legitimacy in criminal justice contexts. Building on some of this other work, much of which has been carried out in prisons,[110] the two authors of this chapter proposed in 2012 that the study of legitimacy in criminal justice contexts needed to move 'beyond procedural justice' as the *dominant* focus of scholarly attention, although we fully endorsed the empirical strength and the theoretical insights of the procedural justice literature.[111] We utilised

[107] TR Tyler, 'Trust and Legitimacy: Policing in the USA and Europe' (2011) 8 *European Journal of Criminology* 254 at 257.

[108] Gilbert, above n 55 at 248.

[109] PAJ Waddington, K Williams and M Wright, 'Dissension in Public Evaluations of the Police' (2015) *Policing and Society* 212; D Harkin, 'Police Legitimacy, Ideology and Qualitative Methods: A Critique of Procedural Justice Theory' (2015) 15 *Criminology and Criminal Justice* 594.

[110] The first major analysis of legitimacy in relation to prisons was offered by Sparks et al, above n 68. More recent work has been produced especially by Alison Liebling: see A Liebling with H Arnold, *Prisons and their Moral Performance: A Study of Values, Quality, and Prison Life* (Oxford, Oxford University Press, 2004); also, summarising later work, A Liebling, 'Appreciative Inquiry, Generative Theory and the "Failed State" Prison', in J Miller and WR Palacios (eds), *Qualitative Research in Criminology* (New Brunswick NJ, Transaction Publishers, 2015).

[111] Bottoms and Tankebe, above n 74. We also cited with approval (at 146) a comment by David Smith that, at this stage in the development of research on legitimacy in criminal justice, care was needed not to infer 'that procedural justice is the sole or central foundation of legitimacy in all societies at all stages of development': D Smith, 'The Foundations of Legitimacy' in TR Tyler (ed), *Legitimacy and Criminal Justice* (New York, Russell Sage Foundation, 2007) 30 at 31–32.

Beetham's conceptualisation of the criteria of legitimacy, and especially his first two criteria of *lawfulness* and *shared values,* as a central focus of our approach. As regards *shared values*, we argued that both procedural fairness and distributive fairness could be seen to be important shared values in relation to criminal justice legitimacy, at least in many situations. Additionally, we agreed with Beetham's view (to be discussed more fully shortly) that 'effectiveness' is an important shared value when assessing state legitimacy.[112] As regards *lawfulness,* we were further persuaded by Beetham's view that a 'first condition of legitimacy' is that, in a state, power must be 'acquired and exercised in accordance with established rules'.[113] Accordingly, we suggested a fourfold conceptualisation of the potential components of criminal justice legitimacy, as viewed by those subject to state power, namely: procedural justice, distributive justice, effectiveness and lawfulness. Two later empirical analyses, based on data from England, Ghana and the United States have supported this fourfold conceptualisation.[114]

In the same paper, we also proposed the adoption of an explicitly *dialogic* conception of legitimacy. We argued that legitimacy is an ongoing dialogue, which begins with power-holders making a claim to exercise legitimate authority. Those without power (whom we called 'audiences') might respond to this claim, power-holders might adjust their claims in the light of audience responses, and so on. Adoption of this view requires one to be alert to the legitimations offered by power-holders, the attributions of legitimacy (or otherwise) made by audiences, and the interactive relationship between them. We were not aware, when we wrote that paper, of Bernard Williams' work on legitimacy, but it will be clear from the discussion in this chapter that his valuable concept of the 'Basic Legitimation Demand' is wholly congruent with a dialogic view of legitimacy; indeed, it enhances our original conception of the 'dialogue' by pointing out that audiences may make reasonable demands on power-holders as to the kinds of legitimations that they (the power-holders) might justifiably offer within the dialogue. A further important feature of the dialogic metaphor is that a single power-holder may need to address several different audiences (the rich and the poor; different ethnic groups; etc); also, audiences may make a significant differentiation in their assessments of the legitimacy of different power-holders (for example, within the police service, the local neighbourhood police and the

[112] Bottoms and Tankebe, above n 74 at 146–47.

[113] Beetham, above n 4 at 64.

[114] J Tankebe, 'Viewing Things Differently: Examining the Dimensions of Public Perceptions of Police Legitimacy' (2013) 51 *Criminology* 103; J Tankebe, M Reisig and XA Wang, 'A Multidimensional Model of Police Legitimacy: A Cross-Cultural Assessment' (2016) 40 *Law and Human Behavior* 11.

specialist drugs squad).[115] Thus, there can be many different dialogues happening simultaneously.[116]

In light of this background, what can be said—as regards police legitimacy—about the content of justifiable responses to the basic legitimation demand? All modern states have created some version of a public police force/service (or forces/services) within their borders, so the basic argument providing a legitimation for the existence of a police service is perhaps not too difficult to make. However, most publics will, rightly, not give their police services *carte blanche* to act as they wish. We believe that the fourfold conceptualisation of 'audience legitimacy' that we identified in our 2012 paper might provide a reasonable description of the main set of practices that the police usually need to offer if they are to provide a justifiable response to the basic legitimation demand, and we shall therefore use this framework as the basis for the remaining discussion in this section. We shall focus especially on the normative dimensions of each of the four suggested requirements, considering why each might be of relevance within realist discussions in which 'what we acknowledge as legitimate, here and now, is what, here and now, makes sense as a legitimation of power as authority'; and remembering also that such discussions 'will be engaged, first-order discussions using our moral, social, interpretive and other concepts'.[117] Precisely which 'moral, social, interpretive and other concepts' will be deployed is of course a contingent matter, varying in different specific contexts, but our suggestion is that there are good normative reasons, supplemented by empirical evidence, to support the view that procedural justice, distributive justice, effectiveness and lawfulness will often be relevant issues in these 'engaged, first-order discussions'.

One further preliminary comment is necessary. Given that it is not too difficult to provide a basic justification for the existence of a police service, and given also that many citizens have only very limited contact with police officers, in practice withdrawal of public support will mostly arise when the police service in a given state or local area *fails* to act in accordance with the public's, or the political elite's, view of how a police service should behave. Thus, substituting 'legitimacy' for 'justice', there is merit in JR Lucas' suggestion that 'we should follow the example of Aristotle[118]

[115] For later research providing evidence for this kind of differentiation, see Waddington et al, above n 109.

[116] Tom Tyler and Jonathan Jackson, in a chapter written partly in response to our 2012 paper (above, n 74) commented that 'the idea that legitimacy is dynamic and interactive' was 'the most important part' of that paper. They also agreed in principle that legitimacy could include dimensions other than procedural justice, but they cautioned that 'the degree to which we move beyond procedural justice is ultimately an empirical issue': T Tyler and J Jackson, 'Future Challenges in the Study of Legitimacy' in Tankebe and Liebling, above n 25 at 94.

[117] Williams, above n 5 at 11.

[118] Aristotle, *The Nicomachean Ethics*, translated by D Ross and edited by L Brown (Oxford, Oxford University Press, 2009) 80.

and adopt a negative approach, discovering what justice is by considering on what occasions we protest at injustice or unfairness'.[119] Following this advice, a key question becomes: why do police services tend to lose legitimacy if their police officers act *unfairly* (procedurally or distributively), or perform their duties *ineffectively*, or *behave unlawfully*?

A. Procedural Justice

Procedural justice (or procedural fairness) has been discussed above, and can be defined as *the fairness of the processes employed to reach specific outcomes or decisions*; it includes both the *quality of decision-making* and the *quality of treatment*. There is no doubt about its empirical importance in relation to police legitimacy; indeed, a powerful conclusion from the existing empirical research is that, when they make overall normative judgements about policing, citizens often prioritise procedural fairness (how they are treated) over the perceived favourability or fairness of the outcome of their encounter with the police.[120]

Given the normative focus of this chapter, we need to ask why procedural justice appears to be so empirically important? The most plausible answer is, stated simply, that *when police actions demonstrate a recognition of an individual's rights* ('quality of decision-making') and *his/her humanity* ('quality of treatment'), then *that individual feels valued*. This answer was first proposed by Lind and Tyler in 1988, and they named it the 'group value model'.[121] Tyler later explained it in the following way in relation to one aspect of the 'quality of decision-making' (willingness to listen):

> People value their participation in organizations and the opportunities that it provides to affirm their status within the group … The willingness of the authority to listen to them and consider their arguments is a recognition of their social standing. If people are not allowed to express their views, they are being denied signs of their standing within the group, as well as opportunities for interaction with authorities that lead to positive beliefs about membership in the group.[122]

Tyler went on to argue that similar issues apply in relation to 'quality of treatment', where, for example, when 'the police harass members of minority groups [or] the poor … they are communicating to those groups that they have marginal … status' within society.[123]

[119] JR Lucas, *On Justice* (Oxford, Clarendon Press, 1980) 4.
[120] TR Tyler and J Fagan, 'Legitimacy and Co-operation: Why Do People Help the Police Fight Crime in their Communities?' (2008) 6 *Ohio State Journal of Criminal Law* 231.
[121] EA Lind and TR Tyler, *The Social Psychology of Procedural Justice* (New York, Plenum, 1988).
[122] Tyler, above n 101 at 175–76.
[123] Ibid at 176.

Interestingly, the group value model seems to have some potential links to Axel Honneth's philosophical work on the 'recognition' of individuals,[124] although as far as we know these links have not yet been explored in the literature on procedural justice.[125] As Christopher Zurn explains, Honneth's 'moral and social theories are founded upon the thesis that personhood is essentially constituted intersubjectively'; and from this base, Honneth postulates that there are 'three forms of intersubjective recognition—love, legal relations and solidarity'—that are vital for healthy human development.[126] These three forms of recognition in turn correspond 'to three forms of practical self-understanding' by the individual subject, namely 'self-confidence, self-respect and self-esteem'.[127] In the present context, it is the second and third of these forms of recognition that are of particular interest. Respectively, these can be summarised as follows:

> [For Honneth] individuals gain a sense of self-respect only through the individual rights that are granted to members of a legal community ... When acknowledged as bearers of legal rights by the other members of their community through their legal status, individuals are able to gain a sense of self-respect, a sense of their inherent dignity as free and equal among others.
>
> Persons ... are positively recognized through the social esteem expressed in solidaristic relations with others ... [E]steem relations extend as far as those who share the same substantive ethical values concerning what is socially worthy ... (what Honneth calls 'communities of value') ... the paradigmatic form of disrespect [for esteem relations is] cultural denigration and insult to ways of life.[128]

These potential links between Honneth's conceptualisation and procedural justice theory clearly require more detailed examination, but the resonances are intriguing.

B. Distributive Justice

In a memorable passage, Dennis Wrong has claimed that

> the problem of order is a ... transhistorical problem rooted in inescapable conflict between the interests and desires of individuals and the requirements of society: to

[124] A Honneth, *The Struggle for Recognition: The Moral Grammar of Social Conflicts*, translated by J Anderson (Cambridge, Polity Press, 1995).

[125] However, Honneth's concepts of recognition and misrecognition were identified as 'core themes in the analysis' in Liebling et al's ethnographic study of the regime of a high security prison in England: A Liebling, H Arnold and C Straub, *An Exploration of Staff-Prisoner Relationships at HMP Whitemoor: 12 Years On* (London, Ministry of Justice, 2011).

[126] CF Zurn, *Axel Honneth: A Critical Theory of the Social* (Cambridge, Polity Press, 2015) 24, 28.

[127] Ibid at 28.

[128] Ibid at 34, 39–40.

> wit, the pacification of violent strife … and the secure establishment of cooperative social relations making possible the pursuit of collective goals.[129]

This 'inescapable conflict' between individual desires and the needs of the collectivity inevitably leads to debates (or worse) about how various goods and services are to be distributed within the collectivity. Such debates can be readily seen in action by watching any group of children at play. Accordingly, it is no surprise that the concept of 'distributive justice' can be traced back historically as far as Aristotle, who defined it as 'manifested in distributions of honour or money or the other things that fall to be divided among those who have a share in the constitution'.[130]

In the context of criminal justice, the outcomes of cases are one manifestation of distributive justice or injustice. We have noted above the common finding, in the general population surveys reported in the procedural justice literature, that how people are treated in their encounters with officials (procedures) seems to shape overall judgements of legitimacy more than the outcome of the encounter. However, this kind of result is not replicated in all contexts. One reason for this is that, as Tyler himself noted in his original publication, in surveys of the general population citizens might well 'lack the information to judge consistency' of outcomes.[131] Also, of course, the more significant the outcome for the individual's life, the more likely it is to affect his/her judgements of legitimacy. Accordingly, Sparks and colleagues found in their study of high security prisons (where sanctions can have relatively severe consequences, and 'news travels specially fast [so] people know about one another's outcomes as well as about procedure') that consistency of outcomes as well as procedural justice was empirically important for legitimacy.[132] Similarly, in a recent study of sentencing in an English Crown Court, the authors commented that their findings supported the hypotheses of procedural justice theory; however, it was also the case that 'in the stark setting of the courtroom, the outcome of a case … is a crucial determinant of court users' perceptions of legitimacy'.[133]

But in any case, the study of outcomes in individual cases is not the only issue of relevance when considering distributive justice. Take, for example, the imaginary case of Courtney, a young black student born in England, who lives in an area of London with a relatively high ethnic minority population. From his studies, he is aware of the official statistics showing that, as at March 2015, blacks in England and Wales were four times more likely than

[129] Wrong, above n 12 at 36.
[130] Aristotle, above n 118 at 84.
[131] Tyler, above n 101 at 153.
[132] Sparks et al, above n 68 at 88–89.
[133] J Jacobson, G Hunter and A Kirby, *Inside Crown Court: Personal Experiences and Questions of Legitimacy* (Bristol, Policy Press, 2015) 166.

whites to be stopped by police:[134] and he is angry about this. One day he is himself stopped by the police. Courtney regards the outcome of his case (no further action) as satisfactory and just. However, he is still angry about the frequency with which black people are stopped, and this delegitimates the police in his eyes. The distributive justice issue that concerns him is, therefore, not the outcome of his case, but the perceived over-enforcement of the law against an ethnic minority.

The perceived excessive use of police powers has often produced resentment among minority communities, sometimes leading to open confrontation between police officers and members of these communities. A well-known English example of this was the riot in Brixton, London, in 1981, sparked by a police stop-and-search operation known as Operation Swamp, which disproportionately targeted black youths.[135] A more recent and more tragic set of examples is to be found in the United States, where there is evidence to show that police shootings are disproportionately focused on African Americans: for example, in 2015 there were 7.22 killings by police officers per million African Americans, compared with 2.94 per million White Americans.[136] A notorious case of a black man being shot by a police officer was the death of Michael Brown in Ferguson, Missouri, in August 2014; we shall shortly explore more fully the contextual background of policing in Ferguson.

Distributive injustice can occur because of the under-enforcement, as well as the over-enforcement, of laws. According to Natapoff:

> Underenforcement is a weak state response to lawbreaking as well as to victimization. It … offers important insights into the government's relationship with vulnerable groups in the context of the criminal system. In practice, underenforcement is often linked with official discrimination, increased violence, legal failure, and the undemocratic treatment of the poor. Underenforcement can also be a form of deprivation, tracking familiar categories of race, gender, class, and political powerlessness. Conceived of as a form of public policy, underenforcement is a crucial distribution mechanism whereby the social good of lawfulness can be withheld.[137]

As Natapoff notes, under-enforcement can involve either a weak response to victimisation or a weak response to certain kinds of lawbreaking (in particular, the failure to pursue lawbreakers who have committed crimes against members of disadvantaged groups). Both kinds of under-enforcement have occurred in England. The first type is exemplified by the Rotherham child

[134] Home Office, 'Police Powers and Procedures England and Wales Year Ending 31 March 2015' (www.gov.uk/government/publications/police-powers-and-procedures-england-andwales-year-ending-31-march-2015/police-powers-and-procedures-england-and-wales-year-ending-31-march-2015#key-findings).

[135] Scarman, above n 46.

[136] *The Guardian*, 'The Counted: People Killed by the Police in the US': www.theguardian.com/us-news/ng-interactive/2015/jun/01/the-counted-police-killings-us-database.

[137] A Natapoff, 'Underenforcement' (2006) 75 *Fordham Law Review* 1715 at 1717.

sex abuse scandal, where, it will be recalled, the police in the area 'regard[ed] many child victims with contempt' and 'gave no priority' to this kind of crime, despite having been made aware of the scale of the problem through three independent reports.[138] As a consequence, those victimised felt desperately unsupported. The second type of under-enforcement (under-enforcement of lawbreaking) became apparent in the case of Stephen Lawrence, a young black man who was murdered in the streets of south London in 1993. A prosecution of suspects initially failed to achieve conviction. Stephen Lawrence's family complained of police racism which, they claimed, had resulted in a failure by the police to take the investigatory process seriously. A commission of inquiry confirmed aspects of the complaints by the family; it found that professional incompetence and institutional racism accounted for the failure of the police to secure convictions for the murder.[139]

Not surprisingly, groups who experience either over-enforcement or under-enforcement of the law tend to blame the police for what they have experienced, so this often leads to a diminution of attributions of legitimacy. Accordingly, distributive fairness is an appropriate and necessary element in the police's response to the public's basic legitimation demand.

C. Effectiveness

In an instructive discussion, David Beetham drew attention to a distinction sometimes made by political scientists between 'legitimacy' (as a normative concept) and effectiveness (which they perceive as an instrumental concept). At one level, he argues, the distinction is valid, because the two concepts 'are not coterminous'. But matters are not as simple as this:

> [T]here is a reciprocal connection between the two [concepts] … [L]egitimacy makes a difference to the effectiveness of a system of power, through the quality of performance it secures from those subordinate to it. Equally importantly, *the performance of government makes a significant difference to, and forms a necessary component of, its legitimacy* … After all, how can the enormous powers of the state be at all justified, or people obliged to obey it, unless it fulfil requirements necessary to the society and their own well being and that it fulfil them effectively?[140]

In the sphere of policing, societies may reasonably differ on what the specific priorities of the police should be—for example, public order, counter-terrorism, property crimes, sex offences or whatever. But whichever priorities are chosen, there will be an expectation by the public that the police

[138] Jay, above n 37.
[139] W Macpherson, *Inquiry into the Matters Arising from the Death of Stephen Lawrence: Final Report* (London, The Stationery Office, 1999).
[140] Beetham, above n 4 at 137 (emphasis added).

should be reasonably successful in achieving results;[141] if they are not, then—on Beetham's analysis—loss of legitimacy may follow.

Extensive research evidence from studies of vigilante violence supports this claim, because vigilantism usually arises in contexts where there is ineffective state policing. For example, Anderson's work in inner cities in the US found that recourse to vigilantism tends to occur in situations where, in a context of weak policing, personal concern for one's safety takes over, culminating in 'people's law', based on 'street justice'.[142] The study also showed that even when the police have the capacity to intervene, they may be unwilling to respond to people's security needs: 'when called, they may not respond, which is one reason many residents feel they must be prepared to take extraordinary measures to defend themselves and their loved ones against those who are inclined to aggression'.[143] Similarly, in Nigeria, a lack of police response against violent robberies contributed to the rise of the Bakassi Boys, a vigilante group that combined torture with occult forces to fight crime.[144]

This direct evidence from vigilantism studies of the relation between police ineffectiveness and low public perceptions of police legitimacy has been interestingly supplemented by survey research in South Africa. South Africa has a high crime rate (in 2011, 50 murders and 100 recorded rapes a day among a population of 50 million), and the purpose of the survey was to test whether, in such a context, procedural justice would feature as prominently as a predictor of legitimacy as it has done in European and North American surveys. The answer was that procedural justice remained important, but was trumped, in these conditions, by effectiveness:

> We find that trust in both police procedural justice and efficacy is correlated to police legitimacy … Yet procedural justice is a less important predictor of legitimacy than in [Anglo-American Democratic Policing] countries, while effectiveness appears to be a stronger predictor of legitimacy than studies conducted in those countries usually find … In South Africa … while fairness is important, effectiveness appears to be more so.[145]

[141] Unless, of course, a completely inappropriate priority is chosen. This happened in Ferguson, Missouri, where an official Federal Government investigation found that the city government had 'consistently set maximizing revenue as the priority for Ferguson's law enforcement activity', and indeed had 'budgeted for, and achieved, significant increases in revenue from municipal code enforcement over the last several years': US Department of Justice Civil Rights Division, *Investigation of the Ferguson Police Department* (Washington DC, Department of Justice, 2015) 9.

[142] E Anderson, *Code of the Street: Decency, Violence, and the Moral Life of the Inner City* (New York, Norton, 1999).

[143] Ibid at 34.

[144] J Harnischfeger, 'The Bakassi Boys: Fighting Crime in Nigeria' (2003) 41 *Journal of Modern African Studies* 23; K Meagher, 'Hijacking Civil Society: The Inside Story of the Bakassi Boys Vigilante Group of South-Eastern Nigeria' (2007) 45 *Journal of Modern African Studies* 89.

[145] B Bradford, A Huq, J Jackson and B Roberts, 'What Price Fairness When Security Is at Stake?: Police Legitimacy in South Africa' (2014) 8 *Regulation and Governance* 246 at 260.

Accordingly, far from being unconnected to legitimacy, police effectiveness can be read as a key measure of the extent to which authorities are able to solve Williams' 'first political question'. As Mulgan notes, this may have consequences well beyond criminal justice:

> [O]rder and safety are essential not just for life to carry on but also for people to live well. The available data suggest that political stability and order, the rule of law and justice, are decisive to happiness ... It is hard to overestimate the value of strong, stable and protective and legitimate governance to human well-being.[146]

Mulgan's reference to 'protective and legitimate governance' raises a further important issue; namely, a possible contrast between the 'protection' offered by public police (that is, by the state) and that offered by vigilante groups or mafias.[147] As Ian Loader has argued, some demands for protection are concerned simply with the prevention of immediate threat, but true security has to go beyond this:

> Security inheres, rather, in the capacity of individuals and groups to feel at ease with the threats that their environment poses, such that they do not, on an everyday basis, have to think about how safe they are, or routinely concern themselves with the effectiveness of the security measures that are in place, or constantly be bothered with whether and how these may need to be bolstered. To be secure, as opposed to simply safe, is to be comfortable in, and with, one's environment and hence free from the burdens of recurring security work.[148]

This conceptualisation helps us to differentiate the role of state policing and the protective activities of organised gangs and similar groups. The state works within the boundaries of normative requirements in which public security is 'a right available, by reason of their membership alone, to all members of that community'.[149] Organised criminal gangs, mafias, or vigilante groups do provide protection, but always partially, and sometimes in a manner that poses a threat to the safety of others, and/or without recognition of notions of justice and accountability.[150] The provision of truly effective security is therefore, in principle, very much an element in the appropriate state response to citizens' basic legitimation demands.[151]

146 G Mulgan, *Good and Bad Power* (London, Penguin, 2007) 45.

147 C Tilly, 'War Making and State Making as Organized Crime' in P Evans, D Rueschemeyer and T Skocpol (eds), *Bringing the State Back In* (Cambridge, Cambridge University Press, 1985).

148 I Loader, 'Policing, Recognition and Belonging' (2006) 605 *Annals of the American Academy of Political and Social Science* 202 at 209.

149 Ibid at 207.

150 Meagher, above n 144; GD Willis, *The Killing Consensus: Police, Organized Crime, and the Regulation of Life and Death in Urban Brazil* (Oakland, University of California Press, 2015).

151 Effectiveness alone is however no guarantee of legitimacy, as is made clear in the quotation from Leslie Green at the beginning of this chapter: Green, above n 1 at 1.

D. Lawfulness, or Rule-governed Power

In Beetham's frequently-reproduced diagram setting out 'the three dimensions of legitimacy', the first of the three 'criteria of legitimacy' is described as 'conformity to rules (legal validity)'.[152] However, later in the same text, in Beetham's fuller description of this criterion, matters become a little more nuanced. Here, it is said that the 'first condition' of the legitimacy of any form of social power is that the power 'should be acquired and exercised in accordance with established rules'.[153] This gives a wider remit to the criterion, because the 'rules' are described as being '*either* customary and conventional in form, *or* … part of a legal order'.[154] Of course, in modern states the rules are very often formally legal, but 'even in the contemporary world the force of convention still exists'.[155]

Both formal legality and informal conventions are therefore relevant to this component of legitimation and legitimacy. Police officers often and rightly appeal to formal legal provisions as the basis for their actions, especially when they make coercive and potentially controversial interventions in people's lives—such as stop and search, arrest, interrogation, communications intercepts, and (in exceptional circumstances) the shooting of a suspect. But, as Beetham points out, if people in power appeal to the law as the justificatory legitimation for their coercive actions, it follows that they must also 'respect [the law] themselves for their legitimacy to be sustained'.[156] More generally (and now embracing conventions as well as formal law), 'it follows from the nature of social rules that in any rule-governed social order the existence and acquisition of power cannot be separated from the normative expectations … by reference to which its possession is justified'.[157]

This set of ideas in turn explains the importance of the concept of the 'rule of law', described by Beetham as (among other things) embracing the view that 'the powerful and their agents, whatever influence they may exercise over the formulation of the law, are themselves subject to it and have to conform to recognised procedures if they wish to change it'.[158] The rule of law has been described by the American legal theorist Brian Tamanaha as 'the dominant legitimating slogan of law at the close of the twentieth century'.[159] At its heart are principles of due process and equality, and an expectation that those who enforce the law, including the police, must do so

[152] Beetham, above n 4 at 20.
[153] Ibid at 64.
[154] Ibid at 65 (emphasis added).
[155] Ibid at 66.
[156] Ibid at 68.
[157] Ibid at 65.
[158] Ibid at 68.
[159] Tamanaha, above n 95 at 98.

in a manner that is 'unbiased, free of passion, prejudice, and arbitrariness, loyal to the law alone'.[160] When these principles are followed, there is of course an overlap between lawfulness, procedural justice and distributive justice.

Unfortunately, however, the police do not always behave in accordance with formal legal requirements, nor with informal conventions as to how law enforcement officials should behave.[161] Such actions can cause (and historically have caused) deep disquiet and a withdrawal of confidence in the police in certain communities, especially underprivileged and/or minority communities, as is illustrated by the investigation by the US Department of Justice into the police department in Ferguson, Missouri, after the shooting of Michael Brown (an incident we have already alluded to above). The Table of Contents at the beginning of the report of this investigation is itself a damning indictment of the Ferguson Police Department (FPD), as the following extracts show:

— FPD Engages in a Pattern of Unconstitutional Stops and Arrests in Violation of the Fourth Amendment [of the US Constitution];
— FPD Engages in a Pattern of Excessive Force in Violation of the Fourth Amendment [of the US Constitution];
— Ferguson Law Enforcement Practices Disproportionately Harm Ferguson's African-American Residents and Are Driven in Part by Racial Bias;
— Ferguson Law Enforcement Practices Erode Community Trust, Especially Among Ferguson's African-American Residents.[162]

The report also shows that these key points are interconnected:

> Our investigation showed that the disconnect and distrust between much of Ferguson's African-American community and FPD is caused largely by years of the unlawful and unfair law enforcement practices by Ferguson's police department ... We heard from African-American residents who told us of Ferguson's 'long history of targeting blacks for harassment and degrading treatment' and who described the steps they take to avoid this—from taking routes to work that skirt Ferguson to moving out of state. An African-American minister of a church in a

[160] B Tamanaha, *On the Rule of Law: History, Politics, Theory* (Cambridge, Cambridge University Press, 2004) 123.

[161] For a remarkable example of a breach of informal conventions, see the evidence of undercover male police officers in England entering into long-term sexual relationships with female political activists, including in some cases fathering children. This evidence was first brought to light by investigative journalists (R Evans and P Lewis, *Undercover: The True Story of Britain's Secret Police* (London, Guardian Books, 2013)), and is now among the matters being considered in a broader judicial inquiry into undercover policing set up in 2015, chaired by Sir Christopher Pitchford.

[162] US Department of Justice Civil Rights Division, above n 141, at i (capitalisation in original).

nearby community told us that he doesn't allow his two sons to drive through Ferguson out of 'fear that they will be targeted for arrest'.[163]

It is worth emphasising that these practices had developed within a country that is rightly proud of its liberal-democratic traditions, and that has enshrined within its constitution a strong Bill of Rights. The stark contrast between the constitutional rhetoric and the actual practices of policing in Ferguson emphasises the need for strong accountability structures for policing within liberal-democratic states.

Of course, police unlawfulness is not always as systematic as it apparently was in Ferguson. For example, on specific occasions a group of officers might be tempted to engage in what has come to be known, rather unfortunately, as 'noble cause corruption'—that is, the use by the police of 'illicit means for organisationally and socially approved ends'.[164] Thus, in a high-profile case, securing conviction of an 'obviously' guilty person might seem to investigating officers to be an act that is clearly in line with the police's mission, and one that will be approved of by the general population. So if the evidence does not seem quite sufficient to achieve a conviction, there might be a temptation to improve it—by, for example, planting or falsifying some evidence, or engaging in unlawful practices of interrogation in order to secure a confession.[165] This is a form of 'cognitive ethical failure', as previously described;[166] but while it might appear to have social benefits, it can also lead to delegitimation if and when the illegality is discovered—especially if the suspected person is convicted, but then found to be innocent, as has happened in some high profile cases.

E. Realism and the 'Basic Legitimation Demand'

We have suggested that the four issues we have identified (procedural justice, distributive justice, effectiveness and lawfulness) are matters that will very often, and quite naturally, be raised within empirically realist discussions of 'what, here and now, makes sense as a legitimation of power'.[167] We do not, of course, claim that all four of them will be raised within every legitimation discussion, because real-world debates do not work like that.

[163] Ibid at 79. The situation was also, of course, exacerbated by the demands of the city authorities in Ferguson for the police to generate additional revenue for the city's budget by an increased use of ticketing for municipal code violations: see above n 141.

[164] Punch, above n 35 at 305.

[165] Sometimes illegalities can also be perpetrated for less 'noble' reasons. For example, in a highly publicised case, police officers in Brooklyn, New York, were convicted for planting narcotics on people when they 'needed a productivity boost': *New York Times* (14 October 2011).

[166] Price, above n 98.

[167] Williams, above n 5 at 11.

Rather, as we have previously suggested, such debates occur especially when there are legitimacy deficits, and they are often heavily influenced by the history and culture of the local situation. Thus, there is much that is contingent about legitimacy debates. Bearing that in mind, our claims are first, that the four issues we have identified are, empirically speaking, not infrequently raised in legitimation discussions; and second, that there are good normative reasons, relating to the concept of justified political authority, why they are regularly raised.

The four issues must, however, always be seen as potentially operating in interaction with one another; and they will not always work in harmony. In particular, there can be tensions between effectiveness and each of the other three matters. The potential tension with lawfulness has been discussed above, but effectiveness can sometimes also seem to conflict with distributive justice (as where a type of crime appears to be committed particularly frequently by a given ethnic group) and with procedural justice (as where, in the wake of terrorist incidents, officers want to concentrate on preventive actions, and so wish to pay less attention to treating everyone with humanity). In dealing with such tensions and conflicts, we suggest that Amartya Sen's 'impartial spectator test' will be a valuable resource, and will help police services to focus on longer-term social consequences, as well as on the immediate situation.

There is also a further point of some theoretical importance that arises from the analysis in this section. Diarmaid Harkin has insightfully pointed out that while there is a general consensus in the academic literature on policing that 'legitimacy is undermined by corruption, brutality and dishonesty', nevertheless, when examples of such behaviour come to light, they 'are rarely *catastrophic* for the police, but contained in their impact'.[168] As a possible explanation of this phenomenon, Harkin draws attention to the potential relevance of John Jost's psychological 'system justification theory', according to which there is 'a general ideological motive to justify the existing social order';[169] but there are at least two other possible, and more sociological, explanations. One would rely on Margaret Gilbert's concept of a 'joint commitment',[170] and the argument would be that many aspects of such a commitment can survive even some major shocks. The second possibility would draw attention to the fact that legitimation and legitimacy are always political issues, and have to be viewed within the context of the particular political system in which they occur.

[168] Harkin, above n 109 at 601.

[169] JT Jost, MR Banaji and B Nosek, 'A Decade of System Justification Theory: Accumulated Evidence of Conscious and Unconscious Bolstering of the Status Quo' (2004) 25 *Political Psychology* 881.

[170] Gilbert, above n 55.

This second possibility is well illustrated by some events in the Republic of Ireland, as described by Vicky Conway (not cited by Harkin).[171] In County Donegal, a disturbing series of allegations about the police emerged from 1996 onwards; these were eventually considered by a tribunal presided over by a High Court judge (Justice Morris), which sat for six years from 2002, and issued eight reports. The findings of the tribunal were 'exceptionally critical' of the police, documenting 'corruption, abuse of power and negligence from management', as well as 'a disregard for procedure at every turn and a belief that this could be done with impunity'.[172] Yet despite all this, a national survey of public confidence in the police showed only a small change from 2002 to 2008 (86 per cent satisfied or very satisfied in 2002; 81 per cent in 2008); and among the 26 counties in the Irish Republic, respondents in Donegal recorded the second highest level of confidence.[173] Conway suggests some reasons for these striking findings, based on Ireland's complex post-colonial history, and the ideological importance of the Irish *gardai* (police) within that history. The details of her discussion need not concern us here, but we do need to note the importance of the historical dimension in this example, because—as previously noted—how people judge the police in a particular situation very often depends upon prior experiences and understandings.[174]

Yet given the dialogic nature of legitimacy, and the existence of multiple dialogues (see above), the lack of impact *on the general public* of events such as those in Donegal might not be the only relevant issue. For example, studies in political science have shown that when a political leader loses the confidence (legitimacy) previously placed in him or her by elites close to the sources of power, this can be fatal for his/her effective continuance in office.[175] Thus, in the policing context, not only public perceptions, but also the state's more formal mechanisms of accountability in relation to the policing function are a vital element in the total set of dialogues about legitimacy.[176] In other words—and unsurprisingly—a realist political analysis of police legitimacy ultimately requires attention to many aspects of state functioning.

The upshot of the discussion in this section is therefore that procedural justice, distributive justice, effectiveness and lawfulness can be empirically

[171] V Conway, *Policing Twentieth Century Ireland: A History of An Garda Siochána* (London, Routledge, 2014) ch 8.

[172] Ibid at 188.

[173] Ibid at 192.

[174] Harkin, above n 109.

[175] R Barker, *Legitimating Identities: The Self-Representation of Rulers and Subjects* (Cambridge, Cambridge University Press, 2001); J Rothschild, 'Observations on Legitimacy in Contemporary Europe' (1977) 92 *Political Science Quarterly* 487.

[176] Conway is highly critical of police accountability mechanisms in the Republic of Ireland, where, she claims, the national government has traditionally held a 'controlling influence over policing': Conway, above n 171 at 217.

identified as important potential contributors to discussions about police legitimation and legitimacy. But these matters can sometimes be in tension with one another; and, given the historical and contextual contingency of legitimacy discussions, in a particular context one or more of them might not have the impact that one would normally anticipate.

As a final comment, the preceding discussion has assumed that the legitimation discussion is taking place within Williams' 'realist' framework, which means that the conception of legitimacy adopted is ultimately empirical. We have argued above that such a framework, although immensely analytically valuable, needs buttressing by some bedrock normative commitments. This is not the place for an extended discussion of what those commitments should be, but in brief we would argue that they should be based on the concept of human rights, and they would therefore be very similar to those contained in the US Bill of Rights or the European Convention on Human Rights. Provisions of this sort would be sufficient to deal with the example that we have used throughout this chapter of the proposal for forced deportation of an ethnic minority in 'Dystopia'; clearly, such a proposal would violate such a Bill or Convention.

VI. CONCLUSION

The analysis in this chapter has, we hope, demonstrated that the legitimacy of the public police is, in contemporary states, an issue of central importance with regard to what Bernard Williams described as 'the first political question' for any state, namely the establishment and maintenance of 'order, protection, safety, trust, and the conditions of co-operation'.[177] Our analysis of this issue has drawn upon prior criminological work on police legitimacy, but it has also considered two concepts from political philosophy not previously discussed within the criminological literature on legitimacy, namely Williams' 'Basic Legitimation Demand' and Amartya Sen's 'impartial spectator'.

Our analysis has been primarily theoretical, but by drawing upon the empirical research literatures on both policing in general, and on the legitimacy of the police in particular, it has sought to remain aware of the day-to-day realities of policing. Indeed, our hope is that some of the central topics discussed here could be of practical assistance to police leaders as they seek to deliver just and legitimate policing. These topics include, first and foremost, Williams' suggestion that there is a need for those, like the police, who are invested with state powers to be able to offer a legitimation *to every subject* as to why the use of those powers is normatively justified.

177 Williams, above n 5 at 3.

Bearing in mind Tom Tyler's concept of the 'teachable moment',[178] we can reasonably add that in principle this requirement needs to be met *on every occasion* that police powers are used. These are stringent requirements, but police officers need to remember that, in the last resort, they are—as Williams crudely but correctly put it—simply 'one lot of people' who have been given power over 'another lot of people'; and, since 'power itself does not justify', the justification of police power is in principle continually necessary.[179] Of course, the sociological reality is—as the events dealt with by the Morris Tribunal in Ireland particularly demonstrate[180]—that sometimes the police can rely on their accumulated public goodwill to retain legitimacy even when they have behaved in unjustifiable ways. But legitimacy is a dialogic process involving many layers, many players, and an unfolding series of events, and it would be an unwise police leader who believes that his or her police service can sustain legitimacy indefinitely in such circumstances. Unwise police leaders do, sadly, exist, but their normative failures are more often, in Terry Price's language, cognitive rather than volitional;[181] and we have suggested that if they were to use Amartya Sen's 'impartial spectator test',[182] the number of such failures would be reduced.

Police officers at all levels are reasonably entitled to ask scholars of policing whether their research and theorisation can offer any practical guidance as to how police legitimacy can be developed and sustained. As we have shown, legitimacy dialogues are always contingent on specific features of the place and time in which they occur, and are influenced by the history and culture of that place and time; and this means that the specifics of legitimation and legitimacy can be very variable. We have however suggested the enduring importance of procedural justice, distributive justice, effectiveness and lawfulness as guides to the delivery of legitimate policing. Perhaps the best way to describe their potential importance as a practical guide is to say, first, that firm evidence can be cited that a failure to deliver any one of these four matters has on some occasions led to a legitimacy deficit for a public police service; but second, there are no reports of a police service that has delivered all four of them, and has lost its legitimacy.

[178] Tyler, above n 107 at 257.
[179] Williams, above n 5 at 5.
[180] Conway, above n 171.
[181] Price, above n 98; Hales et al, above n 99.
[182] Sen, above n 6.

4

Security Against Arbitrary Government in Criminal Justice

LUCIA ZEDNER

> States claim to be entitled to tell you what to do, and to force you to do as you are told. This dual claim to authority and coercion is familiar in the context of the criminal law.[1]

THE CRIMINAL LAW is inherently coercive. Its contravention sanctions the intrusive, rights-eroding and liberty-depriving actions of policing, prosecution and punishment by the state against the individual. The authority of the state to exercise such acute power over individual citizens rests on the presence of sufficient safeguards to protect against unwarranted intrusions on individual liberty. Only where public officials bind themselves to the requirements of the rule of law, abide by principles of due process and uphold fundamental human rights—not least the right to a fair trial—can the authority of the state to promulgate and enforce the criminal law be defended. This is not to propose a purely procedural account; rather, the rule of law requires that the substantive content of the rules themselves must be consistent with justice, fair treatment and fundamental rights.[2] The primary focus of this chapter, however, is on the relationship between criminal law and the requirements of due process, without which there can be no effective limits on the scope of coercive state authority.

The central question addressed by this chapter, therefore, is what is required of the criminal process and how far it can travel from its ideal type before it no longer merits the label of criminal *justice* and the authority it gives to the criminal law is undermined. This question has become all the more urgent in light of recent developments in the UK that seriously erode procedural protections, the right to a fair trial and open justice. New forms

[1] A Ripstein, 'Authority and Coercion' (2004) 32 *Philosophy & Public Affairs* 2. See also RA Duff, *Trials and Punishments* (Cambridge, Cambridge University Press, 1986) 77ff.

[2] See TRS Allan, 'The Rule of Law' in D Dyzenhaus and M Thorburn (eds), *Philosophical Foundations of Constitutional Law* (Oxford, Oxford University Press, 2016) 201.

of summary justice, restrictions on access to justice and the spectre of secret trials subvert basic precepts and principles of due process. In so doing, they impoverish the quality of justice, generate uncertainty and deny defendants the ability to contest the prosecution case fairly and fully. The core contention of this chapter is that these changes to the criminal process threaten the security of the individual against arbitrary government and undermine the authority of the state to enforce the criminal law.

I. STATE AUTHORITY AND THE CRIMINAL PROCESS

To appreciate why departures from due process undermine state authority, we need to examine more closely the relationship between criminal law and criminal procedure. Most recent work in the philosophy of criminal law has focused on questions of criminalisation, its underlying precepts, and the guiding principles that inform the boundaries, structures and constitution of the criminal law.[3] Much of the debate pivots on whether the state has the political authority to make any conduct criminal or whether it is restricted to criminalising conduct on moral grounds, namely that crime involves the infliction of wrongful harms.[4] As such, these discussions lie some way from Glanville Williams' famous definition of crime as an act that can be followed by criminal proceedings, prosecution and, on conviction, punishment:

> A crime must be defined by reference to the legal consequences of the act. We must distinguish, primarily, not between crimes and civil wrongs but between criminal and civil proceedings. A crime then becomes an act that is capable of being followed by criminal proceedings, having one of the types of outcome (punishment etc) known to follow these proceedings.[5]

This definition has been criticised because it side-steps the difficult task of trying to define, classify and defend the enormous variety of disparate conduct (and omissions) that is the subject of criminal prohibition.[6] Something more is required, it is argued, that speaks to the nature of the conduct, the accompanying mental element, the gravity of the harm risked or inflicted,

[3] D Husak, *Overcriminalization: The Limits of the Criminal Law* (Oxford, Oxford University Press, 2008); J Deigh and D Dolinko (eds), *The Oxford Handbook of Philosophy of Criminal Law* (Oxford, Oxford University Press, 2011); RA Duff et al (eds), *The Constitution of the Criminal Law* (Oxford, Oxford University Press, 2013).

[4] See, eg, RA Duff, *Answering for Crime: Responsibility and Liability in the Criminal Law* (Oxford, Hart Publishing, 2007); SP Garvey, 'Was Ellen Wronged? (2013) 7 *Criminal Law & Philosophy* 185. For contrasting views see M Thorburn, 'Criminal Law as Public Law' in RA Duff and SP Green (eds), *Philosophical Foundations of Criminal Law* (Oxford, Oxford University Press, 2011) 21; KW Simons, 'Understanding the Topography of Moral and Criminal Law Norms', in Duff and Green ibid at 228.

[5] G Williams, 'The Definition of a Crime' (1955) 8 *Current Legal Problems* 107 at 123.

[6] G Lamond, 'What Is a Crime?' (2007) 27 *Oxford Journal of Legal Studies* 609 at 610.

and the incursion upon the public interest that it entails.[7] By defining crime as what is followed by criminal proceedings, Williams provides no substantive account of a criminal charge or penal sanction of the sort developed in the jurisprudence of the European Court of Human Rights.[8] Yet the virtue of Williams' definition is that it acknowledges that criminal law is not only, or even primarily, a means by which to classify wrongdoing: it is also the authorisation of a particular response by the state. This second aspect tends to be overlooked in accounts that conceive the criminal law as addressed first and foremost to the putative or actual offender, or to the general public. Whereas to say that crime is 'capable of being followed by criminal proceedings' is to identify another audience—the public officials charged with its implementation. On this second account, by defining and categorising wrongful conduct, criminal law authorises the state to prosecute a suspected offender. Seen this way, criminal laws are instructions to officials to institute and pursue criminal proceedings. Prosecution, trial, conviction and criminal sanction are not merely characteristic of and peculiar to criminal proceedings; they are what define crime as crime.

Williams' characterisation of criminal law as that which is followed by criminal proceedings thus invites closer consideration of the relationship between the criminal law and procedure than is to be found in contemporary debates about criminalisation. In general, criminal law texts have little to say about procedure and works on procedure have even less to say about criminal law so that the interrelation between the two remains underexplored.[9] There are notable exceptions. In *The Criminal Process*, Andrew Ashworth and Mike Redmayne stress their interdependence arguing: 'The criminal process … is the mechanism that authorizes the State to apply the criminal law to its citizens'.[10] For Ashworth and Redmayne, it would appear that a crime is not merely 'followed by criminal proceedings'; rather it is those very proceedings that permit the state to apply the coercive force of prosecution and punishment. This is not to suggest that the authority of the state to criminalise stems solely from the criminal process. Elsewhere, Ashworth acknowledges that this authority derives from the state's larger duty to prevent harm and to provide for security and good order.[11] That state

[7] Though as Simester and colleagues point out, 'the sheer variety of conduct that has been designated a criminal wrong defies reduction to any "essential" minimum'. AP Simester et al, *Simester and Sullivan's Criminal Law* 4th edn (Oxford, Hart Publishing, 2010) 3.

[8] Eg *Engel v Netherlands* (1979–80) 1 EHRR 647; *Welch v United Kingdom* (1995) 20 EHRR 247. See further L Zedner, 'Penal Subversions: When is a Punishment not a Punishment, who Decides, and on what Grounds?' (2016) 20 *Theoretical Criminology* 3.

[9] D Nelken, 'Criminal Law and Criminal Justice: Some Notes on Their Irrelation' in I Dennis (ed), *Criminal Law and Criminal Justice* (London, Sweet & Maxwell, 1987) 139.

[10] A Ashworth and M Redmayne, *The Criminal Process* 4th edn (Oxford, Oxford University Press, 2010) 22.

[11] A Ashworth and L Zedner, *Preventive Justice* (Oxford, Oxford University Press, 2014) 7ff.

authority derives from this larger security obligation is, of course, a central theme in political theory dating back at least to Hobbes,[12] through Locke, Montesquieu, Rousseau and Adam Smith.[13] But, as Locke made clear, the state's exercise of its coercive powers in the name of security itself poses a serious threat to the security of the individual. As he observed, 'Men are so foolish, that they take care to avoid what Mischiefs may be done them by *Pole-Cats*, or *Foxes*, but are content, nay think it Safety, to be devoured by *Lions*'.[14] Given the grave threat to individual liberty posed by an overbearing state, the criminal process, although insufficient in itself to ground state authority, is a necessary condition of the legitimate exercise of the criminal law.

In short, although criminal law licenses state sanction, this licence is not untrammelled. Criminal proceedings are legally constituted to guide and restrain the exercise of state coercive force. Rules of procedure, evidence, sentencing and sanction bind officials to act according to their precepts and to face sanction themselves if they breach these rules. To accept that sanction *ought* to follow breach of criminal laws[15] is thus not only to say that criminal law authorises public officials to prosecute and to impose penal sanctions, it is also to set a limit to that authority.

This dual authorisation of and limit to state authority is important because, were it not so authorised, much of what the state does to enforce criminal laws would itself be wrongful. As Grant Lamond points out, '[w]ithout authorization, for example, an arrest is simply an assault accompanied by false imprisonment'.[16] The acknowledgement that, if not so ratified, the actions of police and punishers would themselves constitute wrongdoing leads David Dixon to conclude that '"police powers" are simply exemptions from criminal or civil liability for what otherwise would be unlawful acts.'[17] Dixon rightly reminds us that, when not carried out in accordance with the law, forcible restraint and detention are crimes; arguably, however, police

[12] T Hobbes, *Leviathan* (London, Penguin Classics, 1651) ch XIII.

[13] On larger questions about the security function of the state see, M Neocleous, *Critique of Security* (Edinburgh, Edinburgh University Press, 2008); L Farmer, 'The Jurisprudence of Security: The Police Power and the Criminal Law' in MD Dubber and M Valverde (eds), *The New Police Science: The Police Power in Domestic and International Perspective* (Stanford CA, Stanford University Press, 2006); I Loader and N Walker, 'Necessary Virtues: The Legitimate Place of the State in the Production of Security' in B Dupont and J Wood (eds), *Democracy, Society and the Governance of Security* (Cambridge, Cambridge University Press, 2005).

[14] J Locke, *Two Treatises of Government* edited by P Laslett (Cambridge, Cambridge University Press, 1960) ch VII 'Of Political or Civil Society' §93.

[15] According to Hans Kelsen, all 'legal norms … are *ought*-statements. They indicate that under certain conditions certain consequences—the sanctions—*ought* to take place.' H Kelsen, 'On the Pure Theory of Law' (1966) 1 *Israeli Law Review* 1 at 3.

[16] G Lamond, 'The Coerciveness of Law' (2000) 20 *Oxford Journal of Legal Studies* 39 at 41–42.

[17] D Dixon, *Law in Policing: Legal Regulation and Police Practices* (Oxford, Clarendon Press, 1997) 64.

stop and search, arrest and interrogation are not merely exempt from designation as wrongful conduct; rather they are positively authorised by and in turn provide authority to the criminal law.[18]

It is worth noting that the centrality Williams accords to criminal proceedings in respect of the criminal law is mirrored in John Rawls' definition of punishment of the same year:

> A person is said to suffer punishment whenever he is legally deprived of some of the normal rights of a citizen on the ground that he has violated the rule of law, the violation having been established by a trial *according to the due process of law*, provided that the deprivation is carried out by the recognised legal authorities of the State, that the rule of law clearly specifies both the offence and the attached penalty, that the courts construe statutes strictly, and that the statute was on the book prior to the time of the offence.[19]

On this account, punishment can legitimately be labelled as such only if it accords with carefully stipulated provisions as to procedure, adherence to the requirements of the rule of law and of legal certainty. Note that Rawls also insists that punishment be carried out only by 'the recognised legal authorities of the State'.[20] Such a claim suggests that a normative account of legal punishment and its justification must be grounded in a larger political theory of the state's role and rightful functions.[21]

II. DUE PROCESS AS PROTECTION BY AND FROM THE STATE

The monopoly of the state to punish has been much explored and the case for its exclusive right to do so has been stoutly defended.[22] For example, Malcolm Thorburn suggests, '[t]he ground of the liberal constitutional state's legitimacy is the simple fact that it—and it alone—can provide the conditions of freedom for all'.[23] To achieve this, the state enacts rules that demarcate the boundaries of acceptable conduct consistent with respect for individual autonomy; ensures compliance with those rules; and sanctions those who do not comply. It follows from this grounding of the state monopoly in the protection of freedom that the state is itself obligated to

[18] Compare also Bottoms' and Tankebe's chapter in this collection.

[19] J Rawls, 'Two Concepts of Rules' (1955) 64 *The Philosophical Review* 3 at 10 (emphasis added).

[20] Ibid. See also N Lacey, *State Punishment: Political Principles and Community Values* (London, Routledge, 1988).

[21] Thorburn, above n 4 at 42–43.

[22] Lacey, above n 20; A Harel, 'Why Only the State May Inflict Criminal Sanctions: The Case against Privately Inflicted Sanctions' (2008) 14 *Legal Theory* 113; M Thorburn, 'Reinventing the Nightwatchman State' (2010) 60 *University of Toronto Law Journal* 425.

[23] M Thorburn, 'Constitutionalism and the Limits of the Criminal Law' in RA Duff et al (eds), *The Structures of the Criminal Law* (Oxford, Oxford University Press, 2011) 85 at 88.

ensure that the process of enforcement protects individual liberty from overreaching through unwarranted coercion or unjustified intrusion by public officials.

Insofar as the state claims the right to enforce the criminal law, it severely limits the right of other social actors to enforce sanctions against wrongdoing (other than through the closely regulated medium of private prosecutions). By preventing individual victims or communities from wreaking vengeance as and when they choose, and by instituting formal proceedings against alleged offenders on behalf of us all, the state also seeks to reduce arbitrariness and injustice. Criminal law delineates the scope of offending behaviour, laws of procedure prescribe official practice and rules of evidence determine which material is legally admissible in the criminal court.[24] Formal laws are underpinned by subsidiary rules, regulations and codes of practice relating to police powers, prosecutorial discretion and the conduct of the trial. As we shall see, in practice these laws are mediated through the discretion exercised by officials at each stage of the criminal justice process, but, in theory at least, this discretion is constrained and guided by a framework of laws pertaining to every aspect of policing, prosecution, trial and sentencing. In short, the criminal process and criminal trial constitute both the authorisation of the state's prerogative to punish and, simultaneously, serve as vital protections against the arbitrary exercise of power over the individual.[25] As TRS Allan observes:

> The justice of the verdict is internally related to the justice of the procedures which produce it: it derives, not simply from the fact that the defendant committed the offence but from the fact that the charge has been proved by a rational process of argument in which the defendant was invited to engage.[26]

For the criminal process and trial to satisfy the requirements of justice and serve as sufficient protection against overreaching of state authority, it must abide by the rule of law. Accounts of the rule of law are heavily contested and vary widely in their content, ambition and the claims made for them;[27]

[24] RA Duff et al, *The Trial on Trial: Truth and Due Process* Vol 1 (Oxford, Hart Publishing, 2004). Especially ch1, RA Duff et al, 'Towards a Normative Theory of the Criminal Trial' and ch 5 MD Dubber, 'The Criminal Trial and the Legitimation of Punishment'.

[25] A contrary view is that 'deviation from standards of justice and legality are not merely the product of informalities and unintended consequences at the level of petty officials, but institutionalised in the formal law of the state': D McBarnet, *Conviction: Law, the State, and the Construction of Justice* (London, Macmillan, 1983) 8.

[26] TRS Allan, *Constitutional Justice: A Liberal Theory of the Rule of Law* (Oxford, Oxford University Press, 2003) 81. See also TRS Allan, 'Procedural Fairness and the Duty of Respect' (1998) 18 *Oxford Journal of Legal Studies* 497.

[27] LL Fuller, *The Morality of Law* (New Haven, Yale University Press, 1964) chs II, V; J Raz, *The Authority of Law* (Oxford, Clarendon Press, 1979) ch 11 'The Rule of Law and its Virtues'; R Barnett, *The Structure of Liberty: Justice and the Rule of Law* (Oxford, Oxford University Press, 1998); G Lamond, 'The Rule of Law' in A Marmor (ed), *The Routledge Companion to Philosophy of Law* (London, Routledge, 2012).

yet, at their core lie some fundamental and commonly accepted tenets. Central rule of law values include certainty, clarity of definition and predictability in the substance and application of laws and, of particular importance to the criminal law, the principle of non-retrospectivity. They contribute to the avoidance of arbitrariness by limiting and guiding the exercise of discretion by criminal justice officials to ensure that they operate 'within a clear and certain framework'.[28] Adherence to procedural fairness and fair warning allow individuals to know what to expect and to be able to recognise when reasonable expectations have been met or breached.[29] Security of expectation depends, therefore, on clarity and consistency of laws, structures and procedures.

A procedural account of the rule of law thus focuses on those rules 'which impose duties instructing the power-holders how to exercise their powers'.[30] This procedural account sets a high bar: the independence of the judiciary and the principles of natural justice require easy access to justice, freedom from long delay and excessive cost; open and fair hearings; accompanied by adequate provision for judicial oversight and review; and, not least, that 'the discretion of the crime-preventing agencies should not be allowed to pervert the law'.[31] Yet Allan proposes an even 'more ambitious, more substantive conception of the rule of law' that goes beyond the fair and impartial administration of law to require that its content also 'embody a coherent and consistent scheme of justice'.[32] Only if the substantive content of law is formulated in such a way as to uphold the same ideals of fairness, impartiality and respect for individual freedom, argues Allan, can the law serve as adequate protection against the exercise of arbitrary power by public officials.

Internal constraints within criminal law, not least via the articulation and application of core principles, contribute to the task of anticipating and avoiding abuse. The principle of maximum certainty is one important principle that seeks to protect against vagueness and to avert arbitrariness in the enforcement of criminal law.[33] Likewise, principles of fairness, transparency and openness help to ensure that the criminal law is applied impartially, justly and without bias, and to provide assurance to the public, and above all to the defendant, that this is so. Such assurance is important because

[28] A Ashworth, 'Preventive Orders and the Rule of Law' in D Baker and J Horder (eds), *The Sanctity of Life and the Criminal Law* (Cambridge, Cambridge University Press, 2013) 45 at 64.
[29] Ibid at 49.
[30] Raz, above n 27 at 216.
[31] Ibid at 218.
[32] Allan, above n 2 at 203.
[33] A Ashworth and J Horder, *Principles of Criminal Law* 7th edn (Oxford, Oxford University Press, 2013) ch 3, 3.5 (on The Rule of Law and Fair Procedures).

legitimacy arguably lies as much in the perception and appreciation of the public as in the workings of the law per se.[34] As Allan observes,

> where justice is not seen to be done, there is an implication that those in authority have little or no regard for the opinions of those affected: the requirement to *justify* their treatment has been implicitly rejected or abandoned. The exercise of authority, in short, has become the exercise of power.[35]

Though it would not do to overplay the disciplinary potential of normative theorising, a thorough delineation of core principles has the potential to provide a working guide for decision-making and to set standards by which to monitor practice, detect and correct unjust derogations and to identify areas for reform.

Vitally important too are the external constraints provided by the fundamental rights defined and protected by the many national and international human rights charters and conventions.[36] Human rights instruments vary in their emphasis but commonly protect the right to legal representation, to open justice in a public hearing and to have one's case heard in a reasonable time by an independent and impartial tribunal. These provisions are addressed both to the defendant as guarantee and assurance and, no less, to public officials in that they articulate the preconditions of, and limits to, their authority.[37] Taken together, these requirements seek to ensure that the legal machinery of law enforcement abides by the fundamental right to a fair trial, and that it is configured so as to minimise the risk of mistake, abuse of power or miscarriage of justice.

To require that fair procedures are consistently applied to all is not to promise, however, that the process will be without fault. As Allan argues, 'There are too many competing demands on limited resources to allow for perfect procedures, even if they could be designed in theory'.[38] In an imperfect process, error will inevitably occur, so the potential for arbitrariness resides not only in the scope of criminal laws, the structures and processes of the criminal justice system; but also in failure to anticipate and protect

[34] T Tyler, *Why People Obey the Law* (New Haven, Yale University Press, 1990); AE Bottoms and J Tankebe, 'Beyond Procedural Justice: A Dialogic Approach to Legitimacy in Criminal Justice' (2012) 102 *Journal of Criminal Law & Criminology* 119.

[35] Allan, 'Procedural Fairness', above n 26 at 506.

[36] As set out, for example, in Art 6 of the European Convention on Human Rights. See further B Emmerson, A Ashworth, and A Macdonald, *Human Rights and Criminal Justice* 3rd edn (London, Sweet & Maxwell, 2012).

[37] Note that Liora Lazarus argues that human rights may also generate obligations in criminal law that require extensions of state power to coerce in the name of providing security, for example, the right to life. See L Lazarus, 'Positive Obligations and Criminal Justice: Duties to Protect or Coerce?' in L Zedner and JV Roberts (eds), *Principles and Values in Criminal Law and Criminal Justice: Essays in Honour of Andrew Ashworth* (Oxford, Oxford University Press 2012) 135.

[38] Allan, 'Procedural Fairness', above n 26 at 512. R Dworkin, *A Matter of Principle* (Oxford, Oxford University Press, 1985) 80–81.

against error and abuse. A criminal justice process worth the name needs to acknowledge that mistakes will inexorably occur and to provide for their remedy when they do.[39] In order to ensure its ability to self-correct, it must incorporate procedures and institutions that permit appeal, provide adequate review of possible miscarriages of justice and redress for those wrongfully convicted.[40]

III. STRAINS IN THE MACHINE: THE RIGHT TO CHALLENGE, DISCRETION AND THE REALITY OF RULES

Despite the high value placed on certainty and consistency, the right of defendants to challenge the case for the prosecution necessarily generates uncertainty. There is a paradox here. On the one hand, as MacCormick observes, 'the Rule of Law … insists on the right of the defence to challenge and rebut the case made against it. There is no security against arbitrary government unless such challenges are freely permitted'.[41] On the other hand, the outcome of the criminal trial is inherently unpredictable. Uncertainty is, therefore, an enduring strain on the application of criminal law. There is an irresolvable tension between security of expectation (embodied in the principle of maximum certainty) and security against arbitrary government (exemplified by the unavoidable uncertainty and unpredictability of the criminal trial). Yet both are important shields for the individual against the unwarranted exercise of coercive power by the state. This observation raises larger issues about the relationship among core principles of criminal law and the difficulty of resolving conflicts between them, which in turn raises questions about the potential of principles alone to guide the decisions of law-maker and law enforcer.[42] In short, although criminal justice principles and human rights are important protections against arbitrary government, it would be naïve to think that their application is in practice unproblematic.

[39] K Roach, 'Wrongful Convictions: Adversarial and Inquisitorial Themes' (2010) 35 *North Carolina Journal of International Law and Commercial Regulation* 388; C Hoyle, 'Compensating Injustice: The Perils of the Innocence Discourse' in J Hunter, P Roberts, S Young and D Dixon (eds), *The Integrity of Criminal Process: From Theory into Practice* (Oxford, Hart Publishing, 2016); C Hoyle, 'Victims of the State: Recognising the Harms Caused by Wrongful Convictions' in M Bosworth, C Hoyle and L Zedner (eds), *Changing Contours of Criminal Justice: Research, Politics and Policy* (Oxford, Oxford University Press, 2016).

[40] For example, the work of the Criminal Cases Review Commission in the UK (www.ccrc.gov.uk/); Innocence projects, often run by university law schools, are another.

[41] N MacCormick, *Rhetoric and the Rule of Law: A Theory of Legal Reasoning* (Oxford, Oxford University Press, 2005) 27.

[42] On the relationship between criminal justice principles, see J Gardner, 'Ashworth on Principles' in Zedner and Roberts, above n 37, 3.

The most problematic aspect of all arises from the obvious fact that the machinery of justice does not run itself. Beneath and beyond the formal structures of substantive and procedural rules, officials exercise discretion and, although the exercise of discretion is essential to the fair application of law, it has the capacity to impair due process.[43] The tension between the necessary exercise of discretion and the overreaching of state authority is an enduring challenge to be managed within any criminal justice system. The greatest uncertainty of the criminal process and the one that raises the most serious risk of arbitrariness is that which results from error, negligence or wilful wrongdoing by criminal justice officials. Criminological research furnishes clear evidence that the criminal process is routinely and radically undermined by the unfair, discriminatory or even errant practices of policing and prosecution.[44] Above it was suggested that the authority of law relies upon the willingness of police and criminal justice officials to abide by the rule of law and conform to principles of due process in order that defendants have the assurance that they are not at the mercy of the unfettered exercise of state coercive power.[45] This perfectionist account stands some way from the realities of police decision-making, as revealed not only by criminological research but also by the dismal record of miscarriages of justice.[46] All too often the exercise of discretion is driven by individual officials' assessment of what they deem to be the 'right' priorities. Officials tend to prefer their conception of the public interest over the defendant's and to privilege the exigencies of the moment over the demands of legality.[47] Such judgement-calls lead officials to fail to inform suspects of their due process rights (for example, to make a phone call from a police station or to access free legal advice) and to override or even disregard fundamental liberties.[48] Excessive discretion oversteps the proper limits of legitimate government and undermines state authority. Criminal procedure must, therefore, not only guide the exercise of discretion but also anticipate error, seek to limit abuse and to provide the means and structures needed to facilitate redress.

[43] See generally Dixon, above n 17.

[44] This literature is vast. See, eg, DJ Smith and J Gray, *Police and People in London* (Aldershot, Gower, 1983); P Manning, *Police Work* (Cambridge MA, MIT Press, 1977); J Chan, 'Changing Police Culture' (1996) 36 *British Journal of Criminology* 109. For an overview, see R Ericson, 'Rules in Policing: Five Perspectives' (2007) 11 *Theoretical Criminology* 367.

[45] Allan, above n 2.

[46] For an overview of this research, see A Sanders and R Young, 'From Suspect to Trial' in M Maguire, R Morgan and R Reiner (eds), *The Oxford Handbook of Criminology* 5th edn (Oxford, Oxford University Press, 2012) 838; Roach, above n 39.

[47] Other, less defensible drivers include the macho imperatives of 'cop culture', racism, sexism, covering for colleagues, and basic disrespect for the rules. See more generally, Ashworth and Redmayne, above n 10 ch 3.

[48] Ibid.

No account of the criminal process can ignore the inherent malleability of rules. Read one way, rules serve as a fetter upon the exercise of discretion and a curb on coercive state powers which, if not so constrained, would profoundly erode civil liberties. *Inhibitory* rules place limits upon the power of the police to stop, search, to arrest, detain and interrogate suspects. Such rules proscribe certain forms of action, oblige officials to justify and account for their decisions and penalise those who transgress. How far these legal limits are effective is another question. Rather than imposing effective controls, purportedly restrictive rules can instead promote adaptive behaviour as criminal justice agents tailor conduct rendered illegal by inhibitory rules. Taking the suspect by the 'scenic route' to the police station to evade rules that require the contemporaneous recording of interviews is just one such well-documented example of rule evasion.

Read another way, the problem lies also in the rules themselves.[49] Some rules, although ostensibly inhibitory, are in fact designed to bring the law into line with existing police or prosecutorial practice and, according to Sanders, Young and Burton, are better understood as *legitimising* rules that work 'by cloaking officers with legal authority'.[50] Still others, for example those concerning police powers to stop and search people on the street also appear to be inhibitory but in fact introduce no new or effective constraint and are more accurately described as *presentational* rules that provide little more than a thin veneer of legality.[51] Most problematic of all are *enabling* rules that furnish the police and other officials with extensive powers exercisable in a wide array of circumstances and thus impose little by way of effective limit.[52] Laws that purport to curb abuses of police powers also provide the authority for the exercise of that power. Rules that appear to restrict the exercise of police power, invariably allow the police to stop, question, search, restrain, arrest and detain within the parameters set out in the rules. For example, the time constraints placed upon the detention of suspects under the UK Police and Criminal Evidence Act (PACE) 1984 actually allow the police to hold suspects up to these limits. Rather than restrain state power, they may in practice extend it. Such laws appear to guide and constrain but are better understood as permissive or enabling, and, as such, act as much as licence as limit. Yet more worrying are the formal, legal derogations from ordinary due process that occur when the state prefers its own interests—be it in efficiency, economy or its own security—over the security

[49] A Sanders and R Young, *Criminal Justice* (London, Butterworths, 2000).
[50] Ibid at 73–74.
[51] DJ Smith, 'The Framework of Law and Policing Practice' in J Benyon and C Bourn (eds), *The Police: Powers, Procedures and Proprieties* (Oxford, Pergamon Press, 1986) 85 at 89.
[52] Sanders and Young, above n 49 at 73–75.

of the individual to whom the process applies. It is to these formal derogations that we turn in the next section.

IV. EROSION OF DUE PROCESS PROTECTIONS

The central contention thus far has been that state authority to promulgate, prosecute and enforce the criminal law resides in no small part in the legitimacy of the criminal process by which it does so. This section explores recent developments in English criminal procedure that constitute such a significant erosion of due process as to call into question whether the resulting downgraded or deformed criminal procedure still serves as an adequate source of state authority for the enforcement of the criminal law. These developments are by no means isolated examples of the attrition that the criminal process in the UK has suffered in recent years.[53] Nevertheless, they repay close investigation because they illustrate the vulnerability of the process to legislative and judicial assault and suggest the precariousness of the structures and procedures upon which state authority to criminalise depends.

A. Access to Justice and Court Charges

Access to justice is a vital precondition of due process and yet in the UK cuts to Legal Aid severely limit that access and the protections that high quality, publically-funded legal representation affords to impoverished defendants. The drive to cut costs also stood behind reduction in the number of magistrates, closure of courts, substantial cuts to the criminal justice budget, and proposals for efficiency reforms such as the 2012 White Paper *Swift and Sure Justice*.[54] So-called 'fiscal imperatives' stand also behind the introduction of court charges, designed to transfer some of the cost of running the criminal justice system to defendants. Court charges in criminal cases are a pervasive feature of many criminal justice systems. For instance, in Germany defendants (unless entitled to legal aid) are, upon conviction, liable to pay court charges, prosecution charges and possible charges for representation of victim-complainants during the trial, on top of the costs of their own defence. Although court charges are widely used in other jurisdictions, they are far from unproblematic. In Germany, even when the prosecution and the

[53] On the wider chronic corrosion of criminal procedure in the UK and greater resort to summary justice see A Ashworth and L Zedner, 'Defending the Criminal Law: Reflections on the Changing Character of Crime, Procedure, and Sanctions' (2008) 2 *Criminal Law and Philosophy* 21.

[54] J Donoghue, 'Reforming the Role of Magistrates: Implications for Summary Justice in England and Wales' (2014) 77 *Modern Law Review* 928 at 929.

court are willing to discontinue proceedings,[55] the 'cost risk' of conviction is a significant disincentive for defendants that may incline them against pursuing a case to trial (in the hope of acquittal)[56] and agree to discontinuance even though this leaves them liable for their own defence costs.

Court charges were introduced in the UK under section 54 of the Criminal Justice and Courts Act 2015.[57] For reasons explored below, the court charge proved to be highly contentious and short-lived. At a time of severe budgetary constraint, the UK Justice Secretary introduced the court charge with the hope of raising £80 million per year ostensibly to cover some of the cost of running criminal trials in England and Wales.[58] Under section 54, convicted criminals were made to pay a charge towards the cost of their case and the running of the court system. Although the charge was defended on the grounds that it would raise additional revenue to support the criminal justice system at large, MPs, magistrates and judges, civil liberty and penal lobby groups immediately raised concerns. Many offenders are impoverished and unable to afford the charge in addition to paying the costs of compensation, the victim surcharge,[59] prosecution costs and fines and, as a result, might be pressed to enter a guilty plea rather than face the possible financial costs of proceeding to trial.[60] The mandatory imposition of a flat rate court charge for a guilty plea, irrespective of the circumstances of the individual or the nature of the case,[61] arguably undermined defendants' right to contest the prosecution case, created perverse incentives to plead guilty and was, therefore, widely regarded as a threat to the presumption of innocence. Where defendants insisted on proceeding to trial and were convicted they risked a higher sentence and a mandatory court charge towards prosecution costs of up to £1,200. Any order as to costs thus risked setting up a defendant to face heavy financial sums, not least in those cases where the defendant already had a number of court-ordered fines or costs outstanding.[62] Small wonder that the human rights organisation Liberty

[55] Permissible on a discretionary basis under ss 153 or 153a of the German Code of Criminal Procedure.

[56] Because on acquittal prosecution and court charges are met by the state.

[57] www.legislation.gov.uk/ukpga/2015/2/part/3/crossheading/costs-of-criminal-courts/enacted.

[58] T Ross, 'Chris Grayling unveils £600 court charge facing all criminals' *The Daily Telegraph* (23 February 2014) www.telegraph.co.uk/news/uknews/crime/10655903/Chris-Grayling-unveils-600-court-charge-facing-all-criminals.html.

[59] Introduced in 2007, the victim surcharge is a charge made upon convicted offenders used to fund victim services through a larger Victim and Witness General Fund: www.sentencingcouncil.org.uk/about-sentencing/types-of-sentence/other-orders-made-on-sentencing/what-is-the-victim-surcharge/.

[60] House of Commons, *Public Bill Committee Criminal Justice and Courts Bill Written Evidence* (London, The Stationery Office, 2014), Submission by The Prison Reform Trust at 20–21.

[61] Of £150 for pleading guilty to a summary offence in the Magistrates Court and £900 for pleading guilty to an indictable offence in the Crown Court.

[62] Ibid, Submission by Criminal Bar Association of England and Wales at 138.

observed, 'This is a shameful state of affairs for a criminal justice system with a proud reputation for fairness and integrity.'[63]

A restriction placed on access to a court or tribunal is not compatible with Article 6(1) of the European Convention of Human Rights (ECHR) (right to a fair trial) unless it pursues a legitimate aim *and* there is a reasonable relationship of proportionality between the means employed and the legitimate aim sought to be achieved. So considerable doubt was expressed as to whether the charge was compatible with human rights,[64] not least because access to justice had already been impaired by swingeing cuts to publicly-funded Legal Aid that pays for legal representation of poor defendants.[65] Further charges were applied under the 2015 Act to those who sought to appeal against conviction, which had the deplorable effect of unfairly dissuading the wrongfully convicted from seeking leave to appeal. Taken together, these financial restrictions on, and, for some, insurmountable hurdles to, access to justice gravely undermined the authority that the criminal process is supposed to lend to the criminal law. For all these reasons, the campaigning organisation, Justice, concluded that, '[w]ith little explanation of how the costs recovery scheme will operate, or any safeguards to protect the integrity of the criminal justice system, we consider the demand for court charges to be unprincipled, unjustified and unnecessary'.[66]

The House of Commons Justice Committee Report, published just six months after the implementation of the court charge, concurred in its conclusion that, 'we have grave misgivings about whether the charge as currently framed is compatible with the principles of justice'.[67] The Justice Committee found that the levels of charge fixed were grossly disproportionate to the means of many offenders, as well as to the gravity of many offences for which they were imposed; that the lack of discretion enjoyed by sentencers to impose or vary the level of charge created injustice; and that its effects were 'inimical to the interests of justice, creating perverse incentives which are affecting defendant and sentencer behaviour'.[68] Resignations by over 100 lay magistrates made in protest against the court charge added weight to these widely held concerns that the charge was a 'tax on justice'.[69] In December 2015, just months after its imposition, the court

[63] Ibid, Submission by Liberty at 69–70.

[64] Ibid, Submission by Justice at 94.

[65] The Legal Aid, Sentencing and Punishment of Offenders Act (LASPO) 2012 sought to cut £350 million from a legal aid budget of roughly £2 billion. F Wilmot-Smith, 'Necessity or Ideology?' (2014) 36(21) *London Review of Books* 15 (www.lrb.co.uk/v36/n21/frederick-wilmot-smith/necessity-or-ideology).

[66] Above n 64 at 96.

[67] House of Commons Justice Committee *Criminal Courts Charge*, HC 586 (London, The Stationery Office, 2015) at 16 (www.publications.parliament.uk/pa/cm201516/cmselect/cmjust/586/586.pdf).

[68] Ibid.

[69] www.independent.co.uk/news/uk/crime/tax-on-justice-michael-gove-scraps-criminal-courts-charges-after-independent-campaign-a6758616.html.

charge was revoked. Although the abolition of the court charge is undoubtedly welcome, the future of court charging may be subject to a review by the Ministry of Justice with a view to reintroduction of 'alternative ways of ensuring that criminals pay their fair share'.[70] Given that we maintain our criminal justice system in the public interest, a powerful counter argument might be that fairness requires it be funded from the public purse.

B. Corrosion of Summary Justice

Lay justice is an important facet of the common law in the United Kingdom. The magistracy is an historic institution dating back to the twelfth century, lauded as the embodiment of democratic accountability, active citizenship, local justice, and social representation in the criminal justice process.[71] Some 97 per cent of criminal cases are heard in magistrates' courts before a panel of three lay magistrates. Of the remaining three per cent of most serious cases heard before a judge in the Crown Court, the vital decision as to criminal liability is made by a jury of 12 lay people. It would not do to over-claim the ubiquity of lay justice; in many large towns and cities lower level courts are now presided over by District Judges who sit without a jury. However, they sit in open court freely accessible to the general public and the press. There is a strongly and widely held view that justice is well served by the openness of the court and the presence of the public, while the transparency and accountability that this ensures is an important check on state power.

Magistrates preside over criminal proceedings for a few hours each month as lay volunteers, they are not legally qualified and have limited training, and, for these reasons, they do not generally make decisions alone. The presence of three magistrates on a panel, who adjudicate in open court with a court clerk offering legal advice, provides some protection for defendants against the risks of inexperience, ignorance of the law, misunderstanding of the evidence, and against discriminatory or otherwise unjust decisions. The fact that decisions are made in open court at which the public and the press may attend offers some limited protection for the individual and ensures that justice is seen to be done. Magistrates perform a role analogous to a jury in the Crown Court in that their job is to reach a collective decision as lay members of the public in respect of a criminal charge against another member of the public. The idea of trial by one's peers is formally enshrined in the requirement under the Magistrates' Courts Act 1980 that trial and sentence be presided over by a court of no fewer than two magistrates.

[70] Written statement by Justice Secretary Michael Gove to the UK Parliament 3 December 2015 (www.gov.uk/government/speeches/courts).

[71] JC Donoghue, 'Reforming the Role of Magistrates: Implications for Summary Justice in England and Wales' (2014) 77 *Modern Law Review* 928.

The right to a 'day in court', while historically entrenched in the UK criminal justice system, is not universally recognised. Some European states allow for trials in absentia if certain conditions are met. German law allows for the disposition of less serious cases by way of a 'penal order' (*Strafbefehl*), which the defendant has to challenge within two weeks to force the state to hold a full trial and which, if unchallenged, counts as a criminal conviction for all purposes. Out-of-court disposals are also an increasing feature of the UK system: the wider use of conditional cautions, warnings, Fixed Penalty Notices (FPNs) and Penalty Notices for Disorder (PNDs), among others, divert many lower level cases away from the court process.[72] Quick and cheap to administer out-of-court disposals now account for about one third of all cases brought to justice.[73] Although not formal convictions they form part of an offender's criminal record and have adverse implications for employment prospects, travel visas, and may be invoked in the case of future offending. Additional problems include the fact that suspects may accept such disposals rather than risk going to court, there is evidence of variation in the deployment of fixed penalties, and concern that such disposals signal a disregard for victim interests; to say nothing of the lack of transparency, police accountability, and magisterial oversight all of which might better serve the interests of justice.

Moves aimed at 'transforming summary justice' apply not only to out-of-court disposals but also to the court process.[74] Sections 46 to 50 of the UK Criminal Justice and Courts Act 2015 radically depart from existing practice by providing for low-level cases to be heard before a single lay magistrate, rather than a bench of three, and for cases to be decided 'on the papers' behind closed doors rather than in open court. The introduction of 'proceedings by way of written charge' is defended on the grounds that it will enable more than three quarters of a million low-level cases to be dealt with more speedily and effectively, on grounds of cost and administrative efficiency. There is something to be said for a reform that promotes access to speedy adjudication and that reduces delay elsewhere in the system. However, opponents point out that such proceedings 'will effectively be a "rubber stamping" procedure and will reduce transparency'.[75] In a written submission to Parliament on the Criminal Justice and Courts Bill, the UK Criminal Bar Association argued, 'we consider that openness of court proceedings is

[72] Ashworth and Zedner, above n 53.

[73] Donoghue, above n 71.

[74] See eg Crown Prosecution Service, *Transforming Summary Justice: a Criminal Justice System-wide Initiative to Improve How Cases are Dealt With in the Magistrates' Courts* (London, Crown Prosecution Service, 2015) www.cps.gov.uk/publications/agencies/transforming_summary_justice_may_2015.html.

[75] Criminal Justice and Courts Bill, Second Reading (*Hansard* 24 Feb 2014 col 64); House of Commons *Public Bill Committee Criminal Justice and Courts Bill*, above n 60, Submission by Public and Commercial Services Union at 35.

an essential safeguard ... proceedings are required to be conducted in open court, to ensure that the judge and clerk are together acting fairly'.[76] This view was echoed by the UK Magistrates' Association, which argued that, 'it is a principle of British justice that cases are heard and the results are made known in public'.[77] The government responded to these criticisms, somewhat weakly with the promise that '[i]n order to preserve open and transparent justice, magistrates' courts will continue to publish daily case lists on the day of the appointed hearings. These lists are currently, and will continue to be, available to local media'.[78] Despite the government's wider transparency agenda and its wish to make court processes more accessible to the public, moving to adjudication of low level criminal cases by a single lay justice behind closed doors provides little assurance of a commitment to open justice. No wonder then that the rights organisation, Liberty, was scathing in its criticism:

> a magistrate deciding cases and sentences while sitting in private, fatally undermines the principle of open justice. The slow erosion of these bedrock principle risks dangerously undermining public trust and confidence in the criminal justice system over the long-term.[79]

Concerns about public trust are compounded by a provision that the procedure may be invoked not only in the case of guilty pleas received but also in cases of non-response by the defendant, even when there is no proof that the accused has actually received the relevant notices that legal proceedings have been instigated against them. It is highly questionable whether such proceedings abide by the Article 6 ECHR right to a fair and public hearing.

The provision for conviction and sentence to be decided by a single lay justice reading the papers alone is, by common consent, therefore a significant erosion of common law principles of openness, transparency and fairness. It seriously undermines the requirement that justice be seen to be done and the assurance of appropriate checks and balances furnished when a decision is reached by consensus in open court. By contrast, paper proceedings are, in the English context, widely viewed as lacking transparency, accountability and adequate public scrutiny. As such, these reforms pose a significant threat to public confidence in the legitimacy of the criminal process. The stripping back of usual due process protections in the interests of economy and speed is by no means confined to this reform. Other changes to summary justice include an expanded role for the police in prosecutorial decisions; the introduction of virtual courts in which offenders are tried by

[76] House of Commons, above n 60, Submission by Criminal Bar Association of England and Wales at 138.
[77] Ibid, Submission by The Magistrates' Association at 60.
[78] Ibid, Submission by The Magistrates' Association at 61.
[79] Ibid, Submission by Liberty at 69.

video-link from the cells of police stations;[80] 'streamlined' procedures; expedited trial of cases involving guilty pleas in dedicated magistrates' courts;[81] and the implementation of a national 'Trial Blitz' to reduce the backlog of cases.[82] Such reforms require investment in training, monitoring and review if they are to be implemented without seriously undermining the protections of due process, but investment is lacking at a time of severe budget cuts to all areas of policing and criminal justice. As a staff writer for the *Law Society Gazette* observed, '"summary justice" has connotations of justice made faster by omitting formalities required by law, which is no justice at all, of course. It also has overtones of vigilante law'.[83]

C. 'Exceptional Measures': Resort to a Partially Secret Trial

The final development to be considered is not legislative but judicial. It pertains to a single case but is of such pivotal importance to the authority of the state to enforce the criminal law that it invites close attention. It has been suggested that state authority to criminalise derives from its fundamental duty to provide security. In no case, one might think, is this authority more clear-cut than with regard to those who threaten the very existence of the state, namely suspected terrorists. And yet, as many academics have observed, the exercise of state powers in the name of security and counter-terrorism raises some of the most acute questions about the extent and limits to state authority.[84] At a time in which recurrent terrorist atrocities and the overwhelming insecurities of mass migration and the refugee crisis place exceptional pressure on governments to ensure security, the temptation to introduce emergency laws, measures and procedures is great—even

[80] J Ward, 'Transforming "Summary Justice" through Police-Led Prosecution and "Virtual Courts"—Is "Procedural Due Process" Being Undermined?' (2015) 55 *British Journal of Criminology* 341.

[81] www.cps.gov.uk/publications/agencies/transforming_summary_justice_may_2015.html#_03.

For critical comment see J Raynor, 'Transforming Summary Justice' *The Law Society Gazette* (18 May 2015)www.lawgazette.co.uk/law/practice-points/transforming-summary-justice/5048839.fullarticle.

[82] H Riddle, 'Get ready for the Trial Blitz' *The Law Society Gazette* (2 March 2015) www.lawgazette.co.uk/analysis/comment-and-opinion/get-ready-for-the-trial-blitz/5047175.fullarticle.

[83] Raynor, above n 81.

[84] B Ackerman, *Before the Next Attack: Preserving Civil Liberties in an Age of Terrorism* (New Haven, Yale University Press, 2006); D Cole and J Dempsey, *Terrorism and the Constitution: Sacrificing Civil Liberties in the Name of National Security* (New York, WW Norton & Co, 2002); R Dworkin, 'Terror and the Attack on Civil Liberties' (2003) 50(17) *The New York Review of Books* 1; O Gross and F Ní Aoláin, *Law in Times of Crisis: Emergency Powers in Theory and Practice* (Cambridge, Cambridge University Press, 2006); K Roach, 'Miscarriages of Justice in the War on Terrorism' (2005) 109 *Penn State Law Review* 967; L Zedner, 'Terrorizing Criminal Law' (2014) 8 *Criminal Law and Philosophy* 99.

where so doing entails derogation from the core protections of the criminal process.

In the UK, a particular area of concern has been the rise and spread of partially closed or entirely secret civil proceedings, most often in immigration and terrorism cases.[85] So-called 'closed material proceedings' are those from which defendants are excluded and at which they are represented by special advocates, that is to say, specially security-cleared lawyers appointed by the Attorney General to act in closed hearings necessitated by the sensitivity of the issues or the intelligence at stake. Special advocates represent those subject to such proceedings but, once they have seen the evidence, are not permitted to communicate with them without special permission. Closed proceedings are problematic because they seriously undermine the ability of those subject to them to know the case against them and hinder their capacity to defend themselves fairly and adequately.[86] Until 2014, closed material proceedings were applied only in civil cases in the UK.

Early in 2014, however, the UK Crown Prosecution Service (CPS) made an unprecedented application on the grounds of 'exceptional circumstances' for a criminal trial of two unnamed defendants known as AB and CD to be held entirely in secret. The two men were charged with collecting or recording information 'likely to be useful to a person committing or preparing an act of terrorism' under section 58 Terrorism Act 2000; one was also charged with making preparations for terrorist activity under section 5(1) Terrorism Act 2006; and the other also with possession of an improperly obtained passport. At an early closed hearing, the judge Mr Justice Nicol had granted the Crown an order that the trial 'should take place entirely in private with the identity of both defendants withheld' and with 'a permanent prohibition on reporting what takes place during the trial and their identities'.[87] The original application was granted on the grounds that without such secrecy the CPS would be unable to proceed to trial and that closed proceedings were necessary to protect the operation of security organisations and security service personnel.

Unsurprisingly, the public announcement that a criminal trial was to be held in secret for the first time in hundreds of years was met by fierce criticism of this 'totally unprecedented departure' from the long-established constitutional principle of open justice.[88] A legal challenge bought by a

[85] Justice, *Secret Evidence* (London, Justice, 2009); A Kavanagh, 'Special Advocates, Control Orders and the Right to a Fair Trial' (2010) 63 *Modern Law Review* 836; A Tomkins, 'National Security and the Due Process of Law' (2011) 64 *Current Legal Problems* 215.

[86] Ibid. See also Ashworth and Zedner, above n 11 at 188.

[87] 'Secret trial plan for English court' *BBC News* (4 June 2014) www.bbc.co.uk/news/uk-27704747.

[88] And not only by the liberal press, see T Whitehead and D Barrett, 'Secret Terror Trial is "Assault" on British Justice' *The Telegraph* (4 June 2014) www.telegraph.co.uk/news/uknews/terrorism-in-the-uk/10876499/Secret-terror-trial-is-assault-on-British-justice.html; P Johnston, 'Secret Trials: "Democracies Die behind Closed Doors"' *The Telegraph* (5 June 2014)

number of media organisations led to a ruling in June 2014 by the Court of Appeal that the identities of the defendants should be made known and that, although the 'core' of the trial was to remain secret, the remainder of the case should be heard in open court, albeit under severe restrictions.[89] The presiding judge, Lord Justice Gross, held that, 'Open justice is both a fundamental principle of the common law and a means of ensuring public confidence in our legal system' and he continued:

> We express grave concern as to the cumulative effects of (1) holding a criminal trial in camera *and* (2) anonymising the Defendants. We find it difficult to conceive of a situation where both departures from open justice will be justified. Suffice to say, we were not persuaded of any such justification in the present case.[90]

The Court of Appeal ordered that the swearing in of the jury and reading the charges; part of the judge's introductory remarks; part of the prosecution opening speech; verdicts and sentencing were to be held in open court. It also ruled that the identities of the defendants and the outcome of the trial should be made public. Significantly, however, there was to be no reporting of the core of the trial and only a small number of court-approved journalists were permitted to attend the closed hearing on the proviso that they surrendered their notebooks at the end of each day.[91]

Although the Court of Appeal ruling was applauded at the time as a victory for open justice by the press and by human rights groups, it was immediately clear that it allowed only parts of the trial to be heard in public. That decision was defended by the former Independent Reviewer of Terrorism Legislation, Lord Carlile, on the grounds that '[m]ost right-thinking members of the public would agree that if national security, particularly people's safety, is affected, then there may well have to be some parts of a trial held in secret'.[92] Such views were criticised by human rights lawyers on the grounds that despite the fact that 'a little bit of transparency is now in the mix', the courts had shown undue deference to ministers' concerns about national security and that the holding of a criminal trial largely in secret constituted 'a very dangerous precedent'.[93] While temporary resort to closed proceedings are a common feature of the criminal trial in the UK—for example, in the case of very young defendants or in cases involving

http://blogs.telegraph.co.uk/news/philipjohnston/100274921/secret-trials-democracies-die-behind-closed-doors/.

[89] *Guardian News and Media Ltd v AB and CD* [2014] EWCA Crim (B1); *Guardian News and Media Ltd & Ors v Incedal* [2014] EWCA Crim 1861, [2016] 1 WLR 1767.

[90] *Guardian v AB and CD*, ibid at [21]; *Guardian News v Incedal*, ibid at [47].

[91] These notes have never been returned to the journalists despite applications for their release.

[92] D Casciani, 'Fully Secret Terror Trial Blocked by Court of Appeal' *BBC News* (12 June 2014) www.bbc.co.uk/news/uk-27806814.

[93] 'Secret Trial Plan "Serious Threat to Justice"' *BBC News* (5 June 2014) www.bbc.co.uk/news/uk-27710985.

serious sexual offences—a wholly secret trial is a very serious erosion of rule of law requirements of open justice, transparency and fairness.

The chilling prospect of a conviction on the basis of evidence that most people, not least the defendants, would not be able to see and could never know about was scarcely mitigated by the small snippets of information that were ultimately released.[94] In the event, after one defendant, now named as Mounir Rarmoul-Bouhadjar, pleaded guilty to the possession offence, the jury acquitted the remaining defendant, law student Erol Incedal, of the more serious charge of preparing an act of terrorism and found him guilty only of the lesser charge of possessing 'a bomb-making document on a memory card likely to be useful to a terrorist'.[95] Incedal was found to have been in possession of a document entitled 'Bomb Making' and labelled as 'Good Stuff' on an SD memory card hidden in the cover of his mobile phone.[96] In the event, more than two-thirds of the trial was held in closed session, attended by only 10 'accredited' journalists who were themselves subject to stringent court orders as to secrecy and who were required to give up all their notes or face contempt of court proceedings. The reasons for continuing secrecy were never reported and, although the Court of Appeal in its ruling had argued that 'from time to time, tensions between the open justice principle and national security will be inevitable', it is very significant that, after the trial was concluded, the Lord Chief Justice, Lord Thomas, announced publicly that:

> We need to get the ground rules straight. We cannot have something like this, in my view, happen again ... The prospect of an anonymous defendant is one that I hope we would never, ever see again in our courts. I really passionately believe in open justice. Justice that is not open is not good justice.[97]

V. CONCLUSION

The criminal law and the authority of the state to enforce it depend upon the fairness, openness and legitimacy of the proceedings by and through which

[94] For example, one defendant used an alleged coded word that referred to 'k 11 22 aaa shhh', which prosecutors alleged may have referred to Kalashnikov rifles. 'Terror Trial: Suspect "had Tony Blair's Address"' *BBC News* (14 October 2014) www.bbc.co.uk/news/uk-29609660.

[95] 'Erol Incedal Secret Terror Trial: Suspect Convicted of Possessing Terrorist Information' *The Telegraph* (7 Nov 2014) www.telegraph.co.uk/news/uknews/terrorism-in-the-uk/11235297/Erol-Incedal-secret-terror-trial-Suspect-convicted-of-possessing-terrorist-information.html.

[96] 'Secret Terror Trial of Erol Incedal is "Exceptional"' *The Telegraph* (30 Oct 2014) www.telegraph.co.uk/news/uknews/terrorism-in-the-uk/11199777/Secret-terror-trial-of-Erol-Incedal-is-exceptional.html.

[97] D Casciani, 'Lord Chief Justice attacks secret trials' *BBC News* (12 November 2014) www.bbc.co.uk/news/uk-30024487.

the criminal law is administered. The tensions between the state's role in providing security through prosecution of criminal conduct and the threat that its actions in so doing may pose to individual security are not easily resolved. Recent developments described in this chapter test the limits of state authority by departing from the ordinary requirements of due process, by restricting access to justice, and by radically curtailing the ability of the individual to challenge the case for the prosecution. Where individuals are denied the protection from the arbitrary exercise of state power that the criminal process is supposed to supply, the rule of law is undermined. Where the courts are directed to sabotage their usual proceedings by recourse to secret hearings in a bid to secure a conviction in a case that might not otherwise be brought to trial, the rule of law is violated. The conclusion of the Lord Chief Justice that 'Justice that is not open is not good justice' is unassailable. The question remains, however, whether it is justice at all.

The nature of the state-citizen relationship; the question of what grounds the authority of the state to exercise coercive power over its citizens; the legitimacy conditions of its policing function; and the protections due to the individual against the arbitrary exercise of state power raise complex political, legal and ethical issues that merit deeper and more considered enquiry than has been possible within the confines of this chapter. Nonetheless it is clear that the legal developments here described test that authority, call into question its legitimacy, and undermine the basic protection of security against the state promised to the individual by the criminal process. The historic 'irrelation' between criminal law and criminal justice scholarship[98] is perhaps partly responsible for diverting academic attention from the fundamental importance of the integrity of the criminal process to the authority of the state to be author and prosecutor of the criminal law. Drawing together these two areas of scholarship might forge a better appreciation of the closely interdependent relationship between the legitimacy of the criminal law and the all too fragile structures, processes and practices by which it is enforced.

[98] Nelken, above n 9 at 139.

5

A Constitutional Perspective on the Criminalisation Process in Sweden

IAIN CAMERON

I. INTRODUCTION

MUCH INK HAS been spilled on the issue of criminalisation.[1] Criminal lawyers in many Western states consider that the criminal law is over-used, or even massively over-used, and they have exerted considerable efforts in trying to devise principles to prevent or limit this.[2] Many of these efforts involve in some way the 'harm principle'.[3] In Mill's words, 'the only purpose for which power can be rightfully exercised over any member of a civilised community, against his will, is to prevent harm to others'.[4] Outside of this area, according to Mill, the individual's freedom ought to be paramount.

The starting point for the present chapter is instead that we should focus on what we are trying to do, which is to restrict the power of democratically elected parliaments to legislate about the use of criminal sanctions.

If this is our aim, we can try to restrain criminalisation by means of constitutional norms (backed up by international commitments, such as under

[1] Criminalisation can be understood in a wider sense, meaning not just making punishable conduct which was not previously punishable, but also increasing sentences for existing offences. Removing discretion from judges in sentencing can have a similar effect. A similar phenomenon is removing jurisdictional limits on the extraterritorial application of the criminal law. I will not go into these more general expressions of an offensive (repressive) criminal law, but focus on criminalisation in its narrow sense.

[2] See, among many sources, D Husak, *Overcriminalization: The Limits of the Criminal Law* (Oxford, Oxford University Press, 2008) and A Simester and A von Hirsch, *Crimes, Harms, and Wrongs: On the Principles of Criminalisation* (Oxford, Hart Publishing, 2011).

[3] See, eg, J Feinberg, *Harm to Others* (Oxford, Oxford University Press, 1984); J Feinberg, *Harm to Self—The Moral Limits of the Criminal Law* (Oxford, Oxford University Press, 1986).

[4] JS Mill, *On Liberty* (Oxford, Oxford University Press, 1859) 14. He continues by stating that '[s]omeone's own physical, psychological or economic good should not be a basis for criminal prohibitions against voluntary behaviour'.

the European Convention on Human Rights (ECHR)). But while catalogues of rights can be seen as expressing the basic values of society, it is difficult to reduce all legitimate use of the criminal law in a complex society to the constitutionally protected rights to life, health etc.[5] Mostly, Western constitutions (and the ECHR) tend to content themselves with setting out criminal procedural limitations and guarantees. Their influence on substantive criminal law is more indirect. Certain things which strike at the heart of a constitutional right may not be criminalised: trade union membership, religious worship etc.[6] But unless it affects a human right, the legislature's ability to criminalise conduct is unrestricted, and even when it does affect a human right, the relative nature of most human rights means that restrictions are permissible if these are foreseeable, necessary in a democratic society etc. Constitutional rights can also forbid the use of certain types of criminal penalties, torture, degrading and inhuman treatment, the death penalty, retroactive criminal law etc.

Another, less ambitious method of using constitutional law to prevent over-criminalisation is to try to put in place rules governing delegation of the power to issue norms, and procedural rules for the preparation of legislation which are designed to facilitate a rational dialogue on the need, or otherwise, for legal reform. As a supplement to these binding general rules, one can attempt to formulate norms designed to operate to limit politicians' tendencies to criminalise conduct. In a democratic *Rechtsstaat*, such external constraints (in Husak's words) operate on a political level and cannot be without exceptions.[7] They can thus only be formulated as principles: what 'ought' to be done. They can be described as moral principles or principles of political philosophy.[8]

To some criminal lawyers, especially from the UK and the USA, where over-criminalisation has been claimed to be a major problem for some years, this second method (general rules promoting good legislation combined with weak principles) might seem useless. Are the politicians not the problem in the first place? Is this not akin to expecting foxes to exercise self-restraint in the chicken coop? Political scientists and constitutional lawyers, on the other hand, believe that rules and institutions (ie the organisations

[5] S Melander,' Kriminaliseringsprinciper och förutsättningar för begränsning av grundläggande fri- och rättigheter' (2002) 89 *Nordisk tidskrift for kriminalvidenskap* 237.

[6] I will not go into the more controversial role of the ECHR in *requiring* criminalisation. See F Tulkens, 'The Paradoxical Relationship between Criminal Law and Human Rights' (2011) 9 *Journal of International Criminal Justice* 577.

[7] See Husak, above n 2. Compare also N Jareborg, 'Criminalization as Last Resort (Ultima Ratio)' (2004) 2 *Ohio State Journal of Criminal Law* 521.

[8] Jareborg ibid. See further K Nuotio, 'Theories of Criminalization and the Limits of Criminal Law: A Legal Cultural Approach' in RA Duff, L Farmer, SE Marshall, M Renzo and V Tadros (eds), *The Boundaries of the Criminal Law* (Oxford, Oxford University Press, 2010).

and mechanisms making them work in practice) matter. Moreover, there is evidence that the relationship between institutions and political culture is not uni-directional, in the sense that one needs a well-functioning political culture before institutions can be said to be meaningful. This is correct, but the relationship is more complex than this: good institutions can foster good political culture, and bad institutions can foster bad political culture.[9] Of course, each state is unique, and one cannot expect that simply transplanting good institutions will transform states with bad criminalisation practices. Still, I think there is undoubtedly something—both positive and negative—to be learnt from the experience of other states.

The object of the present chapter then is to examine the general legal rules in Sweden on preparation of legislation, and the institutions which apply these. Together with the principles of criminalisation adopted by the Swedish parliament in 1994, these have facilitated a rational(ish) dialogue on the need, or lack of need, for criminalisation. As I will show, the dialogue has not always been as rational as one might hope. Twenty years after the adoption of these principles, a Commission of Inquiry on the Use of the Criminal Law published a critical appraisal of the criminalisation process, and put forward a number of proposals designed to strengthen the safeguards against over-criminalisation.[10] I examine the findings of this Commission of Inquiry and its proposals before closing with a number of concluding remarks.

II. THE SWEDISH LEGISLATIVE PROCESS

The Swedish legislative process can be represented graphically in the following way, with three columns, corresponding respectively to the roles of the parliament, government and different expert bodies.[11]

[9] See, eg, S Holmberg and B Rothstein (eds), *Good Government—The Relevance of Political Science* (Cheltenham, Edward Elgar Publishing, 2012); F Fukuyama, *The Origins of Political Order* (New York, Farrar, Straus and Giroux, 2011); D Acemoglu and JA Robinson, *Why Nations Fail: The Origins of Power, Prosperity, and Poverty* (New York, Crown Business, 2012).

[10] *Vad bör straffas?* [What should be punished?] (Statens offentliga utredningar, 2013) 38.

[11] For a more detailed treatment, see T Bull and I Cameron, 'Legislative Review for Human Rights Compatibility: A View from Sweden' in M Hunt, HJ Hooper and P Yowell (eds), *Parliaments and Human Rights: Redressing the Democratic Deficit* (Oxford, Hart Publishing, 2015).

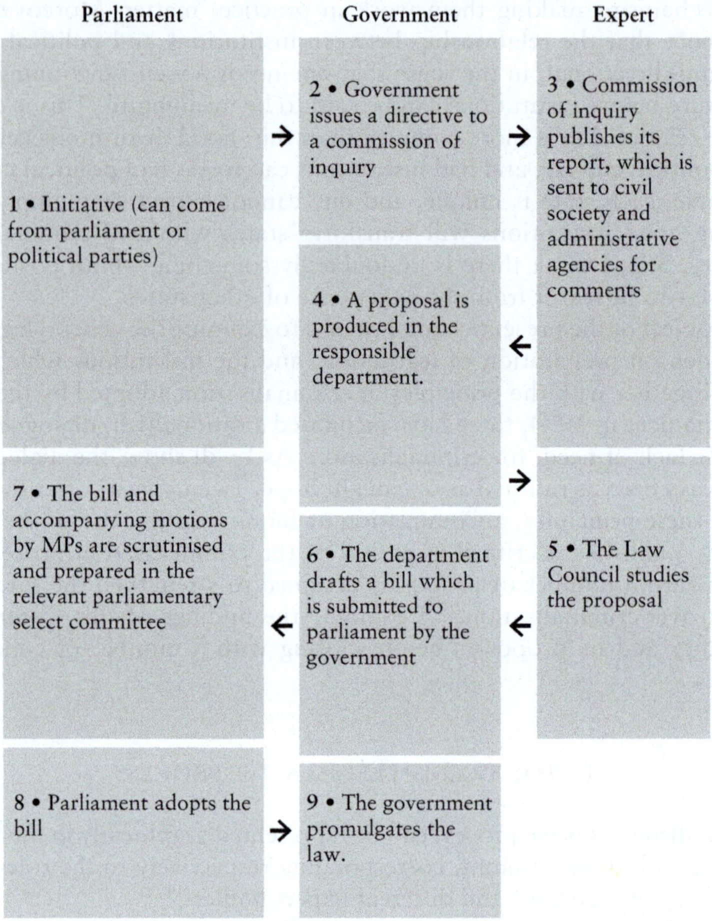

Figure 1: The legislative process in Sweden

Under Chapter 7, section 2 of the Instrument of Government (IG) (*Regeringsformen*),[12] all government decisions, including legislative bills, must be well prepared. This is the first, crucial, part of ensuring a rational legislative process. An initiative for introducing legislation can, exceptionally, be prepared within a parliamentary select committee, but the normal procedure is to appoint a commission of inquiry. A parliamentary commission (now unfortunately a minority of all commissions appointed) is composed

[12] SFS 1974:152. References to the Swedish statute book (*Svensk författningssamling*, SFS) or a government bill (proposition, prop) are by year followed by the relevant number. References to a statutory provision are by chapter and article number. Translations are my own.

of MPs from all parties represented in parliament, usually led by an expert on legislative matters (typically a serving or former Supreme Court judge or a professor of law or political science). As a rule, the commission also has experts from governmental agencies working in the field to be regulated and other experts (most often professors). The need to bring in 'outside' expertise exists because government departments in Sweden are rather small, a by-product of the separation between government and administration. The commission will be given a mandate (which can be broad or narrow) and a deadline for delivering its report containing any proposals deemed necessary for new legislation. Chronologically speaking, the first important factors in securing a rational dialogue are the openness and breadth of the commission's mandate, the person chosen to lead the commission and the time allowed for investigation and production of the report. An open mandate—'identify whether there is a problem, and if so, propose a variety of solutions'—fosters a rational dialogue. A closed and narrow mandate—'we know that X is a serious problem, choose solution A or B to deal with it'—does not. The personal characteristics of the leader of the inquiry are also important: is s/he expert in the relevant area, intelligent and open-minded?

General directives to all commissions are set out in the Ordinance on Commissions of Inquiry (1998:1474). They must take into account the constitutional and financial implications of any proposals made. In particular, under section 15a of the Ordinance, if a report contains proposals for new or amended regulations, the cost of the proposals and other consequences must be specified in the report. Furthermore, the consequences should be specified in a way that meets the requirements for impact assessments set out in sections 6 and 7 of the Ordinance on Impact Assessments of Regulatory Proposals (2007:1244).[13] The latter Ordinance provides in section 6 that an impact assessment, in addition to a description of the problem and the goals to be achieved, should also include a description of the alternative solutions available for achieving the goals, an indication of the consequences of abstaining from regulation, information on the costs and other consequences likely to result from the regulation, and a comparison of these with those of regulatory alternatives.

Every year about 100 commission of inquiry reports are published in the series *Statens offentliga utredningar* (hereafter SOU), some of which attract considerable media coverage. An alternative to a parliamentary commission is a departmental inquiry, usually used for more technical issues of law reform. This can be a one-person inquiry, or it can be conducted by a group

[13] Sweden has been influenced in this respect by the OECD, see OECD, *Regulatory Impact Analysis (RIA) Inventory*, 2005, www.oecd.org/dataoecd/22/9/35258430.pdf.

of persons. Typically, such a group consists only of civil servants from the departments and relevant administrative agencies, but external experts can also be appointed. Departmental inquiries are also published in *Departementserien* (Ds).[14]

Whether the report is published in the SOU or Ds series, it is then sent for consultation (*remiss*) to a wide range of institutions and organisations. This includes governmental agencies, courts and universities, as well as unions and NGOs. These bodies will be given the opportunity (usually within a three-month period) to present written comments on the proposal. These comments can be of any kind, but often end up either approving the proposal (in whole or in part) or recommending that the government refrain from basing any legislation on the commission's proposal. The media can pick up on critical comments. In the area of criminal law, it is not unusual for the parliamentary ombudsman and the government's chief legal officer, the Chancellor of Justice (JK), to criticise proposals for not sufficiently protecting legal certainty (*rättssäkerhet*). Nor is it unusual for the Prosecuting Authority and the Swedish Economic Crime Authority (responsible for investigating economic offences) to oppose new criminalisation proposals.[15] Strong and unified criticism from influential institutions and organisations can lead to changes to the draft bill, or even, though more rarely, to a proposal being quietly dropped. This, then, is another stage for a 'rational checkpoint'; another expression of the rule in IG 7:2 that legislation should be well-prepared.

If the proposal is not dropped, the relevant ministry prepares a draft bill which is sent to the Law Council (*lagrådet*).[16] The Law Council normally consists of six people, of whom four should be sitting judges of the Supreme Courts.[17] The remaining two can be retired judges from the same courts. The courts and not the government choose who to send to the Law Council, and this is usually done so that each judge will take his or her 'turn' of serving two years on the Council. The Law Council normally works in two sections with three members in each.

[14] The published reports for the last few years are: 2007: 53 Ds, 114 SOU, 2008: 53 Ds, 138 SOU, 2009: 69 Ds, 101 SOU, 2010: 46 Ds, 107 SOU, 2011: 49 Ds, 90 SOU, 2012: 56 Ds, 95 SOU, 2013: 87 Ds, 97 SOU, 2014: 66 Ds, 86 SOU, 2015: 109 Ds, 113 SOU. Not all of these inquiries were to investigate the need for new legislation.

[15] While these bodies tend to mention their lack of resources to deal with more work, objections based on ineffective design of offences or on a lack of legal certainty for the accused are not unknown.

[16] For more detail on the Law Council, see T Bull, 'Judges Without a Court: Judicial Preview in Sweden' in T Campbell, KD Ewing and A Tomkins (eds), *The Legal Protection of Human Rights: Sceptical Essays* (Oxford, Oxford University Press, 2011).

[17] The supreme courts, of course, do not permit members who have commented upon draft legislation as members of the Law Council subsequently to participate in a judgment on the constitutionality of that same law.

In accordance with IG 8:19, the Law Council's scrutiny of draft bills is focused on five specific issues: the effect on the Constitution, the coherence of the proposal with the existing system of legal regulation, the likely impact on the principle of legal certainty, whether the law is constructed in a way that will make it possible to achieve its underlying objectives, and, finally, to detect issues that may become problematic in practice. Proposals involving criminal penalties must, as a rule, be sent to the Law Council.[18] The specific issues it focuses on allow the Law Council to comment on how a proposed offence fits with the existing system of the Criminal Code, and on its compliance with accepted standards concerning the structure of offences, including the issues of foreseeability and overbreadth and the important question of whether the proposed offence definition will be effective in reducing the targeted behaviour. Several of these issues overlap with the matters to be considered in accordance with the principles of criminalisation (see below). The Law Council can and does pick up on criticism made during the consultation phase. But whether or not it pays attention to criticism concerning these criminal law issues depends largely on whether the section considering the proposal includes a judge who is an expert in criminal law.

The Law Council can be said to fulfil two different tasks. The first is quite technical, concerning the logic of the law and its effects: ensuring that terms and concepts are consistent with existing law, proposing new wording for individual provisions if they are imprecise or unintelligible, etc. Here one might say that the Law Council works as a highly qualified proofreader. The second task is quite different: checking any upcoming legislation against constitutional law and the principle of legal certainty. This involves the constitutional rules on the delegation of legislative powers to the government and local authorities, the protection of constitutional rights, and the general principle that legislation should be introduced in a foreseeable way. This kind of scrutiny—especially when the principle of proportionality is taken into account—comes much closer to the sensitive boundary between law and politics. Here we can talk about the Law Council as exercising a form of judicial preview.

The Law Council is only an advisory body, and its opinions have no formal legal effect. However, unlike legal advice given within a government department, the views of the Law Council carry special weight both by virtue of being independent and as coming from the highest judges in the

[18] IG 8:21 provides that the opinion of the Law Council should be obtained before the Riksdag takes a decision on inter alia a statute under [8:2] point 2 (see below). IG 8:19 provides that there is no need to send a draft bill to the Law Council if the change in the law in question is of minor importance (ie it is a minor technical issue) or if submitting the draft bill would delay the legislation such that major negative consequences would follow. The latter exception is occasionally invoked regarding taxation legislation.

country. Furthermore, this advice is given in full view of the public, open to all to peruse and discuss, facilitating informed public debate on complicated legal/constitutional issues.[19] The press routinely report on criticism made by the Law Council, and, where there is opposition in the Riksdag (parliament) to the government's proposal, such criticism provides this political opposition with ammunition. Moreover, if the government ignores the Law Council's warning, eg, that the goal of the statute cannot be achieved, or that a particular provision risks being applied in a disproportionate manner, the government knows that there is a clear risk that the courts, in later concrete cases, will take these warnings seriously and interpret the law accordingly.

Most of the 'quality control' of legislation is in fact done outside parliament. However, two further safeguards for a rational dialogue in parliament can be mentioned. The first is that all bills are reported to a parliamentary select committee. The second is that a minority of five members of a select committee may require that additional information be obtained from government agencies unless the resulting delay would have major negative consequences, in which case the majority can overrule the minority.[20] For example, the minority could requests further studies to be made, or perhaps that the Law Council provides its opinion if this has not already been done.

III. CONSTITUTIONAL RULES OF PARTICULAR RELEVANCE TO CRIMINAL LAW

Since compatibility with the Constitution is one of the specific issues the Law Council focuses on, this is a suitable place to discuss how the Instrument of Government regulates the use of the criminal law and the delegation of criminal law competence.

First, the principle of legality is set out IG 1:1. This constitutional rule is supplemented by a more specific criminal law principle forbidding vague criminal law and the use of analogies in criminal law.[21]

Second, custodial sentences involve an interference with a constitutionally protected right, namely that 'everyone shall be protected in their relations with the public institutions against deprivations of personal liberty' (IG 2:8). This is a 'strong' relative right, which may only be restricted by

[19] This is one of the more important features of the system, as it removes the government's 'monopoly' on expert legal opinion and makes it impossible for government to push through legislation without publicly acknowledging constitutional or other problems that might otherwise go unnoticed.

[20] See the Riksdag Act 10:9.

[21] The rule derives from s 5 of the law introducing the Criminal Code (SFS 194:163) but its scope has been developed by case law and influential doctrine. See P Asp, M Ulväng and N Jareborg, *Kriminalrättens grunder* 2nd edn (Uppsala, Iustus Förlag, 2015) 44.

statute after satisfying certain substantive conditions set out in IG 2:20. These provide basically that a restriction may only be imposed for a purpose which is acceptable in a democratic society, it may never exceed the bounds of what is necessary with regard to its purpose (proportionality), it may never go so far as to constitute a threat to freedom of opinion, which is a cornerstone of democracy, and it may never be made only on the basis of a political, religious, cultural or similar belief.

According to influential legal opinion,[22] the constitutional proportionality test should involve three elements, the first two of which are particularly important when it comes to criminalisation. First, it is necessary to pose the question: is the proposed measure capable at all of achieving the supposed goal behind it (prevention/reduction of the undesirable behaviour in question)? Second, are there other, less intrusive means of restricting the right? Both of these questions are empirical in nature. The third element is legal balancing stricto sensu, ie do the advantages of the proposed measure outweigh the disadvantages it entails?[23] Another important requirement, this time implicit in IG 2:20, is that of transparency in presenting arguments in favour of the law reform.[24]

As Asp has noted, there is a difference between the 'forward looking' constitutional principle of proportionality (primarily aimed at the legislature) and the 'backward looking' criminal law proportionality principle, primarily aimed at the courts when determining sentence. I will not go into the links between the two conceptions of proportionality in the present context beyond noting two things. First, notwithstanding the fact that any criminal statute containing a custodial sentence involves a restriction of a constitutional right, in the *travaux préparatoires* to criminal legislation, there is seldom, if ever, a structured application of the proportionality test along the lines advocated above. Such a three stage test would be a way of making the amorphous proportionality principle a bit more concrete. One can see the existing and proposed principles of criminalisation (below) as aiming at the same thing.

Second, it may be that we can expect a more structured application of the proportionality test in the future. The IG has been rewritten to make it more user friendly, and the courts have been explicitly encouraged by parliament to make more reference to it.[25] The Supreme Court, in fact, responded to

[22] T Bull and F Sterzel, *Regeringsformen, en kommentar* (Stockholm, SNS Förlag, 2011). The authors were influenced by R Alexy, *A Theory of Constitutional Rights*, translated by J Rivers (Oxford, Oxford University Press, 2002).

[23] See P Asp, 'Principles of Criminalization—What is "Criminal" in Criminal Law?' in M Ulväng and I Cameron (eds), *Essays on Criminalisation and Sanctions* (Uppsala, Iustus Förlag, 2014) 109.

[24] Bull and Sterzel, above n 22 at 101.

[25] Prop 2009/10:80, s 147.

this encouragement quite recently in a criminal case, acquitting an illustrator of Japanese 'Manga' comics who had, among his large collection of comics, a small number of illustrations in his possession depicting child-like comic characters in pornographic poses.[26] Notwithstanding statements in the *travaux préparatoires* to the legislation indicating that even 'fantasy' child pornography, not involving any real victims, was also covered by the prohibition of possession of child pornography, the Supreme Court employed the principle of proportionality to interpret the provision narrowly, and in the light of the constitutional right of freedom of expression.

Third, as regards fines, the constitutional protection of property IG 2:15 is not a strong relative right, and so does not need to satisfy the requirements of IG 2:20. Moreover, according to the *travaux préparatoires* to the provision, fines are by implication excluded from the scope of the right of property.[27] Nonetheless, the principle of proportionality is also a requirement of Article 1, Protocol 1 ECHR (even if the state's power to use fines is expressly saved, and the state's margin of appreciation is wide). Thus, Convention-based arguments can be made that fines must also be proportionate. And, as already mentioned, proportionality is also a principle of criminal law.

Fourth, a basic requirement for maintaining control over criminalisation is that the number of sovereign bodies capable of passing norms punishable by criminal penalties should be limited. However, the complexity of modern societies means that all states make exceptions to the principle that only the national legislature should criminalise. For example, in the UK, extensive delegation (to the government) and sub-delegation (to local authorities and administrative agencies) of criminal law competence has meant that it is difficult to obtain an answer to the very basic question of how much criminalisation there actually *is*.[28]

There is delegation, and even sub-delegation in Sweden, but it is constitutionally regulated. IG 8:2 provides that 'relations between individuals and the public institutions which relate to the obligations of individuals, or which otherwise encroach on their personal or economic circumstances' shall be adopted by means of a statute. This covers all obligations under public law, not just obligations enforced by specifically criminal penalties. There is an exception in IG 8:3, namely that parliament (Riksdag) may authorise the government to adopt provisions in accordance with IG 8:2

[26] NJA 2012, s 400.

[27] Bull and Sterzel, above n 22 at 89. I have previously criticised the illogical idea of implicit restrictions in constitutional rights which are formulated to contain explicit restrictions: I Cameron,'Vad är en begränsning av en rättighet'? in K Ahman (ed), *Regeringsformen 40 år, De Lege 2014* (Uppsala, Iustus Förlag, 2014).

[28] J Chalmers and F Leverick, 'Tracking the Creation of Criminal Offences' [2013] *Criminal Law Review* 543.

and even authorise the government to sub-delegate this to an administrative authority under IG 8:10. However IG 8:3 also provides that delegated competence may not prescribe 'legal effects of criminal acts other than the imposition of fines'. This means custodial sentences, but also conditional sentences of imprisonment, confiscation etc are excluded. Having said this, this rule is in turn subject to an exception, namely that 'the Riksdag may prescribe legal effects other than fines for contraventions of provisions laid down by the Government in an act of law granting authority under paragraph one'. Still, the result of this basic rule and series of exceptions is that while it is possible to delegate to the government competence to 'fill in', by means of an Ordinance, a criminal law statute containing custodial penalties, sub-delegation by the government of this competence to an administrative authority is not possible. It is possible to sub-delegate the power to prescribe conduct punishable by fines, and there are many such administrative regulations. Nonetheless, the fact that all criminal penalties, even fines, are traceable to a statute, means that it is possible in Sweden to identify the total criminalised area, even if it is still a very large task.[29]

IV. TWO EXAMPLES OF THE LEGISLATIVE PROCESS

I will give two examples of how the legislative process works to prevent over-criminalisation. The first concerns the prohibition of the wearing of masks in public assemblies. This was first proposed by the public inquiry following on the riots in connection with the international summit meeting in Gothenburg in 2001.[30] A new crime was proposed in a departmental report which would have forbidden the concealment of identity when participating in public gatherings. This proposal was heavily criticised during the *remiss* phase, but was taken to the Law Council anyway. The Law Council found that the proposal was unconstitutional, as it in practice prohibited covering one's face (eg, due to the cold) in such mundane circumstances as in a bus queue. It was obviously not proportionate to its purpose.

The government then withdrew its proposal, redrafted it and came back with a more narrowly tailored statute, introducing additional criteria such as the risk of violence, participation in a public assembly (rather than a simple public gathering) and a criminal intent to cause a disturbance of public order. The possibility to apply for advance permission by the police authority was also introduced, as a way of giving persons or groups with legitimate

[29] One can note that the blanket penalty attached to breaching of EU regulations issued in the area of the common agricultural policy adds considerably to this task. This can also be criticised as violating the principle of legality. See Asp et al, above n 22.

[30] See SOU 2002:122.

reasons for hiding their identity while demonstrating advance notice on how they would be perceived by the police. This proposal was approved by the Law Council and thereafter adopted as an Act of Parliament.[31] The example highlights the important role of the Law Council, as it most probably was the negative response from the Council that made the government reconsider its position. This might give rise to the impression that the preceding phase of commentary had no or little impact on the end-result, but this would be a misconception of the situation. The negative response by participants in the *remiss* phase (ie, courts, law faculties and the Bar Council) was in all likelihood instrumental in providing the Law Council with substantive arguments for its conclusion on the issue of constitutionality.

A second example is the legislative process on how to handle photographing in places which violates personal integrity. This has connections to several constitutional issues in Sweden, such as the constitutional protection of gathering information and the particular system of protection of the mass media that exists in our country, which, inter alia, provides for the sole responsibility of the editor for anything published in a periodical.[32] After a rather long period of indecision as to whether to do anything at all in the face of challenges that Swedish law is incompatible with Article 8 of ECHR on protection of private life,[33] the government produced a proposal in early 2011.[34] The proposal was to prohibit photographing people without their implicit or explicit consent, within a dwelling place, or in publicly accessible 'private' situations such as in showers or changing rooms, where this infringed their personal integrity. It also would have criminalised photographing people outdoors, but then only when the photograph would seriously violate their personal integrity. There was a public interest defence. In the *remiss* phase, many institutions (ie, the Parliamentary Ombudsman and the law faculties) as well as representatives of the mass media pointed out that the proposal was difficult to square with the constitutional right of everyone to gather information with the purpose of publishing it.[35] In cases where the photographer claims to have taken the photos with such a purpose, and such a claim would often be difficult to rebut, the law could not be applied. Thus, if no constitutional changes were made, the law would be an empty gesture with little effect on the protection of personal

[31] Prop 2005/06:11, SFS 2005:900.

[32] We can also note that, unlike in the UK, CCTV is relatively limited in Sweden.

[33] See the case of *Söderman v Sweden* No 5786/08, 12 Nov 2013, concerning a woman who was filmed, without her knowledge or consent, in a shower. The Grand Chamber found a violation of Art 8 because Swedish law (at the time) did not criminalise this, or provide for a remedy in damages.

[34] Ds 2011:1.

[35] Set out in the Freedom of the Press Act (TF) 1:1, and the Freedom of Expression Act (YGL) 1:2.

integrity. The government nevertheless went ahead with its proposal, arguing among other things that the constitutional protection of gathering information with the purpose of publishing it was not affected by the proposal. In its view, the constitutional protection did not extend to obtaining information through the commission of criminal acts (eg, burglary, theft) and this proposal would simply add a new exception to this list, making it a criminal act to take certain kinds of photos.[36] When the Law Council in 2012 scrutinised the proposal, it did not find the government's argument convincing, and instead pointed to the very real risk that constitutionally protected behaviour would in fact be criminalised if the law was adopted. The government backed down after that, but returned to the issue in late 2012.[37] The law as passed prohibits photography only in certain specific locations (ie, toilets, showers) when the photos are taken covertly. A general exception applies for acts that are justifiable due to the circumstances, serving as a safety-valve against disproportionate restrictions on the constitutional right to gather information. It is clear that the lengthy and open legislative procedure contributed to the creation of legislation that is much more sensitive to the protection of human rights than would otherwise have been the case.

V. THE CRIMINALISATION PRINCIPLES PRODUCED BY THE COMMISSION OF INQUIRY ON PROSECUTION

The Commission of Inquiry on Prosecution reported in 1992.[38] It considered that the criminal law was being overused and proposed five principles for criminalisation:

1. Before behaviour is prohibited, it should give rise to a concrete damage or danger.
2. Alternative measures to deal with it should either be unavailable, not be rational in the circumstances, or entail disproportionately high costs.
3. A penal sanction should be required in light of the seriousness of the conduct.
4. A penal sanction should be an effective means of countering the undesirable conduct.
5. The criminal justice system must have the resources necessary to deal with the extra burdens following from the criminalisation of the conduct.

[36] Ds 2011:1, pp 22–23.
[37] Proposal sent to the Law Council 20 December, Bill 2012/13:69, SFS 2013:366.
[38] SOU 1992:61.

When parliament adopted reforms to the Code of Judicial Procedure in 1994,[39] it endorsed these principles.[40] While the principles are not in the form of a law, preparatory legislative materials, unlike in the UK, have a high status in Sweden as a source of interpretative data.

Since 1994, the criminalisation principles have sometimes been made an explicit part of the mandates of commissions of inquiry involved in the preparation of criminal legislation.[41] However, there are also directives where these are not mentioned. Some of these directives where no mention is made of the criminalisation principles concern incorporation of treaty provisions,[42] but there are also directives concerning purely 'Swedish' proposals which make no mention of the criminalisation principles.[43]

It is in a commission of inquiry that the main discussion of the need for criminalisation should occur. However, bearing in mind what was said above regarding the restrictions this involves on constitutional rights, it is also necessary for the Riksdag explicitly to show that it has considered the need for criminalisation. Moreover, a more detailed discussion of the bill might be felt to be called for because objections to criminalisation have been raised during the consultation phase and/or by the Law Council. A search I made of the database of government bills (up to January 2015) produced 16 cases where there was explicit discussion of whether or not the principles of criminalisation could be said to be fulfilled.

Opinions differ on whether it is part of the job of the Law Council explicitly to raise concerns as to whether the principles of criminalisation have been followed.[44] Still, it is clear that the Law Council has, on occasion, done exactly this.[45]

[39] Bill 1994/95:23.

[40] SOU 1992:61 at 52–54.

[41] See, eg, Dir 2000:40 'more effective rules for combatting limitations on competition'.

[42] Eg Dir 2014: 155 One can argue that the policy issue of whether or not to criminalise in such cases might already have been determined when the decision was made to ratify or accede to the treaty. However, in most cases, parliament has not first decided to ratify the treaty, and then investigated the need for changes in the law: the two issues are usually dealt with together.

[43] Eg Dir 2015: 96.

[44] Personal communications with former Supreme Court justice Dag Victor and former President of the Supreme Administrative Court, Sten Heckscher.

[45] For a recent example, see 'Criminal responsibility for travelling for the purpose of terrorism' 2015-12-07. It can be noted that two of the members of that particular Law Council, Bo Svensson and Agneta Bäcklund, are experts in criminal law. The Law Council does not always argue against criminalisation. R Lavin, *Lagrådet och den offentliga rätten* (Uppsala, Iustus Förlag, 2009) 102–03, gives the example of a case where the Law Council (not including any criminal lawyers at the time) suggested that the proposed civil fine for unlawfully selling prescription drugs be supplemented with a criminal fine. The government replied that since such a criminalisation had not been the object of consultation, it would be inappropriate to add it to the bill at this late stage (an implicit reference to IG 7:2).

VI. FINDINGS OF THE COMMISSION OF INQUIRY ON THE USE OF THE CRIMINAL LAW

The Commission of Inquiry on the Use of the Criminal Law was established in April 2011 and reported in May 2013.[46] Its mandate was to map out the criminalised area since the entry into force of the Penal Code, to analyse which criteria should apply to criminalisation, to examine whether it is possible to be more restrained in the use of criminal law in various fields, mainly in the special areas of 'ancillary' criminal law, and if so how this can or should be achieved.

The Commission identified four main reasons for continued criminalisation. The first was societal change. The complexity of modern society creates a need for legal regulation. Moreover, the ways in which fraud can be committed or personal integrity can be attacked (eg, by means of the internet) have increased. Second, some criminalisation can be attributed to EU membership or result from international treaty-based obligations. Third, there has been increased criminalisation of inchoate offences involving creation of abstract risks.[47] Fourth, the link which exists between Swedish criminal law and the law of criminal procedure (more extensive investigative measures being available for more serious crime) means that there has been some 'instrumental' criminalisation, and increases in potential sentences, in order to facilitate investigations.

The Commission considered that in the legislative process regarding

> a large number of new criminalisations from the mid-1990s and up until today, there was no discussion of whether or not criminalisation is justified based on the criminalisation criteria. On the contrary, the impression is that in most cases there has been no such consideration whatsoever. Thus, examples of routine criminalisation that the Commission on Inquiry on Prosecution criticized still appear to be present in not insignificant numbers.[48]

In those cases where discussion did take place about whether the criteria for criminalisation were met, the Commission considered that the argumentation had sometimes been adapted to lead to a predetermined conclusion, and not infrequently to the conclusion that it was justified to criminalise the behaviour.[49] The Commission considered that a probable contributing factor was that the criteria devised by the Commission of Inquiry on Prosecution are

[46] *Vad bör straffas?* above n 10 at 38.

[47] See RA Duff and SE Marshall, '"Remote Harms" and the Two Harm Principles' in AP Simester, A du Bois-Pedain and U Neumann (eds), *Liberal Criminal Theory: Essays for Andreas von Hirsch* (Oxford, Hart Publishing, 2014) 205.

[48] *Vad bör straffas?*, above n 10 at 477.

[49] Ibid at 477–78.

> rather vague and capable of being stretched. If there is the will to criminalise certain activities, it seems in most cases to be possible to argue that the criteria are fulfilled. To be effective as a tool to restrict the use of criminal law the criteria need to be made more concrete.[50]

The Commission noted the legal requirement (noted above) that proposals that include the use of criminal law must contain impact assessments. But it considered that

> the impact analysis provided today is often relatively superficial. It is not infrequently stated that a new criminalisation is not expected to result in any additional costs for the legal system. Such a statement appears in the Committee's view directly contradictory because a new criminalisation, if it is to be taken seriously, reasonably must entail increased costs both in terms of criminal investigation and prosecution.[51]

To deal with this problem, the Commission proposed that commissions of inquiry should obtain sufficient evidence in the form of for example empirical studies or surveys by means of questionnaires. For that to happen, the time made available to commissions of inquiry must be adjusted so that they are given the possibility to gather and analyse such material. The Commission considered that it is not until after one has obtained knowledge about the estimated number of times the proposed offence is likely to be committed, that it is possible to make a reasonable assessment of the increased burdens this will entail for the criminal courts. An additional parameter that must be considered is what resources can be expected to be needed to investigate and prosecute infringements in question. One issue that should be addressed, for example, is whether the behaviour to be criminalised is easy to detect or requires more extensive investigative measures. Another relevant question is whether it is possible—with adequate resources—to prove the various constituent elements included in the offence, including the subjective requirements, ie if the perpetrator acted with intent. According to the Commission,

> particular vigilance is warranted when, in order to ensure the effectiveness of criminalisation, it is being advocated that negligent conduct also be criminalised… this jeopardizes the application of the fault principle, as for reasons of efficiency, the requirement of due diligence tends to be set so high that in practice this approaches strict liability. If one believes that setting an intent requirement would make necessary such investigative and prosecutorial resources that it would not be possible to criminalise efficiently, then, in the Commission's view, it would be more reasonable to instead consider other methods to curb the behavior in question.[52]

[50] Ibid.
[51] Ibid at 500.
[52] Ibid at 501.

A. The Criminalisation Principles Proposed

The Commission proposed five principles.

1. The proposed norm for criminalising the conduct in question must concern an identified and concrete interest that is worthy of protection (a protected interest).
2. The behaviour that is intended to be criminalised must be capable of causing injury, or a real risk of injury, to the protected interest.
3. Only those who have shown fault in some way—behaved wrongfully—should be criminally liable.
4. There must not be any sufficiently important countervailing interest.
5. There must not be any alternative method that is sufficiently effective for dealing with the unwanted behaviour. The considerations that should be made with regard to this criterion are:
   a) Is there an existing behaviour-steering rule that is sufficiently effective to counteract the unwanted behaviour?
   b) If a new behaviour-steering rule needs to be introduced, can the unwanted behaviour be countered sufficiently effectively by a rule that is not repressive (eg, a civil law rule providing for damages)?
   c) If it is necessary to impose a repressive behaviour-steering rule action to counteract the unwanted behaviour, the first option to be considered should be a civil fine, an administrative sanction or the revocation of a permit. Criminal punishment should be a last resort.

The following can be said comparing the existing and proposed principles.[53] The first two proposed criteria match the existing first criterion of 'seriousness'. The third criterion involves a new element, namely wrongfulness and the fault principle, which is understandable bearing in mind the special interest the Commission had in offences of strict liability. The fourth criterion refers to 'countervailing interests'; the Commission illustrates this with conduct which results in major harm to society (car accidents, alcohol-related criminality) but where broadly-formulated criminalisation would damage other socially desirable interests (communication, human interaction etc). The fifth proposed principle is a three-stage test: beginning with the need to consider whether new rules are necessary at all, and ending with the ultima ratio rule. The issue of whether or not the criminal justice system has the resources to deal with the new offence is not taken up as such, but in substance should be seen as included in the three-stage test. As noted,

[53] One can also envisage a comparison with Nils Jareborg's influential principles of criminalisation, which also take up other values for criminal legislation—legal certainty, humanity etc (see N Jareborg, *Allmän Kriminalrätt* (Uppsala, Iustus Förlag, 2001)) and with the principles proposed by the European Criminal Policy Initiative, December 2009 www.zis-online.com. For reasons of space I will leave these out of the present discussion.

the Commission considered that the resources argument had been misused: where there was likely to be only a few cases, this was used as an argument that criminalisation would not involve any great additional expenditure, instead of being an argument against criminalisation at all.

B. Analysis of the Commission's Findings and Proposals

The Commission in essence considered that the existing criminalisation principles had not been taken seriously enough. I agree that there have been cases where the need for criminalisation can be questioned, either because of the lack of sufficiently strong interest in criminalisation, or on effectiveness grounds. Even when there are sufficient arguments for criminalisation, objections can be raised regarding the breadth of the criminalisation in question, or the severity of the proposed penalties. For example, the criminalisation of purchasing sexual intercourse in 1998[54]—the Swedish model as it is occasionally called in debates in other countries—has been criticised as not protecting an *individual* interest. While it can be justified on the basis of a *public* interest in protecting sex workers from exploitation, this is in turn open to the attack that it is a form of new moralism.[55] The criminalisation of the possession of pornography depicting children in 1998[56] was supported by all political parties, even if there was a lack of evidence that consuming this type of pornography leads the consumers to commit sexual offences against children. Of course, the interest in preventing sexual offences against children is strong, and producing child pornography means committing very serious offences against children (although these acts were already criminalised and subject to heavy penalties). However, as already mentioned, the Act was framed widely to include possession of 'fantasy' drawings (eg Animé) of child pornographic characters. This could not be justified by the need to protect individuals and the public interest in prohibiting this is much less clear.[57] The introduction of the offence of grooming has also been criticised,[58] as has the reintroduction of the offence of sexual

[54] SFS 1998:408.

[55] P Asp and M Ulväng, 'Tvång, utnyttjande och kriminalisering av sexköp—del I' in P Asp and C Lernestedt (eds), *Josefs resa. Vänbok till Josef Zila* (Uppsala, Iustus Förlag, 2007).

[56] SFS 1998:1444, incorporated in the Penal Code 16:10a.

[57] As noted, the Supreme Court interpreted this provision narrowly, and in the light of the constitutional right of freedom of expression, acquitting a 'Manga' illustrator who had a small number of such illustrations (among a very large number of Manga comics) of criminal responsibility in NJA 2012, s 400.

[58] SFS 2009:343, incorporated in the Penal Code 6:10a. See P Asp,' Grooming—ett got skäl att gorma' in A Møller-Sørensen and A Storgaard (eds), *Jurist uden omsvøb. Festskrift til Gorm Toftegaard Nielsen* (Copenhagen, Christian Ejlers, 2007) 21.

intercourse with animals (*tidelag*),[59] now justified, not on biblical grounds, but on the basis of protection of animals, despite the empirical evidence that there are very few, or no cases to speak of.

The Commission in fact did not make a complete survey of all legislation since 1994 when the principles were, or should have been, invoked.[60] The Commission's findings were clearly influenced by the cases where it considered that the principles of criminalisation had not stopped unnecessary or overbroad or ineffective criminalisation. The preliminary survey I made of databases (noted above) does back up the Commission to some extent. It is true that in the discussion of some of the bills the principles were invoked in a superficial way, and that criminalisation was justified was a foregone conclusion. However, I consider that there were also examples from the legislative process where the principles were invoked against criminalisation, and examples where the invocation of the principles, together with the principle of proportionality, narrowed down the scope of an offence. Moreover, there is a methodological difficulty in measuring impact: a survey of bills, or even directives to commission of inquiries, cannot give a picture of whether the principles might have influenced, or even stopped, certain initiatives even before they got to the stage of a directive. (Of course, the opposite is also true: the mere fact that the principles are invoked as an argument against criminalisation does not mean that they are the real reason. The principles may be invoked when criminalisation is being opposed on other grounds.)

It is admittedly difficult to prove a negative. In any event, it seems clear that the level of criminalisation has been lower than in, eg, the UK. In this context one can note that Swedish politicians are certainly not incapable of coming up with proposals for ineffective, overbroad or just plain stupid criminalisation. Members of parliament can propose bills, by means of a 'motion'. A preliminary search of the database register for motions during 2015 gives a number of examples where criminalisation has been advocated. For example, MPs from the right wing populist party, Swedish Democrats, have advocated criminalisation of insulting the flag or other national symbols. MPs from the Christian Democrat party have advocated criminalisation of drinking alcohol immediately after being involved in a driving accident and removing the double criminality requirement from the

[59] For a—rare—example of a journalistic article questioning this 'politically correct' criminalisation see www.aftonbladet.se/nyheter/kolumnister/oisincantwell/article18401893.ab. The journalist, Oisin Cantwell, has also questioned the point of criminalising travelling for the purpose of terrorism and removing the double criminality requirement on the extraterritorial application of the law on purchasing sex.

[60] Personal communication from Prof Claes Lernestedt, expert in the Commission. Lernestedt's doctoral dissertation was on the issue of criminalisation. *Kriminalisering—Problem och principer* (Uppsala, Iustus Förlag, 2003).

extraterritorial application of the law on purchase of sex. MPs from the Moderate (centre-right) party have advocated criminalisation of escaping from Swedish prisons and purchasing amphetamines (possession and use of these are already criminalised). MPs from the Environmental Party have advocated criminalisation of bullying. Such motions are routinely dismissed by the Justice Committee of the Riksdag. The arguments for dismissing these proposals are usually not the criminalisation principles as such, but instead that the issue has already been examined by a commission of inquiry, and that it considered that criminalisation was not appropriate.[61]

Will the principles advocated by the Commission improve the situation? Probably, but in my opinion they will have only a marginal effect. Impact assessments accord with good legislative technique. But doing proper impact assessments is likely to be too much work and to take too much time: the time available for an inquiry is unlikely to be increased to more than six to seven months. In my opinion, other factors (dealt with in my concluding remarks below) are more important than impact assessments.

VII. CONCLUDING REMARKS

Isolating the impact of the principles of criminalisation from the other, more general factors influencing rational dialogue in the legislative process, and pushing for more sensible criminalisation, is not really possible. In these concluding remarks I will emphasise a number of these other factors at work in Sweden. First, however, I should note the obvious point that the alternatives to criminalisation are not always good. If a criminal penalty is replaced with severe administrative penalties, but without the strong safeguards of the criminal justice process[62] then this can be worse than criminalisation. The desire to remove (expensive) criminal provisions and replace these with cheaper administrative penalties was one of the considerations behind the establishment of the Commission of Inquiry on the Use of the Criminal Law.[63]

[61] See, eg, Justitieutskottets betänkande 2014/15:JuU14, Straffrättsliga frågor.

[62] See, eg, the sanctions set out in EU Directive 2014/56/EU of 16 April 2014, 2006/43/EC OJ L 158/196, 27.5.2014.

[63] I will not go into this issue (where there is a strong European—EU and ECHR—element) beyond noting that principles on when (and how) administrative penalties should be used in Swedish law were set out as long ago as 1982 (prop 1981/82:142). Two of these are of special relevance to criminal law, namely that a system of administrative penalties can offer an appropriate solution in cases of rule violations which are particularly frequent or where particular difficulties exist to calculate the size of the profit or savings that the person violating the rule would achieve in the particular case. Other cases are when the economic advantage to an individual of violating the rule can be considered low, at the same time as general non-compliance with the rule would mean considerable damage to society, so that steps should be taken not only to neutralise any financial benefit in the specific case, but even the prospect of profit or

The first factor, influencing rational dialogue, is particularly relevant to the UK. In my view codification is necessary before one can talk about meaningful restrictions on criminalisation. Nuotio notes that a codified system channels *how* criminalisation occurs,[64] but it does more. Codification makes for a more stable structure of crimes: offences which do not fit into this structure are more easily criticised. Codification allows doctrine to develop a greater value as a source of law, rather than primarily a commentary on case law. As Erik Svensson's chapter in the present volume attests, the significance of legal doctrine is much greater in Sweden than in the UK. Of course, codification in itself is insufficient to act as an obstacle to excessive criminalisation, as shown by the experience of the US and many other states with criminal codes. And the same can be said for states where doctrine has a high status as a source of law: this in itself does not stop over-criminalisation (probably because there is 'over-professorisation' in criminal law—someone can always be found to support any position).

A second very important factor is the constitutional rule that criminalisation with custodial penalties requires a statute. With the exception of the rule that the Riksdag can delegate to the government to 'fill in' elements of such a statute, there is no Swedish equivalent to 'emergency' legislation. The diffusion of the power to enact criminal law, backed by custodial penalties, to administrative authorities and local authorities is a recipe for excessive criminalisation.

A third factor is that Sweden applies the principle of legality of prosecution. This means increased focus on formulating the offence, because it is more difficult to avoid inappropriate prosecutions. The principle of opportunity (discretionary prosecution) in states where it applies is seen as providing a safety valve for inappropriate criminalisation and as such reduces the 'cost' of criminalisation.[65] Again, the principle of legality is not sufficient in itself to reduce over-criminalisation.

A fourth factor is the crucial role of the Ministry of Justice in ensuring that the principles are taken into account—by keeping directives open, referring explicitly to the principles in directives, ensuring that good people sit on commissions of inquiry and that commissions of inquiry have enough time. A commission of inquiry is an ad hoc body: it is the Ministry of Justice

savings. Furthermore, the provisions on calculating the amount of the administrative penalty should be constructed so that they proceed from a measurable and predictable component in the individual case.

[64] Nuotio, above n 8.

[65] In Sweden, under s 9 of the Police Act (1984:387), a police officer may choose not to register an offence, but only in 'insignificant' cases where it is 'manifest' that the offence would only be punishable by a fine.

which is to ensure continuity of expertise. In this respect one should note that the longer the head of the criminal law section in the Ministry remains in office, and the more generally respected s/he is, the more influence s/he can have over the process of criminalisation. The integrity of the civil servants working in the Ministry of Justice is very important. In a democracy, civil servants are supposed to obey the government, but even where the political parties in the government represent the majority of the electorate (which has not been the case for the past two governments in Sweden), this duty of obedience should not, in my view, be 'blind'.

The fifth and final factor is the openness of the legislative process. Politics is not simply (or even mainly) about rationality. What criminal lawyers can hope for is to have rationality checkpoints. If the politicians are so obsessed by their twittering and snap polls that they think that criminalising something is a vote-winner or standing up against it is a vote-loser, then that is what they will do, even if they know it is a waste of time and money. The speed of media discussion, the diminishing importance of formal media ('respectable' newspapers and public broadcast channels) together with the lack of specialisation among journalists (few of whom have, or develop, any expertise in criminal law and criminology) are negative factors in this respect. Even in Sweden, the ability to respond politically to rational arguments against a proposed legislative solution is not always great. Rational discourse can sometimes only go so far. Still, I would argue that a legislative system where multiple voices will be heard in multiple arenas before any final decision is made can be both more rational and more prone to favour legal arguments than a more closed system of legislation.

6

Against the State

ANAT SCOLNICOV

AN OFFENCE OF treason exists in every state, and is often considered the gravest of offences: 'No crime is greater than treason', the US Supreme Court held in 1870.[1] Treason typically carries the most serious punishment—life imprisonment, or death in states which have not abolished capital punishment. In the United States it is the only offence included in the Constitution.[2] In England, treason was the first criminal offence to be enacted in statute, protecting the King's body, and therefore the King's reign.[3] Conviction for treason bears a mark of dishonour conveyed by few other offences. But is this offence just a relic of an older era,[4] or can its existence be justified in a liberal state?

[1] *Haunauer v US* 79 US 342, 347 (1870) (Justice Bradley).

[2] The Constitution of the United States, Art III s 3 provides that: 'Treason against the United States, shall consist only in levying war against them, or in adhering to their enemies, giving them aid and comfort.' See also, 18 USC § 2381: 'Whoever, owing allegiance to the United States, levies war against them or adheres to their enemies, giving them aid and comfort within the United States or elsewhere, is guilty of treason.'

[3] The Treason Act 1351 (amended but still in force today) lays down that: 'Whereas divers Opinions have been before this Time in what Case Treason shall be said, and in what not; the King, at the Request of the Lords and of the Commons, hath made a Declaration in the Manner as hereafter followeth, that is to say; When a Man doth compass or imagine the Death of our Lord the King, or of our Lady his Queen or of their eldest Son and Heir; or if a Man do violate the King's Companion, or the King's eldest Daughter unmarried, or the Wife the King's eldest Son and Heir; or if a Man do levy War against our Lord the King in his Realm, or be adherent to the King's Enemies in his Realm, giving to them Aid and Comfort in the Realm, or elsewhere, and thereof be probably attainted of open Deed by the People of their Condition: … and if a Man slea the Chancellor, Treasurer, or the King's Justices of the one Bench or the other, Justices in Eyre, or Justices of Assise, and all other Justices assigned to hear and determine, being in their Places, doing their Offices: And it is to be understood, that in the Cases above rehearsed, that ought to be judged Treason which extends to our Lord the King, and his Royal Majesty'. See also The Treason Felony Act 1848, s 3, rendering treason a felony punishable by transportation 'beyond the seas for the term or his or her natural life' (today this means life imprisonment for life or a shorter term: Penal Servitude Act 1857, s 2 and Criminal Justice Act 1948, s 1(2)).

[4] In the words of Lord Steyn in *R (on the application of Rusbridger) v Attorney-General* [2003] UKHL 38, [2004] 1 AC 357 [28]: 'The part of section 3 of the 1848 Act which appears

This chapter examines this offence, which, strangely, has not engendered much theoretical discussion. In criminalising the most direct challenge to the authority of the state, treason presents a serious test to any theory of criminalisation as well as to any theory of the state. For the criminal lawyer, it is a matter of concern that the connection to harm to persons is contingent, and often not strong enough to justify the sanctions threatened, and imposed. For the public lawyer, the offence raises fundamental questions about the relationship between the state and its subjects. Does the offence presuppose that legal subjects owe the state loyalty—and is this an obligation that may be enforced coercively?

Prosecutions and convictions for treason are rare. An investigation into the justification of this offence is nevertheless not only of theoretical importance, but also of practical relevance, for several reasons:

First, while no prosecution for treason has taken place in the United Kingdom since the aftermath of World War II,[5] the 'war on terror' after 9/11 has revived the use of indictments for treason (and related offences) in the United States of America. This is exemplified by the case of Adam Gadhan ('Al-Amriki'), an American citizen who posted Al Qaeda videos on YouTube urging war on America. He was indicted for (among other offences) treason, but was killed before he could be brought to trial.[6]

Second, even when prosecution for treason does not take place, the possibility of such a prosecution can serve to paint prosecution for other, lesser offences in more sinister colours. This might, for example, be suggested by the punishment inflicted on Bradley (now Chelsea) Manning, a US soldier who was found to have passed on information to WikiLeaks founder Julian Assange. Manning was charged under the US Military Code with several counts, including 'aiding the enemy'.[7] Although acquitted of this charge, Manning was convicted of various data and computer misuse offences.[8] In the defendant's own view, Manning had not acted in betrayal of the US. The judge appears to have agreed, although it is impossible to know on what grounds, as the judgment was handed down without reasons.

to criminalise the advocacy of republicanism is a relic of a bygone age and does not fit into the fabric of our modern legal system. The idea that section 3 could survive scrutiny under the Human Rights Act is unreal.' The Law Commission in its 2008 *Tenth Programme Of Law Reform* (Law Com No 311) 16 suggested future reform of the offence citing its 1977 Working Paper *Codification of the Criminal Law. Treason, Sedition and Allied Offences* (Law Com WP No 72).

[5] The last being *Joyce v Director of Public Prosecutions* [1946] AC 347 (prosecution of 'Lord Haw-Haw').

[6] First Superseding Indictment, *United States v Gadhan aka Al-Amriki* SA CR 05-254(A) (CD Cal Odt 11, 2006).

[7] Uniform Code of Military Justice 10 USC § 904–Art 104.

[8] *US v Manning* US Army First Judicial Circuit (15 August 2013), available at https://freedom.press/sites/default/files/Manning-verdict-special-findings.pdf.

Notwithstanding Manning's acquittal on the charge of aiding the enemy, a heavy sentence of 35 years' imprisonment was imposed. This may suggest that the colouring of a prosecution with a suggestion of betrayal of the state in itself can turn lesser crimes into heavily sanctioned convictions.

Finally, the gravity of the offence carries an unmistakeable message from the state. Its broad wording, in conjunction with the prominent textual position of the offence, usually towards the beginning of the criminal code,[9] or even in the Constitution,[10] conveys both strong disapproval by the state of behaviour which constitutes treason, and a threat of punishment designed to deter such disloyal behaviour.

In this chapter I will analyse justifications for the offence, both those which have been suggested in the existing literature[11] and others which could be suggested. These are based on harm, duty, loyalty, allegiance, social contract, moral wrongfulness, community and the integrity of the state. In Part I I will examine each of these possible justifications in turn, showing that none of them manages to provide a valid justification for criminalisation of treason in a liberal state. Then, in Part II, I turn to examining the political assumptions regarding the role of the citizen in the state which lie behind the criminalisation of treason. Applying the German *Rechtsgut* analysis to existing treason offences, I demonstrate that the main problem in justifying the offence lies in the difficulty of identifying the social interest protected by the offence. I conclude that the criminalisation of treason cannot be reconciled with the liberal justification of state authority.

I. JUSTIFICATIONS FOR CRIMINALISATION OF TREASON IN A LIBERAL STATE

This section considers the range of justifications which have been put forward in the existing literature. First, however, I should clarify what I mean by 'treason' for the purposes of this discussion. Offences of treason are defined in a variety of ways in different jurisdictions. All of these formulations of the offence include acts that cause harm to others (whether by endangering the

[9] Eg in the Criminal Code of Germany, at the beginning of the Special Part: Ch One, Second Title.

[10] As in the US Constitution, above n 2.

[11] See, eg, A Brudner, 'The Wrong, the Bad, and the Wayward: Liberalism's Mala in Se' in F Tanguay-Renaud and J Stribopoulos (eds), *Rethinking Criminal Law Theory* (Oxford, Hart Publishing, 2012) ch 3; M Gur Arye, 'The Nature of Crime: A Synthesis, Following the Three Perspectives Offered in the Grammar of Criminal Law' (2008) 27 *Criminal Justice Ethics* 91; G Fletcher, *Loyalty: An Essay on the Morality of Relationships* (Oxford, Oxford University Press, 1995); Y Lee, 'Punishing Disloyalty? Treason, Espionage, and the Transgression of Political Boundaries' (2012) 31 *Law and Philosophy* 299.

security of the state's population or similar harm). This type of treason I shall call 'mixed treason'. But many versions of the offence also include actions that do not harm others in any direct sense. An offence of treason which is a pure crime against the state is one where no resulting harm is required, nor even the creation of risk of such harm: the mere act of treason suffices to constitute the offence. An example of pure treason is an announcement of disloyalty to the state and a call on others to follow suit. This I shall refer to as 'pure treason'. In the discussion that follows, I will mainly be concerned with the justification of 'pure' treason offences. I will, however, occasionally refer to differences with the analysis of 'mixed' treason.

A. Harm-based Justification

A good starting point for this inquiry is provided by the liberal justification of criminalisation offered by Hart[12] and based on Mill:[13] a criminal offence is only justified if it prohibits behaviour that causes harm to others.[14] Pure treason, however, is behaviour which causes no such harm. One could, of course, here speak of 'harm to the body politic'.[15] Yet a threat to political stability is not one that the harm principle recognises as harm in the relevant sense. Harm, in this sense, is constituted by a setback to an interest upon which the harmed individual has a normative claim.[16] The harm principle, in other words, protects the resources that individuals have against

[12] HLA Hart, *Law, Liberty and Morality* (Oxford, Oxford University Press, 1963).

[13] JS Mill, *On Liberty* (London, Parker, 1859) ch 1.

[14] Modern liberal writers have relaxed the strictness of the Millean harm principle somewhat. Joel Feinberg (in J Feinberg, *Offense to Others* (New York, Oxford University Press, 1985)) recognises an offence principle alongside a harm principle as providing legitimate grounds for criminalisation, and others give the harm principle a reading where any conduct (whether or not directly harmful) whose prohibition reduces the incidence of harmful events in the future, can be subsumed under it. With such extensive interpretations, it is unsurprising that one writer, B Harcourt, has diagnosed 'The Collapse of the Harm Principle' ((1999) 90 *Journal of Criminal Law and Criminology* 109 at 186). For discussion, see further AP Simester and A von Hirsch, *Crimes, Harms, and Wrongs: On the Principles of Criminalisation* (Oxford, Hart Publishing, 2011) chs 4 and 5; RA Duff and SE Marshall, '"Remote Harms" and the Two Harm Principles' in AP Simester, A du Bois-Pedain and U Neumann (eds), *Liberal Criminal Theory: Essays for Andreas von Hirsch* (Oxford, Hart Publishing, 2014).

[15] Perhaps this thought explains why Hart himself gives treason as a paradigmatic example of harm. I assume he means treason by which harm has been caused in that the state has been put in danger or similar. This type of conduct might, in appropriate cases, come close enough to endangering or causing injury to individuals that it can be classed as 'mixed treason' which is the usual case in which prosecutions for the offence will take place. (HLA Hart, 'Immorality and Treason' *The Listener* (30 July, 1959) 162 reprinted in RA Wasserstrom (ed), *Morality and the Law* (Belmont CA, Wadsworth Publishing, 1971).

[16] Cf J Feinberg, *Harm to Others* (New York, Oxford University Press, 1984) and, for discussion, H Stewart, 'Harms, Wrongs, and Set-backs in Feinberg's "Moral Limits of the Criminal Law"' (2001) 5 *Buffalo Criminal Law Review* 47.

unwarranted invasion by others.[17] So, the harm principle in this simple form cannot justify the criminalisation of treason.

That the offence is not, at heart, concerned with the prevention of harm as such is fortified by an analysis of its scope. Typically, treason can only be committed by persons who have a specified connection to the state. These are usually citizens, although in some states they may include others as well, for instance anyone who owes allegiance to the state such as aliens who are present in the state.[18] (In this chapter I will refer to 'citizens', but this term is to be understood, unless stated otherwise, to refer to the category of actors defined by the treason law as falling within its ambit.)

Just how crucial the relationship of the perpetrator to the target state is to this offence, is evidenced by *Joyce v DPP*,[19] arising from the prosecution of 'Lord Haw-Haw' who broadcast German propaganda in English during World War II; the last prosecution for treason to have taken place in the UK. Here the House of Lords devoted a lengthy discussion to explaining why Joyce had an allegiance to the Crown and therefore could have committed treason, despite the fact that he was not a British subject.[20]

Similarly, in the US prosecutions connected with the 'war on terror', those suspected of potentially treasonous activities have been both citizens of the target state and non-citizens. While there is not much difference between the ideology and self-understanding of citizen and non-citizen terrorists, or between the levels of threat they pose in the target state, treason laws, and the political conception they represent, treat the two types of suspects very differently. So, in the *Gadhan aka Al-Amriki* case mentioned above, the accused was indicted for treason (among other offences) as he was a US citizen and was therefore taken to owe allegiance to the US.[21] Had someone who does not owe allegiance to the US made the videos, the potential threat of harm would have been the same, yet the offence of treason would not have been committed. The elevation of the indicted offence from incitement to terrorism to treason was based solely on the defendant's citizenship.

[17] Simester and von Hirsch, above n 14 at 36–37.

[18] In the US the offence can be committed by anyone owing allegiance to the state—see n 2 above. In the UK the offence is also understood to require allegiance to the Crown: See the discussion of *Joyce v Director of Public Prosecutions* (above n 5) directly below. In Sweden, however, the offence does not appear to require any connection of the perpetrator to Sweden. The Swedish Penal Code, Ch 19 S 1, provides: 'A person who, with the intent that a measure or decision of the Head of State, the Government, Parliament or the supreme judicial bodies be coerced or obstructed with foreign aid, engages in an act involving a danger of this occurring, shall also be sentenced for high treason.'

[19] *Joyce v DPP*, above n 5.

[20] In Canadian law, an offence of treason when committed by a Canadian citizen becomes high treason (carrying a higher sentence): Criminal Code RSC 1985, s 46 (3).

[21] *United States v Gadhan (aka Al-Amriki)*, above n 6.

If any further proof were needed that treason is not predicated on harm, this limitation to a specific category of actors provides it. The danger, or harm, caused by an act such as the publication of an inciting YouTube video is not dependent on the citizenship of the person who posted it. This is further indication that this offence, in contrast to liberal theories of criminalisation, is in some way, which needs to be explored, concerned more with the actor than the action.

Even in the case of 'mixed' treason, harm to others cannot stand on its own as a justification. This is so because the presence of harm still leaves unexplained both the level of punishment threatened and imposed (which is frequently much higher than for a non-treasonous offence of intentional harmdoing), and the restriction of the offence to certain actors only.

B. Duty Justification

If the harm principle cannot supply the main justificatory pillar for the criminalisation of treason, then other justifications, acceptable in a liberal state, should be sought for this offence.

A possibly supplementary, possibly alternative, justification for the criminalisation of treason put forward by Gur Arye[22] is based on a duty of a citizen to his or her state. Whereas a harm principle-based justification cannot explain the limitation of the offence to specific actors, the distinction between citizens and non-citizens would be understandable if duty were the basis of this offence. It is also more plausible to assume that a state might be able to impose specific duties on its citizens (as opposed to non-citizens). A citizen's relation to the state is different from that of a non-citizen. Citizens have legal rights in the state that others do not have, such as a right to enter the state, and different legal obligations towards the state.

Can duty in itself create a justification for a criminal offence? There are indeed offences which are premised on a breach of duty by the actor. But all these offences differ from treason, in that (i) the duty is based on a voluntary undertaking of the duty by the actor, or at least on an implied undertaking of such duty; and (ii) there is still a requirement of harm.

An example of an offence premised on an undertaking of duty by the actor is the offence of embezzlement by an employee. Every employee has chosen to become an employee, thereby undertaking a duty not to embezzle from the employer. An example of an offence premised on an implied undertaking is the offence of parental neglect of a child. Although there is of

[22] Gur-Arye, above n 11.

course no contract of parenthood, by bearing children parents do undertake the duty to look after their children.[23]

If the criminalisation of treason were to be based on breach of duty, it would, however, in most cases be a very different kind of duty from the examples given above. There may be rare occasions where the perpetrator of an offence of treason has previously voluntarily undertaken a specific duty to protect the interests of the state or to maintain confidentiality about its affairs—such is the case, for instance, with members of the armed forces or of the civil service.[24] But were the duty to be grounded simply on citizenship, then it would be unique, since the offence would require no voluntary undertaking of duty, as other duty-based offences do. For most people, citizenship is not a matter of choice, but a product of their birthplace or their parentage.[25] Typically, mere citizenship is indicative neither of a choice nor of any consent to a duty by the actor; and in any event none of the existing treason offences restrict their application to only citizens-by-choice. To criminalise 'pure' treason on the ground of the breach of a duty derived from citizenship would therefore amount to criminalising otherwise legal behaviour on the basis of an involuntary status. This would be incompatible with a liberal understanding of the authority of the state.

C. Allegiance and Loyalty

An alternative to duty-based justifications which has deep historical roots focuses on allegiance or loyalty. In his *Commentaries on the Laws of England*, William Blackstone explains that:

> Natural-born subjects are such as are born within the dominions of the crown of England, that is, within … the allegiance of the king; and aliens, such as are born out of it. Allegiance is the tie, or ligamen, which binds the subject to the king, in return for that protection which the king affords the subject. … Natural allegiance is such as is due from all men born within the king's dominions immediately upon their birth. For, immediately upon their birth, they are under the king's protection; at a time too, when (during their infancy) they are incapable of protecting

[23] It is interesting that in most jurisdictions there is no similar offence of neglect of parents—not a relationship based on choice. 'Due to the lack of enforcement, case law imposing a duty to act on an adult child under a filial responsibility statute is non-existent': L Stiegel, E Klem and J Turner, *Neglect of Older Persons: An Introduction to Legal Issues Related to Caregiver Duty and Liability* (American Bar Association Commission on Law and Aging, 2007) 5.

[24] Note that the Manning case discussed above differs from the typical case of treason under the aspect of duty-based justifications for the offence. Because a soldier voluntarily undertakes a loyalty duty (usually through oath), in these circumstances this duty could be a basis for the criminalisation of treason.

[25] *Jus sanguinis e jus soli.*

> themselves. Natural allegiance is therefore a debt of gratitude; which cannot be forfeited, cancelled, or altered.[26]

Furthermore, it is the King-in-Possession to whom allegiance is owed. As Blackstone asserts:

> [T]hough there be a usurper of the crown, yet it is treason for any subject, while the usurper is in full possession of the sovereignty, to practice anything against his crown and dignity.[27]

This object of allegiance is so confusing that Blackstone deduces the logical but absurd conclusion:

> But, in truth, this seems to be confounding all notions of right and wrong; and the consequence would be that when Cromwell had murdered the elder Charles, and usurped the power (though not the name) of king, the people were bound in duty to hinder the son's restoration.[28]

Alongside 'high treason', the offence of 'petty treason' included treason of a wife against her husband and a servant against his master. Blackstone explains that:

> [T]reason is indeed a general appellation, made use of by the law, to denote not only offences against the king and government, but also that accumulation of guilt which arises whenever a superior reposes a confidence in a subject or inferior, between whom and himself there subsists a natural, a civil, or even a spiritual relation.[29]

Historically, then, the offence of treason was based on subjugation; the relation of allegiance which it presupposed was not a reciprocal, but rather a hierarchical relationship. The subject has a duty of allegiance to his king, and the king offers protection to the subject. Over time, though, the notion at the heart of this relation, that 'a superior reposes a confidence in a subject or inferior, between whom and himself there subsists a natural, a civil, or even a spiritual relation'[30] moved from allegiance to loyalty, as part of an historical development of wider significance and in parallel with linguistic and cultural change. As Benveniste explains, the Latin word for loyalty—fidēs—had undergone a transformation, and 'develop[ed] into a subjective notion, no longer the confidence which is inspired in somebody, but the trust which is placed in somebody'.[31]

[26] W Blackstone, *Commentaries on the Laws of England* (Oxford, Clarendon Press, 1765–1769) Vol 1 at 366.

[27] Blackstone, ibid Vol IV ch 6.

[28] Ibid.

[29] Ibid.

[30] Ibid.

[31] E Benveniste, *Indo-European Language and Society* (Miami, University of Miami Press, 1973) ch 8.

Today, of all these allegiances protected by the criminal law, only that allegiance of the subject to the King remains. Other relationships based on allegiance, such as between husband and wife, which have historically evolved into ones based on loyalty, are considered a private matter and no longer a subject of the criminal law. Allegiance of a subject to a king has developed into a more elusive relationship between citizen and state, and has remained a relationship enforced by the criminal law. This propinquity of the offence to long abolished crimes itself calls into question the validity of the remaining fragment. We now view allegiance or loyalty as a matter of personal choice, not to be enforced by the criminal law.

Nevertheless, a justification based on loyalty has an important advantage over a duty-based justification. While duty is a unilateral relationship, loyalty suggests a reciprocal one. Is it possible that a bond of loyalty ties an individual to the state in a manner which can justify criminal enforcement?

Loyalty is the basis of the justification for this offence offered by Fletcher in his seminal work dealing with treason and related offences.[32] The state, he argues, can demand and enforce a bond of loyalty from its citizens,[33] and can enforce it through the criminal law. In a later work he located this approach within a more general communitarian political theory.[34] Indeed, it may turn out that a treason offence can only be justified in a communitarian theory of the state, but not within a liberal theory of the state. A communitarian theory of the state can value individuals' familial and social connections over individual choices.[35] The individual is considered part of the state not just as a political entity but as a social, communal unit. So the state can protect the cohesion of this communal unit even at the expense of the individual's choice *not* to identify with this community. This is a point I will return to in the next section. At present I want to focus on the idea of loyalty as such.

On what ground can the state demand loyalty? The same difficulties exist here as the previous section identified in the case of duty-based arguments. People do not decide to be born in the state of their birth. Some degree of

[32] Indeed, this is the only theoretical monograph on this offence.

[33] Fletcher, above n 11. See also G Fletcher, 'Ambivalence about Treason' (2003–2004) 82 *North Carolina Law Review* 1611.

[34] G Fletcher, 'Political Theory and Criminal Law' (2006) 25 *Criminal Justice Ethics* 26.

[35] Elsewhere I have distinguished between strong and weak versions of communitarianism. For strong communitarians, such as Alisdair MacIntyre, the self occupies a given social space, and is almost entirely a product of circumstances. For weak communitarians, such as Michael Sandel, the identity of the self is a product of ties and attachments as well as personal choices. Weak communitarians accept that personal choices play a role alongside social connections in forming the identity of individuals. In this, they are different from liberals on the one hand and from strong communitarians on the other. See A Scolnicov, *The Right to Religious Freedom in International Law: Between Group Rights and Individual Rights* (Oxford, Routledge, 2011) 43–45.

choice or agency is exercised in the case of acquired citizenship. But even where citizenship is acquired, it is not necessarily the product of a free choice. For instance, refugees have little choice over their safe haven. Most people are citizens and residents of the state they were born in. Not all of them feel a sense of loyalty to that state. This is particularly true of members of national minorities, disenfranchised groups, and possibly harmless anarchists, but not only those. They are not lesser citizens because they feel no loyalty towards the state.

Moreover, no one in a liberal state should be penalised for their feelings of loyalty or disloyalty, whether or not they make them known. A duty of loyalty is a duty with an affective content. While a just liberal state can demand that one obey its laws (subject to the usual caveats), it cannot demand one's loyalty any more than it can demand one's love. Both are affects, emotions internal to a person, which cannot be externally demanded.

The loyalty-based justification raises two further difficulties. The first is the demand of loyalty to a specific state and the second relates to the more general implications of understanding crime as disloyalty.

The first problem is that it is tricky for a liberal to justify loyalty *to a particular state*. If liberals uphold justice, democracy and respect for human rights, then why should we not owe the same degree of loyalty to any state which respects these? If loyalty to certain values is protected by this offence, then the offence should criminalise disloyalty to *any* liberal-democratic state.[36]

Should a liberal state require loyalty only of its own citizens? Or should it require that every person be equally loyal (or at least respectful) to all liberal states? The answer to this question has varied among liberal writers. Liberal cosmopolitans see no specific value in loyalty to the state of one's nationality, whilst liberal nationalists value such loyalty. A middle approach is taken by Stilz: assuming a democratic and just state, citizens owe allegiance to *their* state of nationality because of the value of cooperation with their fellow citizens in achieving that just state.[37]

That brings us to the second problem with disloyalty as a basis for criminalisation of treason. If *mere* disloyalty can be a justification to criminalise treason, then that entails that disloyalty is a valid reason for criminalisation. That comes uncomfortably close to a general theory of criminalisation based on disloyalty. Compare the concept of treason in liberal states to that

[36] Austria's criminal law is an exception to this state-centric approach to treason. Section 316 of the Austrian Penal Code makes treason against another state (by anyone) an offence, although a lesser one than treason against Austria (the former is punishable by imprisonment of six months to three years).

[37] A Stilz, *Liberal Loyalty: Freedom, Obligation, and the State* (Princeton, Princeton University Press, 2009).

of treason in a Fascist state. As Fletcher notes, the Fascist state treated *all offences*, not only treason, as crimes of disloyalty towards the state. It was the breach of the duty of loyalty towards the state displayed by such acts, rather than the harm caused, which was punished.[38] That is the very essence of a Fascist state: the criminal law serves to uphold loyalty to the regime. But in a liberal state it is difficult to justify loyalty as the criminal law's concern.

D. The Community Justification

Under a communitarian theory of the state, the treason offence can be justified because the state has a reason to demand our loyalty to a *specific* political community rather than to a universal ideal of a liberal community. Alan Brudner has defended such a community-based justification in connection with his broader claim that the state may use the criminal law to protect human dignity.[39] He makes the point, already explored here, that treason[40] is a crime not sufficiently explained by the harm principle. His pertinent example is the criminalisation, as treason, of disclosure of military or scientific secrets to a foreign country that is *not* an enemy state. No harm is caused since the secrets will not be used against the state, but the act still falls under the Canadian treason offence. (In Canada, divulging military or scientific secrets to a foreign state is treason, and if the state is an enemy state the offence becomes high treason).[41]

Therefore, Brudner claims, there must necessarily be another justification for the offence, and he reaches the conclusion that for a liberal:

> Treason is a crime because the life sufficient for dignity is not an imaginary cosmopolis populated by metaphysical agents but an actual political community composed of self-identifying Canadians, Americans, Britons, etc. and distinct from other communities.[42]

Brudner sees the existence of this offence, absent a harm requirement, as indicative of the existence of another basis for legitimate criminalisation: namely, community. Of course, the absence of harm in pure treason could

[38] Fletcher, above n 34. This can perhaps be seen as a specific, corrupted instance of the approach to criminalisation in German criminal law, encapsulated in the notion of the *Rechtsgut*, that all wrongs are public wrongs, although there might also be a private wrong in them. (See further below and K Nuotio, 'Theories of Criminalisation and the Limits of the Criminal Law: A Legal Cultural Approach' in RA Duff et al (eds), *The Boundaries of the Criminal Law* (Oxford, Oxford University Press, 2010) 238.

[39] Brudner, above n 11.

[40] 'Pure treason' in the terms used in this chapter.

[41] Criminal Code RSC 1985, s 46.

[42] Brudner, above n 11.

equally lead to the opposite conclusion: not that there must necessarily exist another justification for treason which therefore must be accepted by liberals as a valid basis for criminalisation, but rather that criminalisation of pure treason is simply not justified in a liberal state.

Brudner's argument relies quite heavily on drawing parallels with offences related to the family, such as prohibitions on polygamy or incest.[43] Even under communitarian theories of the state, however, the community is not equal to the family, even though both have social importance. It is an illiberal conception of the criminal law and an illiberal conception of the citizen in the state to assume that a citizen has a duty to the state akin to the duty one owes to his or her family. 'The public life sufficient for dignity', says Brudner, 'fosters the relationships within which the worth of determinate characters is validated—families, civil associations and political community'.[44] But the relationship between a citizen and the political community (inasmuch as it means the state), is *not* like either the relationship between family members or the relationship between members of civil organisations which those individuals have *chosen* to join.

E. Social Contract Justification

Our examination so far suggests that treason, rather than an offence necessary and justified in a modern liberal state, remains at odds with the development of liberal ideas on the role of the state in enforcing social relationships. But it is worth considering whether the argument that the obligation of loyalty to the state can be enforced by the criminal law, could be bolstered by placing it within the theory of social contract. Matravers has laid the groundwork for a general contractual theory of state regulation of conduct through the criminal law.[45] Although his argument pertains to the system of criminal law as a whole, it is an apt way to view in particular criminalisation of treason.

Matravers follows the accepted categorisation of social contract theories into two views. He provides an account of the criminal law under each of these contractarian views.

The Hobbesian approach[46] views the state as a contract between self-interested agents. Each individual enters into the contract knowing that

[43] Brudner himself says that most 'signpost' laws deal with the family or with sexuality (ibid at 72).
[44] Ibid.
[45] M Matravers, 'Political Theory and the Criminal Law' in RA Duff and S Green (eds), *Philosophical Foundations of Criminal Law* (Oxford, Oxford University Press, 2011) ch 4.
[46] See T Hobbes, *Leviathan* (1651).

s/he can rely on enforcement of others' obligations towards her/him. This accounts for the enforcement of these mutual obligations through the criminal law.

In the Kantian[47] approach the contract is not of self-interested obligations, but of a mutual undertaking to adhere to a moral code. The need for state enforcement under this theory is not to assure self-interest but because each of us wants to know that the others will adhere to the same moral code.

Under this second approach it is fairness that justifies the intervention of the criminal law. Fairness can serve to justify not only enforcement of the moral political contract but also to justify the specific offence of treason. It is not to some elusive 'state' that we owe a legal duty, but to others who have undertaken this duty towards us. There is an obligation of 'fair play' we all owe each other[48] (and for which the existing democratic institutions and processes serve as accepted shorthand).

The social contract theory solves a problem encountered by the loyalty justification. Shifting the relationship protected by criminalising treason, from one of loyalty between citizen and state, to one of *mutual* obligations of citizens, focuses the offence on a relationship that is easier to defend within liberal political theory.

But two further problems would need to be answered by anyone who would advocate a contract theory of criminalisation as a justification for criminalisation of treason:

First, even if as citizens we owe it to our fellow citizens to abide by 'fair play', it still needs to be explained why this principle of political morality can legitimately be enforced by the state specifically through use of the criminal law.

Second, even if a citizen has a moral obligation to 'play fair', a reason is needed as to why this moral consideration should not be balanced against other moral considerations. In some circumstances there might well be countervailing moral reasons for action that outweigh this obligation. Of course, it is true also of other criminal offences that in some situations there might exist countervailing moral considerations, and the justification defences provide scope for considering these. The difference is that the 'fair play' obligation is not particularly strong to begin with and is therefore likely to be outweighed much more frequently.

[47] See I Kant, 'Perpetual Peace: A Philosophical Sketch' [1795] in I Kant, *Kant: Political Writings*, translated and edited by HS Reiss (Cambridge, Cambridge University Press, 1991).

[48] See the discussion of this idea in R Dworkin, *Law's Empire* (Cambridge MA, Harvard University Press, 1986) 195.

F. Wrongfulness

This last point raises more generally the question how the moral wrongfulness of the conduct of the traitor affects the possibility of justification for this offence. It is probably relatively uncontroversial to argue, in principle, for the *moral* wrongfulness of disloyalty, of breaching even an implicit non-binding agreement, or ignoring 'fair play', all accusations which can be levelled at a traitor. Many liberal legal theorists take the view that the moral wrongfulness of an act as such supplies the state with *a* reason in favour of criminalising the behaviour in question[49]—although few theorists, if any, would treat this reason as sufficient on its own.[50] The 'extra element' required on some accounts (at least for an in principle case for criminalisation) appears to be only that the behaviour be a public rather than a private wrong.[51] Other writers insist that the requirements of wrongfulness and harmfulness are cumulative: conduct must be both wrongful and (potentially) harmful in order to make the case for criminalisation.[52]

If behaviour is criminalised on the ground that it is morally wrongful, then this would suggest a need to balance the moral wrongfulness of the betrayal inherent in acts of treason with other possible countervailing moral considerations.[53] Under such a *moral* balancing of wrongs it is not at all clear that loyalty to one's state of citizenship outweighs countervailing moral reasons, such as an imperative to act against some wrong committed by one's state.

Moreover, there may even be a moral duty in some cases to be disloyal to the state. A liberal should demand that one *reject* a despotic government,

[49] See M Thorburn, 'Criminal Law as Public Law' in Duff and Green, above n 45 at 21 (analysing the views of Antony Duff and John Gardner as major proponents of this view). The reliance on wrongfulness is criticised by T Hörnle, '"Rights of Others" in Criminalisation Theory' in Simester, du Bois-Pedain and Neumann, above n 14 ch 9, who prefers to make rights-violation the guiding principle.

[50] This would appear to be the position of Duff, Simester and von Hirsch. The outlier is Michael Moore who rejects such a side-constraint; see MS Moore, *Placing Blame: A General Theory of the Criminal Law* (Oxford, Clarendon Press, 1997).

[51] See RA Duff, 'Towards a Modest Legal Moralism' (2014) 8 *Criminal Law and Philosophy* 217.

[52] Simester and von Hirsch, above n 14 and A von Hirsch, 'Harm and Wrongdoing in Criminalisation Theory' (2014) 8 *Criminal Law and Philosophy* 245.

[53] A simple 'balance of reasons' account of wrongfulness has been put forward by AP Simester, 'Enforcing Morality' in A Marmor (ed), *The Routledge Companion to Philosophy of Law* (New York, Routledge, 2012) 481. Antje du Bois-Pedain argues that, for the purposes of the criminal law, only other-regarding (and in this sense distinctly moral) reasons ought to be taken into account in the balancing process. See A du Bois-Pedain, 'The Wrongfulness Constraint in Criminalisation' (2014) 8 *Criminal Law and Philosophy* 149 and reply by JR Edwards and AP Simester, 'Wrongfulness and Prohibitions' (2014) 8 *Criminal Law and Philosophy* 171.

and *not* be loyal to it.[54] But the proper reaction to a despotic state is an easy case. It is more difficult to determine the apposite response to the many states which are generally benign but fall short of the liberal ideal in many ways. It is much less obvious whether in such cases a liberal should always be loyal to the state, or may betray it when it is acting contrary to liberal ideals.

The important upshot of this discussion is to pose a further challenge to the current scope of the offence. A wrongfulness requirement (which on its own is in any event insufficient justification for the criminalisation of treason) is not satisfied by current formulations of the offence. These leave no room for moral balancing, whereas any morally justifiable definition of treason must take into account a need for such balancing. However, any formulation of a treason offence broad enough to allow such balancing would probably be so vague as to contravene the principle of legality.

G. Upholding the Integrity of the State

The state has a legitimate interest in ensuring its continued smooth operation. A liberal state is justified in requiring its citizens to uphold the continuous existence and operation of the public institutions which support its continued functioning. That is the justification, for instance, for offences involving election fraud.[55] Adherence to the system of government is necessary to its continued operation and may thus be demanded by the state.

However, there are several reasons why this, too, cannot serve as sufficient justification for the offence: first, if this is the justification for the treason offence, it is not clear why the same demand is not also made of anyone who is not a citizen. A non-citizen might perhaps have less opportunity than

[54] Following J Locke, *Second Treatise on Government* (1689) 115–16 (available at www.earlymoderntexts.com/assets/pdfs/locke1689a.pdf). There are modern examples of an explicit recognition of such a right. In 1968, when incorporating emergency powers into the 1949 German Federal Constitution, the memory of the decline of the Weimar republic and of Nazi rule which had relied heavily on emergency powers, persuaded the German parliament to enshrine a right to resist efforts to overthrow the constitutional order (*Grundgesetz für die Bundesrepublik Deutschland*, Art 20(4)). In the immediate phase of political reconstruction after World War II, the constitutional assembly of one of Germany's regional states, Hesse, had drawn an even more radical conclusion from the Nazi experience and given its citizens not just a right but imposed upon them a duty to resist public authority exercised in violation of the Constitution. See du Bois-Pedain, above n 53 at 167 fn19 and *Verfassung des Landes Hessen* of 1 December 1946, Art 147(1).

[55] UK: Representation of the People Act 1983, Electoral Administration Act 2006; US federal offences: 18 USC § 594 (intimidation of voters), 18 USC § 608(b) (vote buying and false registration), 42 USC § 1973i(e) (multiple voting), 42 USC § 1973gg-10(2) (fraudulent voting or registering).

a citizen to participate in election fraud, but has no more *right* to do so than a citizen. Similarly, if treason were truly an offence premised on the protection of public institutions, there would be no requirement that it can only be committed by citizens or others who owe allegiance to the state. But, as has been seen, there is generally some affiliation requirement for the offender.

Second, there is a mismatch, a lack of proportion, between the severity of the punishment (and generally the gravity accorded to this offence), and the rather remote harm to the functioning of the state needed to commit this offence.

More fundamentally, we should ask: the integrity of the state according to whom? Political adversaries will have conflicting opinions as to what preserves the integrity of the state as they conceptualise it. In a liberal state, the criminal law cannot protect the integrity of the state as viewed by the government and the governing party, one side in the democratic political community, over the integrity of the state as viewed by other political parties. In a liberal democracy, the government has a sanctioned monopoly over making *operative decisions* on behalf of the state, and that monopoly can be enforced by the criminal law if anyone tries to interfere with it. But the government does not have a monopoly over *structural questions* concerning the identity of the state, and citizens are no less entitled than their government to hold views on such matters and on what is necessary to preserving its integrity.

Overlooking this is the central weakness of the justification of the treason offence put forward by Youngjae Lee. Lee argues that the basis of treason is the transgression by the actor of the division of power between the citizen and the state.[56] However, the assumption that a person who breaches the delimitation of powers commits treason can be questioned. It is indeed the role of the (legitimate) authorities of the state to decide how the state should act in its relations to other states, and not the role of the citizen. But from a liberal perspective there is no reason why a citizen should not challenge these decisions *merely* because they are within the state's powers. Of course, there may be reasons why a citizen should not act in the realm of the powers of the state, as when doing so causes or threatens harm to others. But a mere breach of this division of power cannot count as a sufficient reason in a liberal state.

II. THE INTEREST PROTECTED BY THE OFFENCE (*RECHTSGUT*)

The elusive character of the offence and the opacity of the interest protected by it, revealed by the discussion so far, were also commented upon by

[56] Y Lee, 'Punishing Disloyalty? Treason, Espionage, and the Transgression of Political Boundaries' (2012) 31 *Law and Philosophy* 299.

Blackstone. Indeed, the need for clarity regarding this crime was precisely the reason why it was the first criminal offence to be enshrined in statute:

> [B]y the antient common law, there was a great latitude left in the breast of the judges, to determine what was treason, or not so: … that is, to raise, by forced and arbitrary constructions, offences into the crime and punishment of treason, which never were suspected to be such. Thus the accroaching, or attempting to exercise, royal power (a very uncertain charge) was in the 21 Edw III held to be treason in a knight of Hertfordshire who forcibly assaulted and detained one of the king's subjects till he paid him ie: a crime, it must be owned, well deserving of punishment; but which seems to be of a complexion very different from that of treason. Killing the king's father, or brother, or even his messenger, has also fallen under the same denomination.[57]

The ominous consequences of an indeterminate criminal offence were not overlooked by Blackstone:

> If the crime of high treason be indeterminate, this alone (says the president Montesquieu) is sufficient to make any government degenerate into arbitrary power. And yet … there was a great latitude left … whereby the creatures of tyrannical princes had opportunity to create abundance of constructive treasons… [t]o prevent the inconveniences which began to arise in England from this multitude of constructive treasons, the statute 25 Edw III c 2 was made; which defines what offences only for the future should be held to be treason.[58]

The uncertainty concerning what conduct amounts to treason was removed to some extent by the legislation Blackstone refers to, but a lack of clarity as to who or what is *protected* by the criminalisation of treason remains to this day.

What is ambiguous about the treason offence, and has been lacking in its analysis, can be brought to the fore by making use of a concept of German criminal law—the *Rechtsgut*.[59] This refers, literally, to the 'legal good', or the interest or value, protected by the offence, and in Germany is used to analyse and assist the interpretation of each criminal offence.

Although English law does not employ such a concept, and therefore does not include anything like this among the elements of a criminal offence, the

[57] Blackstone, above n 27 Vol IV ch 6. See also the opening words of the Treason Act 1351, above n 3.

[58] Ibid.

[59] For a brief explanation of the *Rechtsgut* concept see the 'Editors' Introduction' to Simester, du Bois-Pedain and Neumann (eds), above n 14 at xxiii–xxiv. See further on the difference between German and English criminal law in approaching the interpretation and justification of offences, O Lagodny, 'Basic Rights And Substantive Criminal Law: The Incest Case' (2011) 61 *University of Toronto Law Journal* 761; MD Dubber, 'Theories of Crime and Punishment in German Criminal Law' (2005) 53 *American Journal of Comparative Law* 679, and more generally, M Bohlander, *Principles of German Criminal Law* (Oxford, Hart Publishing, 2009) 19.

notion that criminalisation serves to protect *Rechtsgüter* is illuminating.[60] Analysis of the treason offence in terms of the *Rechtsgut* protected has the advantage of drawing attention to criminalisation as an exercise of public law. As Nuotio notes, in German law, all criminalised conduct is understood as a 'public wrong' (although there may be a private wrong involved as well) because offences are understood to criminalise violations of interests judged to be of sufficient significance to require protection through the criminal law.[61] In a *Rechtsgut*-based penal system, the wrong involved in any offence is thus always a legal wrong (although it may simultaneously be a physical wrong, as in the case of offences requiring bodily harm etc.) as it involves violation of a legally protected interest. This scheme of analysis does not remove the need to justify the treason offence within liberal principles, as it still requires an explanation of the significance of the interest being protected, but it does assist in understanding what is at stake in doing so.

If we approach existing treason offences from this perspective, then it becomes clear that one of the main difficulties with this offence is that the social value or legal interest that is protected thereby remains obscure.[62]

In its origin, the offence protected both the physical king, and the King as corporation sole,[63] as they were one. That is not the case today, either in republics or in constitutional monarchies. In constitutional monarchies, such as the UK, there is a distinction between the physical person who is a monarch, and the office of the Crown. The protected interest has thus changed, both in republics and in constitutional monarchies. The wording of the offence has undergone changes which reflect this, in republics eliminating the reference to a monarch. But the result is that the very concrete object protected by the offence has disappeared, and it is not clear what interest is protected in its place by this offence.

This lack of a clear protected interest can be seen if we consider the following example: if D were to kill the Queen for the purpose of robbery, D would have committed the actus reus of treason accompanied by a specific intent to kill her. Compare this with E who kills the Queen for the purpose of destabilising her rule. In English law both defendants would have committed treason. However, a distinction between D and E can be observed when one specifies the protected interest in the elements of the offence.

[60] For a discussions comparing the two concepts, see N Persak, *Criminalising Harmful Conduct: The Harm Principle, its Limits and Continental Counterparts* (New York, Springer, 2010).

[61] Nuotio, above n 38.

[62] This is true also in Germany, where the German Criminal Code includes treason in the offences against national security, yet not all treasonous acts necessarily undermine national security.

[63] The corporation sole of the monarch (a peculiar entity in English law), is the incorporated office of the monarch, occupied by the physical person who is the king or queen.

If the protected interest in treason is identified as the stability of the state, E would have committed treason, but D would not have done so. Recourse to identification of a protected interest thus both defines the treason offence and restricts its reach. In this way, a *Rechtsgut* approach can also help to render it more justifiable in a liberal state.

This can, however, only be achieved if we are able to identify which interest is protected by modern treason laws, and against what.

In a republic there is no physical being against whom treason is committed. It is committed against a legal entity.[64] That in itself is not problematic, as there are also offences against corporations.[65] In offences against corporations, a readily identifiable social interest is however protected, typically the right to property. But in the case of treason, it cannot credibly be claimed that it is the property of the state that is being protected.

What then *is* the interest protected in the treason offence? The territorial sovereignty of the state? The constitutional values of the state? The integrity of the state? Even if we could identify the protected interest as the integrity of the state, we should, as was noted in the previous section, still ask: the integrity of the state according to whom? As was pointed out above, this raises particular difficulties in a liberal state where citizens are free to hold and promote their own views about how the state should be structured. This leads us towards considering a different protected interest: constitutional integrity rather than governmental stability. Germany again offers a telling example, as its Constitution stipulates that citizens have 'the right to resist any person seeking to abolish this constitutional order, if no other remedy is available'.[66] Under this conception it is the duty of a citizen to protect constitutional governmental institutions rather than all governmental institutions.

In protecting the constitutional order, the German high treason offence (*Hochverrat*) protects the constitutional values of the state as well as its security.[67] The German Criminal Code defines 'high treason' as undertaking with force or through threat of force to undermine the continued existence

[64] Although in the Criminal Code of Estonia an attack against life or health of higher state public servants is an offence included in the same chapter as treason and punishable by the same sentence (s 244).

[65] Such as theft from an employer, usually a corporation.

[66] *Grundgesetz,* Art 20(4).

[67] The German Criminal Code, s 81 provides as follows: '(I) Whosoever undertakes, by force or through threat of force, (1) to undermine the continued existence of the Federal Republic of Germany; or (2) to change the constitutional order based on the *Grundgesetz* of the Federal Republic of Germany, shall be liable to imprisonment for life or for not less than ten years. (II) In less serious cases the penalty shall be imprisonment from one to ten years.' On protection of the constitution as a *Rechtsgut* see Dubber, above n 59.

of the Federal Republic of Germany or to change the constitutional order based on the Basic Law of the Federal Republic of Germany. So, although the German Criminal Code includes treason in the 'offences against the security of the state' we can surmise that state security is not the only protected legal good, but so are its constitutional values.

Although it is only in Germany that protection of the Constitution is expressly included in the definition of treason, the protection of the Constitution can perhaps also in other states be seen as the interest or value protected by treason offences.

In certain cases, the criminalisation of treason has indeed been used to advance such values. The post-war de-Nazification war crimes law in Austria (*Kriegsverbrechergesetz*) included an offence of high treason against the Austrian people, which was made retroactive to cover the Nazi period.[68] Such an offence cannot be understood as a crime directed against the state as a sovereign territorial entity. It can only be understood as a crime whose protected interest is a certain set of values of the state. In this case, even agents of the state going about state business can be held responsible for treason.

While the discussion so far suggests that the protection of constitutional values may be a legitimate object of the treason offence, the dangers of this view should not be overlooked. The values of the state being protected by the criminalisation of treason can be morally good or bad. In both liberal states, such as Germany, and dictatorial states, such as the Soviet Union during the 'red terror', the treason offence protects, or protected, loyalty to the values of the state. Communist states had a treason offence, but the protected interest in this offence was class loyalty—the offence being its betrayal—rather than national loyalty. The 1922 Penal Code of the Russian Federative Socialist Republic defined treason in Article 57 as:

> Efforts to overthrow the power of the Soviets, and assistance to the part of the international bourgeoisie that does not accept the equality of the communist principles of property and seeks to overthrow it by intervention, blockade, espionage, financing of mass media, or other means.

About four million people were convicted of this and related offences during the years of the 'Red Terror' (1937–1939).[69]

Thus treason can vary between protecting the smooth operation of the state, or its existing values, or new changed values. These can be compatible

[68] K Eisterer, 'Austria Under Allied Occupation' in R Steininger, G Bischof and M Gehler (eds), *Austria in the Twentieth Century* (New Jersey, Transaction Publishers, 2009) 190 at 207.
[69] C Pitts and A Ovnyannikova, 'New Treason Statute, Anti-NGO and Other Repressive Laws: "Sovereign Democracy" or Renewed Autocracy' (2015) 37 *Houston Journal of International Law* 83 at 102.

with liberal commitments, but this is not necessarily the case. Examining the treason offences of the UK, the US, Canada and Germany from the perspective developed in this section, a variety of protected interests emerge: security, territorial integrity, the monarch (UK), and constitutional values (Germany). Moreover, within the same state, for instance the UK, the protected interest can be seen to have changed over time, although the wording of the offence has remained unaltered. Today even in the UK the offence cannot be understood as merely protecting the monarchy, as it also serves to protect the state in its other aspects. Such broad and disparate protected interests casts further doubt about the appropriateness of this offence to a liberal state and even about its compatibility with the principle of legality.

III. CONCLUSION(S)

The offence of treason is not a disused relic but alive and present in recent enactments.[70] Although little used in prosecutions, it has real and far-reaching implications.

Meir Dan-Cohen wrote of a 'wall of acoustic separation'[71] between two functions of the criminal law: modifying behaviour and prosecuting offenders. Criminal laws can modify behaviour even when prosecution seldom takes place. The offence of treason casts a long shadow, its very existence bringing about modifications in behaviour. The mere suggestion that one is a 'traitor' confers an ominous tint, even where the actual indictment—or eventual conviction—is for lesser offences.

As has been seen, none of the justifications for criminalising treason are compatible with a liberal theory of the state. The fundamental problem is that the offence of treason postulates not just a specific duty of the citizen towards the state, such as paying taxes or obeying criminal prohibitions enacted by law, but a general duty. Such a duty is to the liberal mind both over- and under-inclusive. It suggests that the citizen always has a duty of loyalty towards the state, when such duty should exist only when the state is (or its actions are) more-or-less benign by broadly universal liberal constitutional values (justice, democracy, rule of law and human rights). Moreover, in a global liberal society, the 'global citizen' should have an equal duty towards all more-or-less good states, and a right, even a duty, to be disloyal to all corrupt states (or at least to their corrupt governments).

[70] See, eg, Criminal Code of Canada RSC 1985.

[71] M Dan-Cohen, 'Decisions Rules and Conduct Rules: On Acoustic Separation in Criminal Law' (1984) 107 *Harvard Law Review* 625.

Since no state can credibly claim to be a perfect state, no state can legitimately take judgements of political morality out of the hands of its citizens. The most one could justify is a much more circumscribed offence protecting the broadly universal liberal constitutional values just mentioned. But that would be an altogether different offence.

These conclusions also hold more general lessons:

The existence of this offence has important implications for the theory of the state: The challenge that citizenship poses for any liberal theory of the state is heightened by the existence of the treason offence. With this offence on the statute book citizenship is not merely a criterion for benefits conferred by the state (such as a right to enter the state), but also a criterion for criminal responsibility and punishment.

The existence of this offence has important implications for the theory of criminalisation: The analysis of the treason offence should give pause for thought to any liberal theory of criminalisation. This is an offence which cannot be sufficiently accounted for by any of the existing theories of criminalisation. There may be other offences which also do not fit neatly into any theory. That does not necessarily mean the theory is wrong, however; it might well mean that the offence cannot be justified in a liberal state.

Perhaps the continuing existence of the offence shows us that even in liberal states criminal law is premised on theories of the state and of criminalisation that are less firmly rooted in liberalism than we would like to believe.

7

Legal Dogmatics, Theory and the Limits of Criminal Law

ERIK SVENSSON*

I. INTRODUCTION

IN DISCUSSIONS CONCERNING criminal law and the authority of the state, one frequently comes across statements such as 'criminal law constitutes the state's most radical exercise of power over individual citizens'. At least in some respects, this is certainly true. Within the framework of criminal law, the state deprives citizens of their freedom, physical as well as economic, for reasons that involve laying claim to moral authority and/or the social necessity of imposing hard treatment to convey censure. The purposes for which criminal law is used are not straightforwardly benevolent, aimed at enabling legal subjects to lead better, safer and more successful lives, and the same is true of the purposes for which punishment is inflicted on those who violate the criminal law's prohibitions. Criminal law, in this sense, is repressive.[1] Repressive measures cannot be accepted unless there is sufficient justification to use them. The exercise of power must be grounded on the same values and principles upon which such power is justified. This is true for individual cases as well as on a structural level: the criminal law enterprise must be justified as a whole, as an integral part of any theory of the state, as well as in every specific case where it expresses itself as an exercise of power. For these reasons, it is important that a principled approach be adopted in criminal law matters.

In this chapter, I will not address the issue of how criminal law can be justified as a whole, but instead concentrate on how it could be justified

* For helpful comments and suggestions, I owe gratitude to Gustaf Almkvist, Petter Asp, Iain Cameron, Norah Lind and Johanna Chamberlain.

[1] The repressive nature of criminal law is, for example, stressed by M Ulväng, 'Criminal Law and Civil Peace' in M Del Mar and Z Bankowski (eds), *Law as Institutional Normative Order* (Farnham, Ashgate, 2009) 131 at 134.

in individual cases. The first of these questions belongs to the subject of political philosophy. Criminal law is thus reviewed externally, from the perspective of for example a liberal conception of the state. The question of how criminal law can be justified in individual cases can be discussed externally or internally. When discussed externally, it has to do with why the practice of punishment is justified as such. Answers to this question could relate to for example general prevention or retributivism. These are arguments external to a particular set of rules which might be used to review any system of criminal law. When discussed internally, the question of justification relates to the scope of the law's application. The criminal law itself, as a system of norms, provides the framework for an internal discussion. Questions are posed and answered within the given system of norms.

In what follows, I will address the role that legal science has to play in this latter kind of justification process. In my opinion, the importance of scholarly work in the legal field goes beyond accurate description of the law. Legal scholarship—in the form of 'legal dogmatics'—is the institution whereby the often fuzzy and sometimes incoherent elements of the law are shaped into a (somewhat) coherent structure. More specifically, I make a distinction between legal dogmatics and legal theory. In my opinion, internal questions of how the scope of criminal law could be justified should be characterised as dogmatic rather than theoretical. I will use some of my own research concerning parties to a crime to illustrate this point.[2] In doing so, I suggest that dogmatics has a central role to play in justifying the actual use of punishment in individual cases.

II. THE CONCEPT OF LEGAL DOGMATICS

The term 'legal dogmatics' (*Rechtsdogmatik* in German, *rättsdogmatik* in Swedish), as well as the concept that the term refers to, is rarely seen in Anglo-American literature. 'Doctrine' is sometimes used as a translation, but this can be confusing. In Germany as well as in the Nordic countries, legal doctrine and legal dogmatics are two distinct concepts. Legal doctrine, in these contexts, refers to a body of literature that pursues the orderly presentation and interpretation of posited legal norms. This can include descriptive expositions of some part of the law (for example the Swedish legislation on tax fraud), textbooks intended to be used at universities, collections of case law including comments on certain cases, as well as monographs that

[2] E Svensson, *Gärningsmannaskap vid fleras deltagande i brott* (Uppsala, Iustus Förlag, 2016).

are the result of several years of scholarly work. Doctrinal scholarship helps to set out and explain 'what the law is'.

Legal dogmatics shares its subject matter with legal doctrine: legal norms. Dogmatics is distinguished from legal doctrine mainly by the claims and ambitions that are found in the former. Dogmatics is not only about describing the law, but also about forming the legal material (statutes, case law, and from a Swedish perspective usually the *travaux préparatoires*) into a coherent structure. Neil MacCormick speaks of legal dogmatics as

> the production of clear and systematic statements of legal doctrine, accounting for statute law and case law in terms of organising principles, relating actual or hypothetical decisions both to their factual bases and to governing norms elaborated out of the authoritative materials.[3]

The production of such statements is part of what MacCormick calls a *rational reconstruction* of the legal system.[4] According to the German legal theorist Robert Alexy legal dogmatics consist of propositions that (i) could form a basis for a legal argument, (ii) relate to positive law (chiefly enacted norms and case law) which (iii) make up a coherently interrelated whole, (iv) are part of an institutionalised legal science, and (v) have normative content.[5]

These criteria are important in understanding the sense in which legal dogmatics can lay claim to the designation of being 'scientific'. As Nils Jareborg explains:

> A successful scientific investigation has the form of 'This is how it should be!', that is, there are good reasons to think about (an aspect of) the world in this way, there are good reasons to use this model of reality, this theory, this set of concepts, and so on, given the purposes of [our investigation].[6]

Scientific inquiry, Jareborg maintains, aims not at knowledge or information simpliciter but at insight and understanding. It involves a 'creative reworking' in that '[t]he results of research—knowledge, information, data—must be structured, synthesized, systematized and summarized into some form

[3] N MacCormick, 'Reconstruction after Deconstruction. A Response to CLS' (1990) 10 *Oxford Journal of Legal Studies* 556.

[4] From a Swedish perspective, Nils Jareborg has expressed the same opinion (with reference to MacCormick). See N Jareborg, 'Legal Dogmatics and the Concept of Science' in G Freund, U Murmann, R Bloy and W Perron (eds), *Grundlagen und Dogmatik des gesamten Strafrechtssystems. Festschrift für Wolfgang Frisch zum 70. Geburtstag* (Berlin, Duncker & Humblot, 2013) 49.

[5] R Alexy, *A Theory of Legal Argumentation* (Oxford, Oxford University Press, 1989) 253. This book was originally written in German (*Theorie der juristischen Argumentation*). In the English translation by Ruth Adler and Neil MacCormick, the German word 'Rechtsdogmatik' is translated as 'legal dogmatics'.

[6] Jareborg, above n 4 at 51.

of (re-)construction of (a tiny bit of) some sort of reality'.[7] Legal dogmatics thus 'primarily concerns … reconstruction of actual legal systems', which means that it is 'in principle bound by authoritative decisions by legislators and courts'. This, as Jareborg further explains,

> does not mean that scientific argumentation is limited to such decisions or that a legal dogmatist cannot widen her perspective beyond that of valid law. … Still, a connection to some form of political power must be kept, because otherwise we cannot talk about a legal system. … In this sense, legal dogmatics is a system-internal science, in contrast to other legal sciences which look at law from an external perspective.[8]

All of these writers seem to regard dogmatics as an activity, something that can be *done* with statutes and case law. Alexy speaks of constructing legal norms into a coherent whole; MacCormick of developing organising principles and of engaging in rational reconstruction; Jareborg of a creative reworking. The task for dogmatics seems to be the formation of legal norms into some kind of system. From this it is possible to distinguish between two different parts of dogmatics: *interpretation* of the legal norms, and the *systematisation* of these norms. Ideals of *coherence* and *rationality* serve as guiding principles in both parts.

Dogmatics in this sense can be distinguished from *legal theory* (or legal philosophy), in that the subject of dogmatics is *legal norms* as such. Theory (as the concept is used here), however, is not about specific norms, but works on a more abstract level. It is thus possible to have a theory about anything: agency, the function of norms, the state, et cetera.

A norm 'comes to life' only when it is used in a particular case. Every case is unique, and the applicable norm must always be interpreted anew. These are basic hermeneutical insights. Still, it is possible to discuss the interpretation of statutes in a more general fashion. This includes analysing the concepts that are used in different statutes, clarifying how a certain statute is related to other parts of the law, etc. In criminal law, it is common to divide dogmatics into the *general part* ('Allgemeiner Teil des Strafrechts' in German) and the *specific part* ('Besonderer Teil des Strafrechts' in German). The former concept refers to norms about the application of statutes that are common to all, or at least most, of the specific offence descriptions. Within the scope of the general part issues of ie agency, causation, mens rea, defences and excuses are dealt with. The second concept refers to norms about how certain statutes should typically be interpreted.

[7] Ibid at 50.

[8] Ibid at 53. The external perspective is taken, for instance, by legal sociology, including by the highly influential systems theory approach to legal systems developed first by Luhmann and later Teubner.

In any legal system that works with a Penal Code, all criminal acts are defined in statutes. A large part of any Penal Code consists of offence definitions; effectively a list of criminalised acts. The criminal acts are defined in a more or less abstract and synthetic (as opposed to casuistic) language. Even when the principle of legality is respected, and statutes are only interpreted within the scope of their meaning, many acts that would not normally lead to criminal liability could be subsumed under a statute as constituting a crime, if interpretation was only about applying this specific statute. Dogmatics is the doctrinal elaboration of these norms, referring to both the general and the specific part of criminal law.

Thus, it is fair to say that while the offence definitions contained in specific statutes widen the scope of criminal law, legal dogmatics relating to both the general and the specific part of criminal law *limits* this scope. In what follows I will argue that legal scholarship has an important role to play in this limitation process.

III. ILLUSTRATION: THEORIES OF CAUSATION AND PARTIES TO A CRIME

A. Introduction

In section II above, I suggested that dogmatics can be distinguished from theory by virtue of its subject matter: legal norms. Even if this is true, any 'rational reconstruction' of some part of the law rests upon notions that could be described as theoretical: from the perspective of criminal law, for example, it is necessary to have some notion of basic philosophical issues such as human agency, causation and the like. Having said this, I believe there is sometimes a tendency to overestimate the importance of theory and to underestimate the importance of legal dogmatics when developing arguments about the limits of criminal law.

In the next section I will attempt to substantiate this claim by drawing on my previous research concerning parties to crime.[9] Parts of the research focused on how the distinction between liability as a principal offender of a crime and liability as a secondary party to a crime should be drawn. This distinction is important in any system of criminal law, for conceptual reasons. To decide whether someone has aided or abetted a crime, it is necessary to identify the 'complicity object'[10]—the act that is aided or abetted.

[9] Svensson, above n 2.

[10] This is the felicitous term used by CE Herlitz, *Parties to a Crime and the Notion of a Complicity Object. A Comparative Study of the Alternatives Provided by the Model Penal Code, Swedish Law and Claus Roxin* (Uppsala, Iustus Förlag, 1992).

Responsibility as a secondary party to a crime presupposes that it is a criminalised act that is aided and abetted. Whether or not the distinction between principal and secondary liability has an effect on eg the level of punishment, the two kinds of criminal liability are conceptually interrelated.

When working on my doctoral thesis, I discovered that the specific legal question of the distinction between primary and secondary liability is usually framed in a general, theoretical fashion, in the sense that different authors set out to construct abstract theories, external to a specific set of rules, that could be used to decide the specific cases that might appear within a system of criminal law. This approach gives the impression of a search for some external, theoretical framework that could explain what the distinction between different forms of criminal responsibility 'really is about'. I noticed that many scholars start by developing the theory, and *then* ask the legal questions which the theory is supposed to answer. This could be used as an example of a broader tendency to frame questions of criminal responsibility as theoretical questions. In my opinion, this way of framing the question creates the risk of discussing something other than questions of criminal responsibility, namely the theory itself, with no basis in the specific legal discourse in which the questions are posed. A theory transcends any specific system of criminal law, but questions of liability presuppose such a system.

In the following sections, I will draw on an example to illustrate this point. Imagine that A is frustrated because his neighbour's apple trees are casting shade over his garden. He wants to get rid of the trees. To do this, he calls a gardening service provider, B, to ask for help. A describes the location of the trees to B and asks for the trees to be cut down, without telling B that the trees in question belong to a neighbour. One hour later, B cuts down the neighbour's trees. Would it be right to hold A, or B, or both, criminally liable for cutting down the trees? The cutting could be described as inflicting damage, the way this crime is defined in Chapter 12 § 1 of the Swedish Penal Code.[11] If so, who is the primary and who is the secondary party? This is a question of the scope of criminal law's application. At first glance, it might look like we need some kind of theory of how the two forms of liability should be distinguished.

As was mentioned above, there are several theories that address on an abstract, 'transcendental' level how the distinction between primary and secondary liability should be drawn. In this section, I shall discuss a couple of theories that are based on the concept of causality. In Anglo-American literature, such theories, very similar to those that have been advocated in

[11] The statute provides as follows (in the wording of the official English translation): 'A person who destroys or damages property, real or moveable, to the detriment of another's right thereto, shall be sentenced for *inflicting damage* to a fine or imprisonment for at most six months'.

Germany and the Nordic countries for a long time (at least since the mid-nineteenth century), have recently been suggested again.[12] I will use two of these theories to illustrate the limited usefulness of extra-legal theories for restricting the application of criminal law to cases where this is reasonable.

B. Michael S Moore's Causation-based Rejection of the Distinction between Primary and Secondary Liability

According to the American scholar Michael S Moore, the question of causality is central to every assessment of moral as well as legal responsibility.[13] Moore makes clear that when he speaks of the concept of causality, he seeks to identify the 'nature' of causality, something that is independent of how the concept is used in language.[14] The criterion for the correct use of the concept in (for example) criminal law is therefore that it conforms to the 'metaphysics' of causality.[15] These 'metaphysics' are, according to Moore, to be found in 'science'.[16] In 'science' causality is no more and no less than 'a natural relation that holds between events or states of affairs'.[17] In this way, the starting point for discussions about moral and legal responsibility is a 'metaphysical' notion of causality.[18]

[12] In German doctrine, it is common to categorise these theories, according to type. In a somewhat simplified fashion, they could be described as follows. 'Formal objective' theories ('formal-objektive Theorien') means that only the person who has committed an act that in the formal sense could be described using the wording of a statute is a perpetrator. By contrast, different forms of 'substantive objective theories' ('materiell-objektive Theorien') focus on the 'substantive' perpetration of a crime. Different kinds of 'subjective' theories ('subjektive Theorien') focus on the mens rea of the people involved, and regard the perpetrator as the person who has looked upon the criminal act as his own. An overview is provided in, among others, G Jakobs, *Strafrecht. Allgemeiner Teil. Die Grundlagen und die Zurechnungslehre* (Berlin, De Gruyter, 1993) ch 21 III.C and C Roxin, *Täterschaft und Tatherrschaft* 9th edn (Berlin, De Gruyter, 2015) ch 2. From a Nordic perspective, see Herlitz, above n 10. Claus Roxin, to take one example, categorises theories based on causation as 'materiell objektive Theorien'. See further Roxin, ibid.

[13] M Moore, *Causation and Responsibility: An Essay in Law, Morals, and Metaphysics* (Oxford, Oxford University Press 2009) 20: 'causation is a prerequisite of legal liability.'

[14] Ibid at 288: 'If criminal liability is to track moral responsibility, the law … must discover, not stipulate, what causation is'.

[15] Ibid at 230, where he stresses the importance, in criminal law, that its notion of causality 'corresponds to a pre-legal, metaphysical notion of … causation' and that it is 'metaphysics, not legal policy that tells us when action *causes* a certain harm'.

[16] Ibid at 5 where Moore claims that his notions are based on a 'scientific view of the world'.

[17] Ibid at 5. In another article, Moore has claimed that causality is governed by 'a metaphysics of force and energy': M Moore, 'The Metaphysics of Causal Intervention' (2000) 88 *California Law Review* 827 at 877.

[18] It is quite hard to follow how Moore gets to this point. Stapleton remarks: 'Moore adopts an odd strategy to find a pre-legal notion of cause: he constructs an account that inexplicably draws on alleged patterns of causal usage (in the Law no less!) which he seems to assume reflect moral concerns, and then claims this provides an avenue to a sound *metaphysical* account

This starting point has a decisive impact on how Moore sees the distinction between perpetrator and accomplice liability (or, in other terms, primary and secondary liability). Based on a theory of what causality 'really is' Moore claims to be able to demonstrate that there really is no difference between the two. Accomplice liability is 'superfluous' in any system of criminal law.[19] There is only one way of making something happen, namely to contribute causally to the event. What is to be counted as a cause is ultimately determined by the laws that govern the physical universe.

According to Moore, a cause for an event can be either strong or weak.[20] In his analysis, causality therefore becomes a 'scalar' concept. The person who loads a gun has contributed to the fact that this gun is fired in the same way as the person firing the gun, but to a lesser degree.[21] The fact that the person firing the gun in some jurisdictions is held liable as a principal offender, and the person loading the gun is held liable as a secondary party, proves that this jurisdiction is not adjusted to the metaphysics of reality, but rather is based on mistaken notions. Moore claims that,

> [w]hatever is sufficient causal contribution for liability as a principal … should be sufficient for liability as an accomplice, and vice versa. Causal accomplices should again be treated like principals, because both groups equally cause harm.[22]

Moore also claims that there are three other grounds for moral and legal responsibility, in addition to causal responsibility. First, one can be held responsible for an omission, if the omission has been a necessary condition for a certain harm to occur.[23] Second, one can be held liable if one's action has been 'chance-raising' in respect of a certain event.[24] Third, one can be held liable for some failed attempts to cause something. Moore calls this third ground for responsibility 'subjective culpability'.[25] None of these other grounds of responsibility, however, allow for a distinction between primary and secondary liability to be made.[26]

In Moore's writings, a certain notion of 'metaphysics' provides the framework for questions posed within criminal law. Moore seems to believe that

of causation': J Stapleton, 'Choosing What We Mean by Causation in the Law' (2008) 73 *Missouri Law Review* 433 at 466.

19 Moore, above n 13 ch 13 and M Moore, 'Causing, Aiding and the Superfluity of Accomplice Liability' (2007–2008) 156 *University of Pennsylvania Law Review* 827.

20 See Moore, above n 13 at 118.

21 Ibid at 299.

22 Ibid at 300.

23 Ibid at 302.

24 Ibid at 307.

25 Ibid at 314. For a critical analysis of 'chance-raising' and 'subjective culpability', see RA Duff, 'Is Accomplice Liability Superfluous?' (2007–2008) 156 *University of Pennsylvania Law Review* 432 at 444.

26 Moore, above n 13 at 320.

the concept of causality *always* means something like a scalar natural relation governed by the natural laws of force and energy, and *this* conception of causality leads him to the conclusion that the distinction between primary and secondary liability is based on an illusion and ought to be abandoned. There is 'really' no difference between the ways in which people causally contribute to harm. In legal discourse, however, the question is not so much *whether* concepts like primary and secondary liability track any pre-legal, metaphysical reality but what function they perform in the practice where they are used. If one is to decide how the distinction between primary and secondary liability is to be drawn in a specific case, one is not helped by theories of what the concept of causation 'really is' on a 'metaphysical' level. The distinction is not drawn on this level, but within the practice of criminal law.

C. Sanford H Kadish's Causation-based Defence of the Distinction between Primary and Secondary Liability

One reason why Moore founds his attack on the distinction between primary and secondary parties on a theory of causality is that he writes in a tradition where causality has been put forward as the basis of the opposing view.[27] A particularly influential philosophical-theoretical approach to causation grounding the distinction between primary and secondary parties was presented by Sanford Kadish in the mid-1980s.[28]

Kadish's argument is based on the premise that there is a crucial conceptual distinction between, on the one hand, causing something by moving things physically, and, on the other hand, providing reasons for other people to act in a certain way.[29] According to Kadish, this distinction refers to a distinction between the physical world and human agency that is essential to criminal law as such.[30] If A influences B in a way that makes B commit X, it is only B that causes X. From this, Kadish draws the conclusion that the distinction between primary liability ('perpetration') and secondary liability ('accomplice liability') lies in the fact that primary liability is causal, while secondary liability is not.[31]

[27] See also GP Fletcher, *Rethinking Criminal Law* (Boston, Little, Brown, 1978) 634.

[28] SH Kadish, 'Complicity, Cause and Blame: A Study in the Interpretation of Doctrine' (1985) 73 *California Law Review* 323.

[29] Kadish claims that his arguments are not bound by any relationship to a specific legal order, but are on a general, theoretical level, see ibid at 324.

[30] Ibid at 326: 'Central among the beliefs that underlie the criminal law is the distinction between nature and will, between the physical world and the world of voluntary action. Events in the physical world follow one another with an inevitability, or natural necessity, that is conspicuously absent from our view of voluntary action.'

[31] Ibid at 327.

According to Kadish, there is causality between X and Y if X has been a necessary condition for Y.[32] In addition to this he builds his analysis of causality on Hart's and Honoré's *Causation in the Law*.[33] Just as Hart and Honoré, Kadish claims that every voluntary human action starts a new causal chain no matter what influenced this voluntary action.[34] In aiding and abetting a crime, the actions of at least two persons are involved. If one of these persons acts through the other, in the sense that she persuades the person 'in front' to commit voluntary actions, the person 'behind' has not caused the effects of these actions. Only the actions of the person in front stand in a causal relationship to these effects.[35] On this view, there are two different kinds of moral and legal responsibility: perpetration, grounded on what one has caused, and accomplice liability, grounded on something other than causality. The person 'behind' has only provided another person with reasons for causing something.

The concept of causality is, according to Kadish, part of the 'natural world', and cannot be used to explain voluntary human action. It is not possible to be certain about what the person in front would have done if the person behind had not influenced her.[36] Everyone who acts voluntarily is a 'wild card'.[37] Thus, theories of causality cannot be used to explain why people are held criminally liable for aiding and abetting crimes committed

[32] Ibid at 360: 'In causation, proof of a but-for-relationship is required.'

[33] The book was initially published in 1959, and a revised second edition was published in 1985. Hart and Honoré treat causality by analysing the notions of causality that appear in everyday language. One issue discussed is how far a causal chain can be extended and still be relevant in the moral and legal context. Their argument on this point has been very influential in British and American doctrine. The theory is that no causal chain runs through an independently acting individual: the causal chain leading from a person's deed ceases when a person breaks this causal chain with his own deed. The conclusions on this issue are brought out in the following quote from HLA Hart and T Honoré, *Causation in the Law* 2nd edn (Oxford, Oxford University Press, 1985) at 42: '[A] voluntary human action intended to bring about what in fact happens, and in the manner in which it happens, has a special place in causal inquiries; not so much because this, if present among a set of conditions required for the production of the effect, is often treated as the cause (though this is true), but because, when the question is how far back a cause shall be traced through a number of intervening causes, such a voluntary action is often regarded both as a limit and also as still the cause even though other abnormal occurrences have provisionally been recognized as causes.'

[34] Kadish quotes the following passage from Hart and Honoré, above n 33 first edn at 41: 'A deliberate human act is therefore most often a barrier and a goal in tracing back causes in such inquiries: it is something *through* which we do not trace the cause of a later event and something *to* which we do trace the cause through intervening causes of other kinds.' See Kadish, above n 28 at 335 fn 11.

[35] Kadish, above n 28 at 335: 'What results from the second actor's action is something the second actor causes, and no one else can be said to have caused it through him'.

[36] Ibid at 335: 'No matter how well or fully we learn the antecedent facts, we can never say of voluntary action that it had to be the case that the person would choose to act in a certain way'.

[37] Ibid at 360.

by other people. Instead, there are two separate kinds of liability in criminal law: liability for causing something and liability for providing reasons for someone else to cause something.[38] The distinction between primary and secondary liability responds to this distinction.

If Kadish's analysis was right, and accomplice liability has to do with providing reasons for action rather than causing effects, then we would have reason to restrict accomplice liability to aiding and abetting by psychological means. This would lead us to some rather strange positions. If someone provides a gun to a shooter—what many would consider a paradigm case of secondary participation—we would, if we follow Kadish's approach, only be able to retain that classification by saying that this person is held liable for the shooting because by providing the gun he created a reason for the shooter to use it. However, we think of this person as being held liable for the 'physical' action of providing the gun. It is also the case that many crimes are defined in such a way that they are necessarily committed by providing reasons for action, rather than manipulating the natural world of cause and effect. One example is fraud. In Chapter 9 § 1 of the Swedish Criminal Code it is stated that '[i]f a person by deception induces someone to commit or omit to commit some act which involves gain for the accused and loss for the deceived or someone represented by the latter', this person should be held liable for fraud. Using Kadish's theory, it would not be possible to make a distinction between primary and secondary liability when it comes to crimes like this. Kadish's theory might be plausible on an abstract, theoretical level, but is not very useful in practice. It could not do the work it is set up to do: provide reasons for how the distinction between primary and secondary liability is to be drawn (eg in a case of fraud).

IV. THEORY AND LEGAL DOGMATICS

I find it an odd strategy to use theories of *causation* to create answers to questions of *criminal liability*. When treating specific problems of criminal law as theoretical problems, the interpretation of norms—which is always the starting point in practical criminal law—is left out of the picture. It is possible that Moore's analysis of causation is right, or that Kadish's is right, but this will not solve puzzles of responsibility. People could agree or disagree on what causality means or 'really is'. Whatever view people take on that issue, the questions of criminal liability remain unanswered.

[38] Ibid at 333: '[T]he criminal law has developed two separate doctrines for fixing blame. The doctrine of causation deals with fixing blame for natural events. The doctrine of complicity deals with fixing blame for the criminal action of another person'.

In criminal law, the issue of for example causality usually has its origin in a question of whether someone should be held liable for a certain act or not. The interpretation of events in a legal context is dependent on the design of the law. No matter how advanced or sophisticated a model one manages to create in order to determine whether causality exists in a particular case (or not), legal questions are *always* about resolving specific legal problems.[39] Models of causality could not, in themselves, be used to find answers to questions of criminal liability. Such questions are always posed within the specific discourse of criminal law. One arrives at theoretical issues from a particular question formulated within a system of norms. When questions of criminal responsibility are treated as if they were theoretical questions with no reference to a specific system of norms, the doctrinal issues—issues tied to specific legal statutes or other forms of norms—are neglected. This is the flaw of Moore's and Kadish's theory-driven approaches to distinguishing between primary and secondary liability, and a common phenomenon in legal scholarship in general. In my experience, it has the consequence that questions of responsibility are treated on too high a level of abstraction.

To categorise a certain act in terms of criminal responsibility is not a question of applying a certain theory 'from above'. Rather, I would argue that the opposite approach is preferable: in deciding a case at hand, it might be necessary to discuss some of the theoretical underpinnings of criminal law. In this sense theoretical issues are approached 'from below'. It is not a question of creating a theoretical blueprint for solving puzzles of responsibility, but rather a question of sometimes deciding a certain case with reference to arguments that presuppose theoretical understanding. Formulated in a different way: the question is not 'is this system of norms coherent with my theory?' but rather 'what theory is needed to apply this system of norms in a coherent way?'

Discussions of theoretical issues always take place on a theoretical level, but the application of law is a practical enterprise. If legal scholarship is to be of any help when it comes to giving the law a structure, something is needed that is closer to the specific legal norms than is the case with theory, and, at the same time, is more principled than doctrine. In my opinion, legal dogmatics can provide this bridge between, or synthesis of, theoretical and doctrinal questions.

The dogmatic question could be formulated as: 'what is the law in this case?' This is a practical rather than a theoretical question. Scholarly dogmatic reasoning is much like practical legal reasoning in this sense. The

[39] Peter Cane is of the same opinion. See P Cane, *Responsibility in Law and Morality* (Oxford, Hart Publishing, 2002) 116: 'It does not follow, of course, that "C caused O" is synonymous with "C is responsible for O".'

difference is mainly that the scholar usually formulates her question in a more abstract fashion than the practitioner. Reasons for or against a certain answer are found in the sources of law; that is, eg, enacted laws, case law and doctrine. As mentioned above, the *travaux préparatoires* are also an important source of law in Sweden. What I have just said does not mean, of course, that the law is 'collected' in specific sources; rather the law has to be reconstructed with reference to the legal material. To answer the question of what the law is in a specific case is to provide reasons that are recognised within the system of norms that is criminal law, and could be tied to the values and principles upon which the system of norms rests. When a system of norms is established, questions posed within this system can be answered internally. The reasons in favour of a specific solution should be produced with reference to the system as such.

Legal dogmatics is, in other words, a tool by which problems can be solved from a legal point of view. Within dogmatics, the law is reconstructed in a systemic fashion. This involves issues on how different rules relate to each other, how different precedents should be interpreted, et cetera. It involves conceptual analysis and the creation of distinctions and definitions. It is thus possible to distinguish between cases that should be decided differently and to explain why other cases should be treated alike.

The 'gardener case' mentioned above could again be used to illustrate this. This case gives rise to a specific question of how the law should be limited in its application. In legal practice, all questions of criminal law's limits appear in this way: 'how should *this* case be decided?' In the specific case of the gardener, the question could be formulated as: 'should A or B, or both, be held liable as a perpetrator or not?' On a superficial level, both Moore's and Kadish's theories could be said to provide answers to this question. From both Moore's and Kadish's points of view, B is a perpetrator, since he 'caused' the trees to be cut down, regardless of whether one follows Moore's view on causation or decides to go with Kadish's view on the same issue. It is thus possible to say things like, 'according to Kadish's causality driven theory on the distinction between primary and secondary liability, B is a perpetrator'. From a *legal* perspective, though, there are other reasons for not holding B responsible as a perpetrator. One obvious reason for not holding B responsible as a perpetrator is that B did not act with the proper mens rea, since he did not realise that he was damaging the property of A's neighbour. In other words: important factors come into play that are not a part of eg Kadish's theory.

It is also possible that the theories discussed above would give different results in a specific case, although they are both based on the concept of causation. When it comes to A's responsibility, Moore and Kadish would take different positions on whether he is a perpetrator or an accomplice. According to Kadish's theory, A gave the gardener reasons to cut down the trees and is thus an accomplice. According to Moore's, we have no reason to draw any distinction at all between perpetrators and accomplices. However, the person who asks herself how the specific gardener case should be *decided*, is not interested in the theories as such. The theories are external to the law, and have no legal implications. Dogmatics, on the other hand, is internal in the sense that it finds its arguments in rules and principles within the same system of norms that the question is posed in, in the first place.

When such an approach is followed, the discussion regarding whether A is a perpetrator or not would proceed along the following lines. From the perspective of a civil law system, crimes are always defined in statutes. The scope of criminal responsibility is thus, first and foremost, determined by how these statutes are constructed. In the gardener case, it might be counterintuitive to hold A responsible as a perpetrator, since it was in fact B who physically cut down the apple trees. However, the issue here is not who cut down the trees physically, but whether A can be said to have damaged the property of another person. We are not asking ourselves the general, abstract question of what, for example, causation means, or what it means to act, but the *specific* question of whether what A actually did could be described as damaging property. This is because we are, at this point, only interested in the question of whether Chapter 12 § 1 of the Swedish Penal Code is applicable or not. To do this we have to think about what 'inflicting damage' means in Swedish criminal law. Could this be done by telling someone else to do something? If A used his trained monkey to damage the trees of his neighbour, it seems clear that A could be held liable for damaging property. Is the unknowing, misinformed B to be compared with a trained monkey in this case? To answer this question, we have to look for other cases in which damage was inflicted, compare the case at hand to these cases, look for clues on how the statute should be interpreted in the *travaux préparatoires* and in legal doctrine, think about the principles specified in the general part of criminal law, et cetera. This process is partly about deciding what the law is *in abstracto*, and partly about explaining why the law is applicable *in concreto* in this specific case. The decision should be coherent with what is found. It is justified with regard to existing criminal law, but it also reconstructs the law anew, since every case is unique. In this process, several different kinds of arguments and considerations, working in different directions, might be of importance.

Legal decision-making is, in this sense at least, more complicated than theoretical speculation. When deciding whether A is a perpetrator or not, the entire dogmatic structure of (in this case) Swedish criminal law will come into play. It is the task of legal scholarship to provide this dogmatic structure. By reconstructing the law, legal scholarship in the form of dogmatics ideally provides arguments enabling courts to come to coherent decisions in specific cases, *and* works as a touchstone of rationality for new statutes. Dogmatics is not so much a *theory* of what the law should be, as a *framework for reasoning* about it.

The map of criminal law will always have blank spaces. The task for legal dogmatics is to reconstruct the different sources of law into a coherent structure. It is possible to use this structure to provide reasons for how to navigate in the blank spaces on the map. In this sense the limits of criminal law, and thus the limits of state authority in criminal law matters, is to a large extent identified and set through legal dogmatics.

8

The State's Obligation to Provide a Coherent System of Remedies Across Crime and Tort

MATTHEW DYSON

VIRTUALLY ALL MODERN legal systems distinguish between those wrongs enforceable by a private party—torts, and other civil wrongs outside the scope of this chapter—and those where the state is involved in detection, investigation, prosecution and/or sanctioning—crimes. Once crime and tort are treated as separate components of the legal system, the remedies for the two types of wrong tend to diverge. Some force other than the substantive unity of the subject area—such as a concern with providing the victims of certain wrongs with appropriate avenues of redress—is then required to keep the remedies coherent across those components. Such remedial coherence is important from the perspective of the users of the legal system, the victims of crimes and torts, the prosecutors and the defendants. For them, the legal categorisation of crime and tort might be interesting, but not what matters.

This chapter addresses the minimum remedial mechanisms that the state should provide linking crime and tort. It does so from a launch pad of the Victim's Rights Directive 2012/29/EU of 25 October 2012,[1] which in its core remedial provisions provides as follows:

> Article 11
>
> 1. Member States shall ensure that victims, in accordance with their role in the relevant criminal justice system, have the right to a review of a decision not to

[1] The run-up to this Directive lasted about 30 years. The Council of Europe and the UN took a particular interest in victims' rights during the 1980s. After some earlier measures, International Recommendation (85)11 of the Council of Europe (1985) on the position of the victim in criminal law and procedure gave 16 guidelines for promoting the victim's role in the justice system. The UN Victims' Declaration of 1985 covered a number of procedural and protective rights, including 'fair restitution' covering compensation and recovery of property: General

prosecute. The procedural rules for such a review shall be determined by national law. [...]

Article 15

Member States shall ensure that, following a decision by a competent authority, recoverable property which is seised in the course of criminal proceedings is returned to victims without delay [unless required for a prosecution and in any case as determined by national law].

Article 16

1. Member States shall ensure that, in the course of criminal proceedings, victims are entitled to obtain a decision on compensation by the offender, within a reasonable time, except where national law provides for such a decision to be made in other legal proceedings.

2. Member States shall promote measures to encourage offenders to provide adequate compensation to victims.

The Directive's core remedial rights can be summarised as *review* of a decision not to prosecute, *restoration* of property and *compensation*, to which Article 13 adds the provision of legal aid, and Article 14, reimbursement of costs. However, since each right extends only as far as national law allows, the Directive gives no detail on their content. Building on recent work comparing the relationship between crime and tort in a range of legal systems,[2] this chapter investigates what remedial framework national law must provide across crime and tort in order to be logically and practically coherent.

The chapter starts, in Part I, with a clarification of the distinction between tort and crime and a brief historical sketch of its evolution. In Part II it argues that although a range of legal actors are typically involved in generating the norms, the state has a default obligation to provide a coherent system of remedies. In Part III it turns its attention to how a state may do so adequately. Here it argues that a minimum list of remedial questions have to be addressed, but there are many roads to remedial heaven: each question on this list can be answered in different ways as long as the system

Assembly, Declaration of Basic Principles of Justice for Victims of Crime and Abuse of Power, A/RES/40/34 of 29 November 1985. The European Union has also been active, both through the European Court of Justice, such as Case 186/87 *Cowan v Tresor Public* [1990] 2 CMLR 613, and through legislation. Legislative efforts began with Council Framework Decision 2001/220/JHA of 15 March 2001 on the standing of victims in criminal proceedings. This gave rights to information, protection, participation and compensation (specifically, under Art 10, within a reasonable time, adequate and including the recovery of property). Implementation of this measure was unimpressive, so after the Lisbon Treaty gave the EU greater legislative powers over justice matters, 'Directive 2012/29/EU of the European Parliament and of the Council of 25 October 2012 establishing minimum standards on the rights, support and protection of victims of crime' was passed in 2012.

[2] M Dyson (ed), *Comparing Tort and Crime: Learning from across and within Legal Systems* (Cambridge, Cambridge University Press, 2015).

still functions effectively as part of a wider structure of compatible answers. Part IV shows that while there are competing considerations underlying the various answers to these questions, the most important considerations are practical, focusing on legal actors' approaches and the efficiency of the system. It also discerns a common pattern: for the most part, criminal justice is taken as the starting point of the remedial framework, onto which civil law interests are added and around which further enabling rules are set to facilitate that prioritisation.

I. TORT AND CRIME: CLARIFYING THE DISTINCTION

Before we begin our discussion, it is helpful to remind ourselves of the basis and the history of the distinction between tort and crime. On a classificatory level, the distinction between the two might usefully be drawn on the basis of four overlapping and contradictory indicia:[3]

1. moral or natural description of the wrong;
2. characterisation of the process of remedying the wrong being of public concern rather than merely private;
3. the presence of 'penalty' or compensation; and
4. a positivist approach of some kind, focusing on the process of creating the legal classifications and thus their resulting form.

None alone seems conclusive and this is not the place to go into the competing claims.[4] More important here is the simple and known, if rarely openly acknowledged fact, that the distinction is not obvious. Historically, less trouble was taken to differentiate criminal and civil laws. A simple remedial structure covering both was, typically, already in place through normal procedural rules. To begin with, attempts to classify ancient laws are fraught with difficulty.[5] For instance, many of what might be regarded as ancient *civil* law systems contained *penal* elements and this is particularly evident in Roman law. In the early common law, 'crime' and 'tort', as we call them now, were equally valid ways for a victim to pursue justice for a wrongful act.[6] The choice seems to have been between *compensation* and *vengeance*,

[3] There are many ways to slice this particular cake. See, in particular, the helpful analysis in KW Simons, 'The Crime/Tort Distinction: Legal Doctrine and Normative Perspectives' (2007–2008) 17 *Widener Law Journal* 719; J Lindgren, 'Why the Ancients May Not Have Needed a System of Criminal Law' (1996) 76 *Boston University Law Review* 29, 36; WH Hitchler, 'Crime and Civil Injuries' (1934–1935) 39 *Dickinson Law Review* 23, 23–29.

[4] See further, M Dyson, 'Tortious Apples and Criminal Oranges' in Dyson, above n 2, 416 at 419–21.

[5] See Lindgren, above n 3.

[6] M Dyson and J Randall, 'England's Splendid Isolation' in Dyson, above n 2, 18 at 18–19. See generally, DJ Seipp, 'The Distinction between Crime and Tort in the Early Common

and this choice was one for the victim.[7] It is hard to be clear on when the need for a distinction, using the ideas behind 'tort' and 'crime', if not those terms, was recognised. Certainly by the end of the eighteenth century, Lord Mansfield felt confident enough of it to say '[T]here is no distinction better known, than the distinction between civil and criminal law'.[8] However, even if the need for a distinction was known by then, its edges were uncertain.[9] As it developed, the rule clearly shows the language moving from 'private' and 'public' wrongs, to 'tort' and 'crime'. Similarly, French law did not at first make a distinction between civil and criminal.[10] Of course, modern language like *responsabilité* was not then known; indeed, in that period one might realistically speak of *repression pénale* and *réparation civile*, that is, a focus on process or outcome, rather than doctrinal arrangement.[11] By some German writers, the distinction between private law and criminal law is even said to be one of the great achievements of the nineteenth century.[12] Two smaller European legal systems recognised this distinction also quite late. Medieval Swedish law did not distinguish between crime and tort per se, but between wrongs to individuals and wrongs to society. This system remained in the landmark Law Code of 1734, though academic literature began to refer separately to civil and criminal law and procedure.[13] It is only in the last hundred years or so that Scotland has developed completely separate jurisdictions, procedures and penalties for crime and tort, which in turn has led to some differences of substantive legal rules.[14]

The more complicated legal framework that results from this process of differentiation can make it harder for users of the legal system to navigate the legal environment. Remedies available through the 'tort' route, and those available through the criminal law, now tend to diverge and,

Law' (1996) 17 *Boston University Law Review* 59; JB Ames, *Lectures on Legal History and Miscellaneous Legal Essays* (Cambridge MA, Harvard University Press, 1913) chs II, III and IV.

[7] For Spain, see M Roig Torres *La reparación del daño causado por el delito (aspectos civiles y penales)* (Valencia, Tirant lo Blanch, 2000) 32–38.

[8] *Atcheson v Everitt* (1775) I Cowp 382 at 391; 98 ER 1142 at 1147 (Lord Mansfield).

[9] As they were in *Atcheson v Everitt* ibid.

[10] O Descamps, *Les origines de la responsabilité pour faute personnelle dans le Code civil de 1804* (Paris, Librairie générale de droit et de jurisprudence, 2005) 204–13; J Bell and D Ibbetson, *European Legal Development: The Case of Tort* (Cambridge, Cambridge University Press, 2012) 72–73.

[11] See, eg, G Viney, *Introduction à la responsabilité* 3rd edn (Paris, Librairie générale de droit et de jurisprudence, 2008) 162–63.

[12] P Hellwege and P Wittig, 'Delictual and Criminal Liability in Germany' in Dyson, above n 2, 123 at 124.

[13] See generally, S Friberg and M Sunnqvist, 'Crime and Tort in Sweden: Theoretical Distinction, Practical Connection' in Dyson, above n 2, 173 at 174–76.

[14] J Blackie and J Chalmers, 'Mixing and Matching in Scottish Delict and Crime' in Dyson, above n 2, 271 at 286–315.

for this reason, must be co-ordinated in some way to avoid interference or contradiction.[15]

II. THE STATE'S ROLE IN REMEDIES ACROSS CRIME AND TORT

What is the state's role in creating a remedial framework across crime and tort? It might easily be taken for granted that the state is the primary determiner of the remedial content of the legal system. There are some important philosophical questions over the location of sovereignty and law-making power underlying this assumption which could be explored if space permitted. For our purposes, however, in the absence of a realistic alternative, the issue is not whether the state is the right body, but exactly the mechanism by which the state should do so. As the Victim's Rights Directive shows, even states themselves typically view the state as the legal actor in a position to affect the remedial sphere and thus it is the legal actor which should be put under an obligation to do so.

One simple way to justify the state's involvement is to do as the Victim's Rights Directive has done, and view the effect of a crime on the victim as a state's concern, thereby tapping into the foundational interest the state has in the criminal law. While 'victim' and 'tort claimant' will not be precisely contiguous, this approach will largely justify the state's role across the whole framework. Since justifying the coercive power of the state is the subject of another chapter in this volume, it will not be attempted here.[16] Instead, this chapter approaches the framework across crime and tort as a matter that should be looked at overall rather than as two separate and unconnected remedial frameworks, crime and tort. This does not require defining the framework as 'criminal' in order to justify state involvement but simply relies on the practical argument that the state should be interested in the effective resolution of disputes amongst its citizens.

The state is most obviously involved with the remedial framework through its underlying code or legislative framework and the decisions of its judiciary. The state should set out the appropriate rules and make them accessible. Many of the attendant requirements are commonly thought to be inherent in the principle of *legal certainty* or the *Rule of Law*, depending on the national tradition in question. This includes such basic aspects as clear and accessible legislation, funding and staffing the courts to resolve disputes about the rules, and publicising those decisions. The content of those rules is

[15] For the purposes of the chapter, 'remedial' is given a wide meaning, as including those legal aspects other than substantive law which might affect how legal actors behave across crime and tort.

[16] See Malcolm Thorburn's chapter in this volume.

another matter: this chapter argues that the framework must answer certain questions (Part III) and that certain combinations of answers are most effective in promoting certain ends (Part IV).

That said, the state is rightly able to delegate *some* parts of the generation of remedial rules to others, including private parties. The difficult question is about which parts of the system may be delegated and how the delegation takes place. This is not to say that the *enforcement* of the criminal law should be delegated (or abrogated) to private parties. That question is discussed in another chapter in this volume.[17] Rather, the state has the default obligation to ensure a framework for remedies across crime and tort which answers certain fundamental questions but those answers might, in fact, have been generated by private parties.

A legal system can still function even where the state has not given a specific answer to a remedial question. In such situations, a legislative or judicial answer is often set down, or substituted, by legal actors. Even today, legal questions can be answered by the assumptions of those in practice, with lawyers shaping litigation whether through assumptions, best guesses or calculations based on the risk of being wrong when advising their clients. In addition, some questions appear not to impair the functioning of the system when they are left without an answer, the remedial question perhaps not even being seen. One likely explanation is that a system may be structured in a way to prevent an individual remedial question being active: where the wider shape of its remedial structures provides an 'answer' to that question through its answers to the other remedial questions. This is more likely the more matters dealt with by civil courts are also dealt with by the criminal courts, sufficiently quickly, cheaply, effectively and permanently.

III. MINIMUM REMEDIAL QUESTIONS ACROSS CRIME AND TORT

There are six basic issues concerning the remedial framework provided by crime and tort that a legal system must address:

1. parallel proceedings
2. prior determinations
3. relative procedural advantages
4. prosecutorial triggers
5. remedial availability
6. remedial priority

It will be seen immediately that these extend beyond the three basic rights described in the Victims' Rights Directive: *review* of a decision not to

[17] See Alon Harel's chapter in this volume.

prosecute, *restoration* of property and *compensation*. Rather, those three questions in fact lock in with the others, producing a set of questions of primary importance to the relationship of remedies across crime and tort.

A. Parallel Proceedings

Should concurrent and parallel proceedings in both crime and tort be possible? The remedial implications of any answer to this question are significant, as such a rule could delay either a civil claim or a criminal prosecution. In practice, where a timing rule does impose a priority, it is the criminal action which will be prioritised, putting the state's interests over those of the private individual. Is such a rule right? Should a claimant have to wait before seeking compensation, potentially suffering economic or other losses in the meantime and potentially jeopardising the ultimate claim itself? However, if a civil claim were able to proceed before a conviction, it could impact on how the criminal trial proceeded:

1. investigatively, with difficulties of evidence-gathering in the face of the ongoing civil proceedings;
2. procedurally, such as when:
   (a) a defendant might have to disclose defences relevant to the criminal trial already during the civil proceedings and thus earlier than desired; or
   (b) a jury or other fact-finder interprets the testimony of witnesses who are financially interested in the civil claim; or
   (c) there is uncertainty about the process by which a prior civil judgment could be admissible in a criminal prosecution;
3. substantively, such as where if the first court were to make a determination, that determination might conflict with a point of law relevant to the other court. This applies both to findings of fact and to legal characterisations of those facts.
4. In terms of efficiency, concurrent proceedings may well be a waste of resources.

These examples show why a legal system must consider this issue, but currently legal systems respond in very different ways. Many legal systems have adopted a formal rule to suspend a civil claim while a criminal prosecution is pending or ongoing. The suspension is mandatory in France[18] and

[18] V Malabat and V Wester-Ouisse, 'The Quest for Balance between Tort and Crime in French Law' in Dyson, above n 2, 73 at 89–91.

Spain,[19] whereas there is a discretion to suspend in England,[20] Germany,[21] Sweden,[22] Australia[23] and the Netherlands.[24] That discretion is exercised commonly in the Netherlands but less frequently in Australia and even less frequently in England. It is interesting that some states expressly note the link between a civil court suspending to allow a criminal prosecution to go forward and the reverse, a criminal court suspending in order for an important matter of civil law to be determined. In Germany, for example, the criminal court can so suspend its proceedings, but even where it does, it need not follow the civil court's judgment.

In practice, criminal justice is typically faster than civil justice, so even if the civil claim is brought first or soon after the criminal prosecution is begun, it is likely that the prosecution would conclude first. In any case, it will normally be in the claimant's interests to wait for the criminal prosecution to be complete: they might benefit from a compensation vehicle in those proceedings and they can at the very least use evidence and arguments deployed in the criminal trial and in some cases the conviction itself.

There are many reasons for why a country has adopted a particular rule. One reason is to avoid the risk of conflicting judgments: in France this is commonly put as 'guarantee[ing] compatibility',[25] in Spain avoiding '*resoluciones contradictorias*'.[26] This is not a reason in the Netherlands, which seems to be more pragmatic, noting that criminal justice is faster and might provide compensation if desired anyway, that a conviction would provide compelling evidence in any later civil claim and that it is effective case management.[27] Another possible reason is institutional competence, in that matters of criminal law inherent in a claim should be decided by a criminal court. English law has a particular history which continues to play a role in the present.[28] There, all a convicted felon's property was forfeited to the Crown until 1870; the state was therefore financially interested in private persons

[19] L Bachmaier Winter, C Gómez-Jara Díez and A Ruda-Gonzáles, 'Blurred Borders in Spanish Tort and Crime' in Dyson, above n 2, 223 at 240–41 (noting the interesting divergence between the civil and the criminal procedure rules).

[20] Civil Procedure Rules 1998, *Practice Direction 23A—Applications*, rules 11A.1 to 11A.4. For detail, see M Dyson, 'The Timing of Tortious and Criminal Actions for the Same Wrong' (2012) 71 *Cambridge Law Journal* 86.

[21] Hellwege and Wittig, above n 12 at 168.

[22] Friberg and Sunnqvist, above n 13 at 216.

[23] K Burns, A Loughnan, M Lunney and S Wills, 'Australia: a Land of Plenty (of Legislative Regimes)' in Dyson, above n 2, 367 at 401–02.

[24] I Giesen, F Kristen and R Kool, 'The Dutch Crush on Compensating Crime Victims', in Dyson, above n 2, 316 at 347–48.

[25] Malabat and Wester-Ouisse, above n 18 at 89.

[26] Eg, N Reynal Querol, *La prejudicialidad en el proceso civil* (Barcelona, JM Bosch, 2006) 141–42.

[27] Giesen, Kristen and Kool, above n 24 at 347–48.

[28] See generally, Dyson, above n 20.

prosecuting as well as being interested for the sake of society itself. This all shifted in the twentieth century. First, the mandatory suspension rule, which had only ever applied to the more serious crimes (felonies), was abolished when the distinction between misdemeanour and felony was removed in 1967. However, 12 years later, under the influence of Australian case law, a remarkable shift happened and a rule on the same question was created which gave a discretion to suspend the civil claim. In particular, a defendant should be protected from having to reveal his defence in a civil case instead of saving it for the criminal trial. This ultimately brings the common law into the same balancing act at play in many other jurisdictions: a suspension should not be used as a tactical tool to pressure the defendant by extending litigation, nor should a civil claim impede the criminal court from doing its duty.

The exception to this established position is Scotland,[29] where it seems that no rule on timing exists. There it appears that the issue has never arisen before a court in a way that required a rule to exist, nor has it been legislated on. The answer appears to be that there is a presumed position, perhaps that it would follow English law, and no one has challenged it in court. In particular, the size of the Scottish system has meant that some important questions throughout the law have not been answered, or answered to the satisfaction of all legal actors. As a result of the relatively longstanding and rapid investigations of the Scots Sheriffs, there appears to have been less need for civil claimants to bring such actions prior to the completion of the criminal prosecution. The absence of forfeiture of property for serious crimes may also have reduced the pressure for a distinct answer to this legal question.

B. Prior Determinations

Assuming that in practice, or by the force of a rule of law, a criminal procedure will precede a civil claim, what effect should the outcome of the criminal trial have on the civil proceedings?

Here we face one primary issue of substance. What would the prior determination show were it to be relevant? In the common law, criminal offences and civil wrongs overlap at times, but there is no overarching structure to equate or translate them. Whether a civil wrong and a criminal offence overlap or are identical is a matter largely of historical development. For this reason, the value of prior determinations will vary. There is a strong argument that this arrangement is unprincipled and that English law should reconsider the apparent allure of difference. Within other legal traditions,

[29] Blackie and Chalmers, above n 14 at 278–80 and 314ff.

many criminal offences are automatically civil wrongs where certain minimum conditions are met. The Brazilian and Dutch systems, for instance, link up civil and criminal wrongs. Dutch law's key definition of an unlawful act is, amongst other things, 'an act or omission in violation of a duty imposed by written law' and all criminal laws must be in written form.[30] Brazilian civil law defines an unlawful act as the starting point of civil liability in tort, under Article 186 of the Civil Code, and a criminal wrong is an unlawful act. French law famously held on to a principle of unity of civil and criminal fault for some decades, also making prior determinations more relevant to later actions.[31]

Assuming that a civil and a criminal court might well speak to the same substantive issues, the value of what the court speaking first says may vary according to the formal outcome of the case. Assuming that, as will usually be the case, it is the criminal court which decides first, the possible outcomes are: a conviction, an acquittal or some other determination.

The simplest case is where the criminal court has *convicted* the defendant and the conviction is in issue in later civil proceedings. On the one hand, where the procedural safeguards of the criminal justice system have been followed, there is a strong argument that the state's willingness to censure through the conviction and, where appropriate, punish, should mark the events in a way which is relevant to a later civil court. This may appear particularly relevant where there is a higher standard of proof in the criminal proceedings than the civil ones. There are five options:

1. *Independence*: ignore the conviction and decide the matter entirely on its own. This is rare. Some Australian jurisdictions do this, but even there the defendant's admissions in a criminal court can be tendered as evidence of the content of those admissions.[32]
2. *Evidential*: admit the conviction as evidence of the facts upon which it must have been found. This is the (statutory) position in England and Scotland.[33] Since tortious and criminal wrongs are not normally substantively aligned, a conviction cannot normally bind a later court about liability itself. There is a further difficulty in jurisdictions, like England and Australia, which use juries, since juries do not specify what

[30] Giesen, Kristen and Kool, above n 24 at 320–26. In addition, breaching social standards of due care also generates liability.

[31] Malabat and Wester-Ouisse, above n 18 at 92–94.

[32] NSW, Victoria, Tasmania, ACT and the Commonwealth pursuant to the uniform evidence legislation, ss 91 and 92. Conversely, the Northern Territory, Queensland and South Australia admit evidence of convictions in subsequent civil proceedings. In fact, Queensland goes even further, creating a rebuttable presumption that the conviction proves facts and the defendant's state of mind: K Burns et al, above n 23 at 404–06.

[33] At common law a conviction is not even admissible: it is treated as a *res inter alios acta*: Dyson and Randall, above n 6 at 60–61; Blackie and Chalmers, above n 14 at 281.

facts they find when they give their verdict. However, if the judge's directions are clear, it should be possible to establish what the jury must have found in order to convict.

3. *Persuasive*: the conviction represents a competent judicial investigation of the facts, comity suggests the second court should have respect for the outcome of that investigation. The conviction will have a 'very strong influence' (Sweden)[34] or serve as 'compelling evidence' (the Netherlands)[35] on potentially all the determinations of the civil court (substantive and factual). In Germany, while the formal rule is that the two cases are independent and the civil judge must decide each case according to his or her own conviction,[36] if a criminal judgment gives a detailed account of the facts that the criminal court found, then this increases the amount of detail that is expected from a party in a civil case who wants to challenge these facts.[37]
4. *Binding*: the conviction binds a later civil court, for instance, by *res judicata*. This is normally positive as in France,[38] but in Spain[39] it can also be negative: a criminal court can determine that the defendant did not commit the crime or that the crime itself did not happen at all. In France the conviction is binding in regard to substantive and factual elements: the existence of a causal link between the defendant's act and the harm to the victim, of intentional or negligent misconduct, of the specific harm and of various material facts. In Spain, only findings of fact are binding so the modern position is that their rules are not 'full' *res judicata*.
5. *Differentiation*: whatever general position is adopted, certain wrongs are treated differently. For instance, in an English defamation case, a conviction is irrebuttably presumed to be proof of the facts upon which it must be founded.

Weaker effects tend to have more practical reasons, such as the wasted costs of re-litigating, though they can include the risk of implied criticism of the

[34] Friberg and Sunnqvist, above n 13 at 217.

[35] Giesen, Kristen and Kool, above n 24 at 354.

[36] The relevant provisions are German Code of Civil Procedure (Zivilprozessordnung), § 286 and § 287. They describe the court as deciding 'at its discretion and conviction, and taking account of the entire content of the hearings and the results obtained by evidence being taken, if any, whether an allegation as to fact is to be deemed true or untrue' (§ 286) while for the amount of damage suffered from an act so proved, the court has what is regarded as a wider discretion on all the circumstances (§ 287). In any case, under § 286, a court is not bound by statutory rules of evidence unless the code so specifies in other provisions. It is difficult to say how persuasive the prior conviction will be, and it will depend on each judge's interpretation, including how convincing on the facts the conviction is. It appears likely that the conviction will, outside minor cases, often be persuasive.

[37] See BGH NJW-RR 05, 1024; OLG München, judgment of 16 April 2007 – 9 U 3865/06.

[38] Malabat and Wester-Ouisse, above n 18 at 88.

[39] Bachmaier Winter et al, above n 19 at 252–53.

criminal justice process should a civil judge find differently to the conviction. The decisive factor in the common law was whether the public would perceive a civil judgment as undermining a criminal conviction. Stronger effects tend to have further or other justifications, such as the pre-eminence of the criminal system and its methods, as in France, or perhaps the unity of the legal system or its cohesion and efficiency, as in the Netherlands.

Where there was no conviction, the most common determination is of the equivalent of 'not guilty'. In this form, there is typically nothing that could affect a later civil action, since no positive finding has been made by the criminal court, only that the evidence does not show the guilt of the accused. The mere fact of being accused of conduct which is criminal does not raise a principled problem of *ne bis in idem*, known to common lawyers as autrefois acquit or autrefois convict or the rule against double jeopardy. Scots law has an additional determination available, of 'not proven'. This is often taken to signal that the jury did not believe that the accused was innocent but found the evidence too weak to establish his guilt.[40] For the purposes of a later civil claim, 'not proven' might be taken as evidence supporting the claim though it would be very difficult to show how much evidence it should be, if any. There is a further determination available in some countries, such as Spain, and apparently Italy, whereby the criminal court makes a positive determination that either the relevant acts complained of did not occur, or that the defendant did not do them. This determination is binding on later civil courts in Spain.[41]

In the reverse situation, should a civil case come before a criminal one, an unlikely possibility normally, the judgment is never treated as authoritative on the facts, though in practice the process of gathering evidence for the civil case may make a later criminal prosecution easier to substantiate. It also appears that procedural methods to prevent 'collateral attacks', civil claims which undermine an earlier determination of a criminal court, are a significant development of the common law.[42]

C. Relative Procedural Advantages

There are many procedural aspects of civil and criminal procedure that affect the remedial outcomes across crime and tort. This chapter can only

[40] For a recent analysis, see J Chalmers, F Leverick and A Shaw (eds), 'Post-Corroboration Safeguards Review. Report of the Academic Expert Group' (August 2014), para 13.8, available at www.gov.scot/Resource/0046/00460650.pdf.

[41] Article 116 Ley de Enjuiciamiento Criminal, though it does so rarely; this is obviously far more than the mere acquittal, for instance, through failing to persuade the judge of the charge.

[42] See generally, M Dyson and J Randall QC, 'Criminal Convictions and the Civil Courts' (2015) 74 *Cambridge Law Journal* 78.

highlight some instances where differences between them are of importance to the existence of a coherent remedial framework. In particular, where a choice of mechanism is possible, tort or crime may offer particular advantages which could change how legal actors behave. Here we note four examples.

First, there may be differences in the rules of evidence, such as who may give evidence and what powers exist to force that evidence. In some cases, the state has extensive investigative powers which civil parties envy; at the same time, there are typically procedural protections for the defendant to criminal investigations designed to protect against the very same powerful state. The sum of these differences could incentivise preference for one form of remedy over another by suggesting the greater likelihood of success by that route rather than another.

The importance of these procedural rules is seen in how much legal actors can seek to benefit from adjusting them. The avoidance of procedural protections by using civil mechanisms is not a technique restricted to private parties. The state may be interested in achieving policy aims without the difficulties of the criminal law and this can lead to hybridisation. A famous example in England has been the Anti-Social Behaviour Order (ASBO): orders were often made by civil courts, breach of which was then dealt with by a criminal court.[43] ASBOs effectively tailor the criminal law to individuals, without legislating new rules for everyone. ASBOs were also until recently made by criminal courts as adjuncts to traditional sentencing, extending the prospective powers of the criminal courts dramatically without apparently having to compromise on the principles of criminal law underpinning them. Professor Andrew Ashworth, who has been a leading commentator on ASBOs, summarises them as

> hybrid legal order[s] … intended to achieve (a) the admissibility of evidence according to rules of civil evidence and procedure; (b) the assessment of the evidence by reference to the civil standard of proof; (c) the making of a civil order, whose terms would not be restricted to desistance from the conduct established in court; (d) the threat of a criminal offence for breach of the civil order, with a substantial maximum penalty; and (e) sentencing on breach that takes account of earlier conduct not proven or admitted in a criminal court.[44]

[43] ASBOs were introduced by the Crime and Disorder Act 1998, ss 1–4. For more detail, see A Millie, *Anti-Social Behaviour* (Maidenhead, Open University Press, 2009) ch 6; E Burney, *Making People Behave: Anti-social Behaviour, Politics and Policy* 2nd edn (Devon, Willan, 2005) ch 5.

[44] A Ashworth, 'Social Control and '*Anti-Social* Behaviour': The Subversion of Human Rights?' (2004) 120 *Law Quarterly Review* 263 at 289. See also, A Ashworth, 'Conceptions of Overcriminalisation' (2007–2008) 5 *Ohio State Journal of Criminal Law* 407 at 418.

Under the Anti-social Behaviour, Crime and Policing Act 2014, ASBOs have morphed into Injunctions to Prevent Nuisance and Annoyance; after conviction for a criminal offence, ASBOs have now been replaced by Criminal Behaviour Orders but the fundamental purpose has not changed significantly. Hybridisation like this is also well known in the USA, in the contrast between procedural 'due process' protection in criminal law and weaker civil protections: for example, the controversial area of 'civil penalties', where the state pursues what are in fact penalties without meeting the stricter demands of criminal proof.[45]

Second, differences in prescription periods affect the relative merits of civil and criminal claims. In Spain, this has had a distinct impact depending on whether the civil or the criminal chamber of the Supreme Court was hearing the claim.[46] In England and Wales, only tortious claims, not criminal actions (other than the less serious offences tried by the magistrates' courts) have limitation periods. A classic recent example of the significance of this difference is the litigation over whether a convicted sex offender's sudden riches from winning the lottery on day release from prison are relevant to extending the tortious limitation period.[47] By comparison, if the individual had only been found and convicted after the lottery had been won, a compensation order would easily have been made when a civil claim was long time barred (unless the discretion to extend that period was used).

Third, the cost of litigation, whether civil or criminal, could have a significant impact on the relative use of tort or crime. The state is directly involved in this not only in setting the fees and liability for costs for litigation, but also in providing legal aid. It is far more common for a state to provide legal aid to a defendant to criminal charges than to support civil claimants for harm they have suffered, or, indeed, to support defendants to civil claims. Conceivably, this could encourage wealthy claimants to ignore any possibility to claim compensation for losses within the criminal proceedings, where such a possibility exists, in order to decrease the litigation strength of a defendant who in civil proceedings would be either unrepresented or have to pay for his or her own defence. It similarly matters what the rules are for recovering costs in private prosecutions, if permitted, and whether litigation funding by third parties is permitted.

Fourth and finally, how civil and criminal orders are enforced constitutes a significant difference across crime and tort. Generally civil orders are enforced by the claimant while criminal orders are enforced by the state.

[45] See, eg, J Morris Clark, 'Civil and Criminal Penalties and Forfeitures: A Framework for Constitutional Analysis' (1975–1976) 60 *Minnesota Law Review* 379.

[46] M Dyson, 'Connecting Tort and Crime: Comparative Legal History in England and Spain since 1850' (2009) 11 *Cambridge Yearbook of European Legal Studies* 247 at 280.

[47] *A v Hoare* [2008] UKHL 6, [2008] AC 844.

However, the state can also affect the civil side, with one obvious example being insurance. The ability of a defendant to satisfy a claim for compensation will very often depend on the availability of insurance. This is something the state can influence. On the one hand, it can require third party insurance, as states typically do for motor vehicles and harm to employees; on the other hand, it can affect the behaviour of insurance companies, such as by requiring them to insure certain persons, even those who commit crimes. In England, the Motor Insurer's Bureau, a conglomeration of private insurers, is obliged to cover harm caused to third parties by uninsured drivers and untraced drivers.[48]

D. Prosecutorial Triggers

The decision to prosecute is a classic instance of interplay between tort claimants and the status of the victim employed within the criminal process.[49] Legal systems tend to elevate the public prosecutor as the primary prosecuting authority, using the resources of the state to enforce the criminal law. This often involves formally recognised discretion on when to prosecute, as exists in the common law, Scotland, France and the Netherlands. Sweden is slightly unusual in having a rule requiring prosecutions, but allowing exceptions where the public interest in proceedings is not strong enough, narrowly defined.[50] Two countries where there is a strong rule against any discretion in prosecution are Germany and Spain. There, the principle of legality is taken to mean that no state actor, neither prosecutor nor judge, can deviate from the clear rules for the commencement, scope and continuation of criminal procedure. That said, it would be possible for legislative provisions to grant discretion in specific areas, as indeed happens in, for instance, Germany. In countries which grant the prosecutor a formal discretion on whether to prosecute, the effects might be widespread. In particular, this might tend to encourage expansive criminalisation by leaving it to prosecutorial discretion to avoid too much enforcement of the rules. As Douglas Husak has argued, prosecutorial discretion offers one of the only ways of narrowing criminal liability, particularly in the modern world. He suggests that statutes are in effect menus from which prosecutors choose.[51]

[48] See R Merkin and J Steele, 'Policing Tort and Crime with the MIB: Remedies, Penalties and the Duty to Insure' in M Dyson (ed), *Unravelling Tort and Crime* (Cambridge, Cambridge University Press, 2014) 22 at 27–28, 30–35.

[49] Some further insight can be gained from E Hoegen and M Brienen, *Victims of Crime in 22 European Criminal Justice Systems* (Nijmegen, Justitie, 2000).

[50] Friberg and Sunnqvist, above n 13 at 186 fn 43.

[51] D Husak, *Overcriminalization: The Limits of the Criminal Law* (Oxford, Oxford University Press, 2008) esp 26.

However, there must be some discretion, even informal, in determining whether there is sufficient evidence of a crime, and reasonable people might disagree in assessing that evidence. In Germany, review of a decision not to prosecute is possible both at the level of the prosecuting authority and, if that fails, a court. This *Klageerzwingungsverfahren* seems to be an example of German thoroughness, perceiving the risk, however slight, that the public prosecutor might not assess the facts and evidence in the right way.[52]

There are therefore four levels of victim involvement in the decision to prosecute:

1. *No review*: outside of the European Union, it would be possible to have a system where the victim has no formal right to obtain a review of the prosecutor's decision on whether to prosecute.
2. *Light*: for example, in England there is now a right to request that the prosecuting authority review its decision not to prosecute.
3. *Medium*: a right to review by a court. In Germany, the first review is by the prosecuting authority, but this can be followed by a court hearing. In the Netherlands, the victim can request a review by the Court of Appeal; that court is selected as it is hierarchically superior to the Public Prosecution Service, which in this context is treated as equivalent to a first instance court.[53]
4. *Strong*: a right to force a prosecution by becoming a civil party *par voie d'action* and indeed, require the public prosecutor to carry out the prosecution. This makes French law quite exceptional. That said, there are safeguards: it is available only in the Police Court, the Neighbourhood Court[54] or the Correctional Court,[55] which excludes more serious crimes.

Of course, informal pressure, or political pressure, might be applied to encourage the public prosecutor to prosecute and perhaps even not to prosecute.

The alternative to affecting the prosecutor's decision whether to prosecute, is for the victim to prosecute. Such a right is rarely exercised in the common law, perhaps more commonly in England than in Australia, though it is practically unknown in Scotland.[56] In England, it has been variously described as a constitutional safeguard and as an anachronism.[57] Even if a

[52] Hellwege and Wittig, above n 12 at 166–67.
[53] Giesen, Kristen and Kool, above n 24 at 336, noting other related rights.
[54] Art 531 CPP.
[55] Art 388 CPP.
[56] Blackie and Chalmers, above n 14 at 280.
[57] *Gouriet v Union of Post Office Workers* [1978] AC 435 at 476–77; cf *Jones v Whalley* [2006] UKHL 41, [2007] 1 AC 63 at [16].

private person brings a private prosecution, in both England and Australia, the state can take over a private prosecution and then discontinue it, so the right is somewhat illusory.[58] In France, there is much less call for private prosecutions given the strong right of review, but even so in recent decades independent administrative authorities and sometimes even private persons have been given the right to prosecute.[59] The right exists in Germany in respect of minor crimes, but apparently not to enhance the position of the victim, rather to relieve the state of the burden of such prosecutions.[60] In Sweden, the *målsägande*, 'the person who owns the case', if she has been personally harmed, can prosecute cases, support the prosecution, appeal an acquittal against which the prosecutor does not appeal, and act as a party claiming damages; however in practice the *målsägande* rarely prosecutes, given the generous state provision for prosecution and assisting the victim.[61] In Spain, the right of every citizen to prosecute, the *acción popular*, is thought to be an important constitutional safeguard, but again is rare, being used in not more than three per cent of all criminal cases.[62] There is no right to private prosecution in the Netherlands.

Private prosecutions do not appear to be common. The high costs, as well as the investigative and evidential burdens, tend to discourage the use of such a right. However, some administrative bodies and large corporations, such as media companies, are willing to turn to private prosecutions in sufficiently significant cases, particularly in England. One of the more significant questions here, is whether the private prosecutor's costs can and should be paid by the state or by the defendant, and whether and if so, how, when and for what reasons the state should be able to intervene and take over such a private prosecution, particularly where the intention is then to terminate it. There has been a significant growth in commercial parties bringing private prosecutions in England as well as seeking to avail themselves of the state's other mechanisms for enforcing the law, whether investigative or procedural.[63]

E. Remedial Availability

Legal systems must decide which parts of the system will offer the appropriate remedies for harm suffered by a victim. If we assume that there are

[58] Dyson and Randall, above n 6 at 59; Dyson, above n 4 at 447.
[59] Malabat and Wester-Ouisse, above n 18 at 79–81.
[60] Hellwege and Wittig, above n 12 at 168.
[61] Friberg and Sunnqvist, above n 13 at 187–88.
[62] Bachmaier Winter et al, above n 19 at 239.
[63] See generally, M Dyson and P Jarvis, 'Remedies of the Criminal Courts' in G Virgo and S Worthington (eds), *Commercial Remedies: Resolving Controversies* (Cambridge, Cambridge University Press, forthcoming).

two sets of interests, the state's and the victim's, in many instances, those interests will coincide and the legal body meeting them might most sensibly be the same. The two private interests most relevant here are the interests in compensation and in the restoration of property.

i. Compensation

One of the primary interests someone injured by a criminal wrong will have is to obtain compensation with the minimum effort, particularly where the state prosecutes the defendant. Three aspects of this question will be examined: the nature of any such claim, how it is opened and closed and its limits.

a. Nature of the Claim

Legal systems have to decide how to offer compensation to the victim of a crime which is also a tort. The vehicle for obtaining compensation for the aggrieved party could take a number of forms, but its nature could be one of three things: criminal, civil or a hybrid.

An autonomous criminal compensation vehicle would be difficult to create and maintain, since direct comparisons with civil law would be so obvious and would need constant reasoned rejection.

A pure civil compensation vehicle embedded in the criminal process is theoretically the case in many systems but it is hard to say that it will come to the same outcome as a civil court would.

As for hybrid rules, like those in the compensation orders of the common law and Scotland, the links between crime and tort are unclear. There seems to be a focus on the practical utility of the order to criminal courts, avoiding complicating criminal adjudication by attempts to get the civil law perfect.[64] One tricky example is Spain: it does not use the 'pure' civil rules from the civil code, but, at least in modern legal theory, is or should be using 'civil' rules, albeit that they appear to deviate towards criminal goals or forms in some ways.[65]

b. Opening and Closing

Any vehicle for compensation must be opened, whether by the victim or not, and once triggered, have sufficient evidence of the harm to be compensated.

[64] Other attempts to peg compensation to tort standards, like some state compensation funds, may face a similar problem, often leading to cheaper and more efficient tariff-based systems; Dutch and Swedish state guarantees for criminal compensative vehicles are similar.

[65] See generally, Dyson, above n 46.

Here formal rules blend into practice, since even where an application by the victim is required the state may try to obtain it, such as through the police, prosecutors and victim support organisations. In any case, the formal opening of a criminal prosecution is a condition to civil claims being brought within the criminal process.

As for closing the compensatory process, there are again formal and informal mechanisms. Formally, it seems more likely where it is a fully civil process, like the *partie civile*, that the claim might be settled and leave the criminal process. For instance, in Germany, uncharacteristically for a criminal court, the parties can suggest, or ask the court to propose, a settlement.[66] Conversely, in hybrid vehicles there may be less opportunity to do so, especially where the victim did not apply in the first place. In England or Scotland there is no such chance to ask the court to propose a settlement. However, the party aggrieved, or the prosecution, could decline to offer the necessary evidence and no order would be made. The result, an acquittal, would not formally jeopardise a later civil claim.

c. Limits

Limits on the vehicle for compensation are common. They can be divided into restrictions on bringing the compensation vehicle, and costs and risks for using it. In both cases, there can be formal and informal limitations. In ascending order of limitations:

1. Spanish law has the fewest limitations of any kind. Prosecutors must claim on behalf of the victim, the claim cannot be rejected once made and there are no cost or risk implications for making the claim. This open door policy has led to an over-reliance on the criminal law to solve what might best be characterised as civil disputes.[67]
2. French law freely allows compensation claims, not other actions with civil ends, but does put some risks on *parties civiles* who tread close to malicious or unfounded claims: if the civil party forces an abusive or dilatory prosecution, he can be fined and is liable to pay damages.[68]
3. Swedish law has light formal limits:[69] claims which are 'clearly unjustified' or impose a 'significant inconvenience' on the prosecutor putting it forward will be rejected. However, the criminal court is incentivised to hear the claim in that event, as otherwise it would simply be postponed to the same judges sitting in a different capacity where the victim will

[66] § 405 StPO.
[67] Bachmaier Winter et al, above n 19 at 241ff.
[68] Malabat and Wester-Ouisse, above n 18 at 81–82.
[69] Friberg and Sunnqvist, above n 13 at 212–16.

only have free legal advice if an aggrieved party counsel had already been appointed in the criminal trial.

4. Formally a German criminal court can reject a claim if inadmissible, without merit or if, after taking all legitimate factors into consideration, the claim seems inappropriate for resolution in a criminal court (for instance, it would prolong the trial substantially).[70] The criminal court can also determine liability, and perhaps certain facts, but leave the exact quantification to civil courts. However, the informal limits are more significant. Lawyers resist using this mechanism because they maintain the strict separation between criminal and civil law instilled at university and prefer specialised civil judges to hear the claim; criminal judges might fear that they will be overburdened by having to deal with complex issues of civil law.[71] Furthermore, and more mundanely, the lawyer's fees will be lower. Finally, there are fears about how insurance cover may operate, particularly because a finding of no civil liability will prevent another claim against the offender's compulsory insurance. That, of course, is a particular problem where the legal system does not automatically equate criminal wrongs with civil ones.
5. The English, Australians, Scottish and Dutch have admissions limits but little risk. For example, in England, only 'clear cases' will be dealt with by the criminal court, though the criminal court has developed its own more simple rules in some areas of law, like causation, which may help to keep cases 'clear'.[72] One important limit is that the compensation order is set partly by the defendant's means so is unlikely to compensate fully. In addition, compensation orders require the judge to convict, therefore the standard of proof is 'beyond reasonable doubt'; it is slightly unclear whether all the facts justifying compensation have to be proven to that standard, but it seems likely they have to be.

These limits seem to exist for divergent reasons. Spain puts no limits because of its view of the obligations of the state to right wrongs and punish the guilty. French law accepts that the ability to force a prosecution is exceptional and should at least have protections against abuse, such as it only being available outside the most serious crimes and liability for abusive claims. It may also be a constitutional protection, to ensure that prosecutors exercise their discretion to prosecute properly lest a victim intervene and force them to do so. On the other hand, internal admissions limits are

[70] Hellwege and Wittig, above n 12 at 165ff.

[71] E Siegismund, 'Ancillary (Adhesion) Proceedings in Germany as Shaped by the First Victim Protection Law: An Attempt To Take Stock' in H Iitsuka and R Findlay-Debeck (eds), *Resource Material Series No 56* (Tokyo, United Nations Asia and Far East Institute for the Prevention of Crime and Treatment of Offenders, 2000) 102 at 108–09.

[72] Dyson and Randall, above n 6 at 55ff.

more generally justified as attempts to avoid overburdening the criminal justice system, or, to protect defendants' rights to justice. They can also be linked to a concept of constitutional or institutional competence: that criminal courts are not the best places to determine all civil claims. Finally, systems which have a separate hybrid order, like the English, have concerns about consistency since those orders typically need not match an underlying civil wrong.[73]

ii. Restoration of Property

A second civil purpose which easily coincides with the criminal law is the restoration of property. In English law, for instance, criminal powers to restore property have been very significant.[74] Civil courts have generally found it more convenient to order the value of the property to be paid, particularly given the difficulty of identifying and enforcing orders against specific property where not already held by a court or the police. Criminal courts have, however, had various powers to restore specific property from at least 1529. These have been used extensively, particularly in low level theft cases. It seems likely that these powers in the Crown Court and Magistrates courts have taken the pressure off the need for a civil power to restore specific property since the most obvious instance (identifiable, movable property in the hands of a state agent) is regulated by the criminal law. In some other countries such claims cannot take place within a criminal procedure.[75] The availability of such a remedy is particularly interesting because the definition of property and the role of property offences is controversial in some common law legal systems, such as the English,[76] while apparently not controversial elsewhere.[77]

F. Remedial Priority

At their simplest, remedies applied by civil and criminal courts will often have the same practical outcomes: the payment of money or the requirement to do or not to do certain things. The primary civil remedy in practice is based in money, whether in liquidated damages or the payment of a debt,

[73] Whenever non-civil law limits are put on the compensation vehicle, it moves closer to being a hybrid, or a criminal vehicle.

[74] See generally, M Dyson and S Green, 'The Properties of the Law: Restoring Personal Property through Crime and Tort' in Dyson, above n 48, 389.

[75] Eg, Malabat and Wester-Ouisse, above n 18 at 82ff; Blackie and Chalmers, above n 14 at 282 fn 73 other than through the action of 'spuilzie': ibid at 287.

[76] Dyson and Randall, above n 6 at 48–49.

[77] Eg, Bachmaier Winter et al, above n 19 at 229.

with some form of injunction or requirement to do or abstain from doing certain things constituting the secondary remedy in practice. Proprietary remedies do have some significance for rare or particularly valuable property but there is typically significant benefit to satisfaction in money terms for ease of enforcement if for no other reason. In the criminal law, the range of orders tends to be much wider. They reach from the highly invasive, such as imprisonment, the variable, like the drug rehabilitation orders, to the generally less invasive, like community service orders. They also include monetary awards, particularly in fines to the state, costs awards and, in systems with criminal or hybrid compensation models, compensation to the victim. There may also be proprietary orders, such as confiscation of property used in the commission of crimes.

The practical impact of one form of order on the possibility of complying with the other type is of great significance to the victim as well as the defendant and requires a priority between the different remedies. Such a priority must cover all the types of orders. Even the distinction between orders relating to conduct and to money tends to unravel in practice, since enforcing the majority of the conduct orders inhibits the defendant's ability to earn money to satisfy a monetary order. Surprisingly, having a more integrated system of civil and criminal orders does not necessarily result in more integrated formal rules. For many systems, a criminal court when awarding compensation is making a civil order whose enforcement is left up to civil courts, and thus the state might choose to leave the matter to private hands.

In England, where the criminal courts are making criminal orders to compensate, and do so for practical reasons to ease the burden on victims, such an order of priority is essential. If a defendant cannot satisfy all the orders that could be made against him, the criminal courts must prioritise in the following way.

First, a compensation order takes priority over a fine;[78] where compensation and confiscation are ordered 'back-to-back' the compensation order will first be paid out of the confiscation order, and any remaining assets go to satisfy the confiscation order.[79] Someone who has received a compensation order can still bring a claim in tort or contract later, and be awarded damages in full, but they will not *recover* any sum already paid under the order.[80] *However*, if a confiscation order has already been given effect, there is no retroactive reallocation of those assets in order to satisfy a later compensation order or later civil claim,[81] the only hope would be a variance of the confiscation order before full enforcement.

[78] S 130(12) PCC(S)A 2000.
[79] POCA, s 13(5)–(6).
[80] See s 134.
[81] See, eg, *R (Faithfull) v Crown Court at Ipswich* [2008] 1 WLR 1636.

Second, between a fine and confiscation, the difference is rather in the mode of calculation (statutory versus the defendant's gain), the mode of application (sentencing versus by the prosecutor's application) and the ultimate allocation within the criminal justice system (state versus state agencies).

Both these sets of priority are premised on the priority of orders once they have been made; they do not instruct the judge which orders to make in the first place. There are some mandatory sentencing ranges and some rules in England, as in many systems, although the trial judge also has significant discretion. Compensation orders may be used instead of other punishments, as may fines, though they are typically additional to other dispositions save in minor cases. Confiscation is technically not regarded as a sentence or 'punishment' per se,[82] so will not affect other personal sanctions, such as imprisonment. The reality appears to be that informal calculations by judges provide the bulk of English remedial priority, often without formal authority and operated largely through the sentencing discretion granted to judges.

IV. SETTING APPROPRIATE REMEDIAL MECHANISMS

These six remedial questions must be answered, directly or indirectly, in every legal system. By answering them, the state can create an infrastructure to express both criminal and tortious components of the law. However, the variety of answers legal systems have adopted highlights the difficult issue of what are the 'best' answers. 'Best' here will depend on how much any one answer *and* the answers as a whole promote the values deemed the most important in that legal system. This chapter cannot unpack all those values in different systems, but it will draw on the reasoning described above to categorise the values legal systems appear to be using.

First, there are *internal norms*, reasons which relate to the shape of the legal system. The most significant such reason is the importance attached to the homogeneity and intelligibility of the legal system. This can be expressed in a variety of ways, but is most commonly seen in some form of 'unity' or 'coherence'. This chapter has used 'coherent' to describe a minimum level of matching concepts, processes and outcomes. However, the term is often used within legal systems, though rarely to explain components of the system and their relation to each other, but more in jurisprudential discussion of the coherence of the system itself. It is therefore not surprising that the normative coherence of a single remedial framework across crime and tort has not been the centre of how the remedial questions are answered. This

[82] Save in terms of appeal jurisdiction: *R (Faithfull) v Crown Court at Ipswich* [2008] 1 WLR 1636.

is regrettable since the more commonality across the system is preserved, the less pressure there is to fragment and complicate the system itself. In addition, doing so better represents the view of legal actors that the system's different avenues are there to be chosen from, while still decreasing the uncertainty and ambiguity for those less versed in that system. One place where coherence, or perhaps even unity, is seen is in systems which have considered how different substantive legal components across different fields of law compare with each other. Thus, the Dutch and Brazilians use the same concept of unlawful acts in crime and tort; the French and Spanish have had similar unifying conceptions of many of their underlying concepts, most famously in the French concept of the unity of civil and criminal fault: all this in turn simplifies how they apply remedies for those acts.

Second, there are *external norms*: calls to higher level principles regarding how specific interactions should take place. Classic examples of such principles include 'fairness', 'certainty' and 'intellectual robustness'. Again, these reasons tend not to provide most of the inspiration for how legal systems answer the core remedial questions across crime and tort. Certainly these reasons can be seen, but they tend not to be seen as norms, but more in the form of the next category of reasons, practical impact. When they are visible, it is often in the form of fairness and certainty, such as in the consideration whether it is fair that a defendant should be forced to reveal, in a civil claim, those matters which might found his defence to a criminal charge.

Third, there are *instrumental* reasons for the particular remedial framework: where the interaction is guided by the outcomes to be achieved. The most common forms of this are efficiency and regulation. Typically the law is used directly to achieve an end, but a side-constraint is the operative capacity of the law itself. This category therefore includes perceptions of non-legal actors of the law itself, a factor in how much the law is esteemed and respected. This seems to be the most significant single group of reasons shaping how remedies across crime and tort are structured. Remedies themselves naturally promote instrumental ends, specifically, the enforcement of the underlying primary obligations breached. More than this, though, the choice of remedy across crime and tort seems particularly influenced by the practical costs of the alternatives to a unified system.

Fourth, there are *institutional* factors affecting the remedial framework: reasons why an institution, either a framework with associated norms or, more often, a legal actor, is suited to a particular task. The most common form of this is competence, whether the framework or legal actor can process the interaction (cardinal competence) and whether it can do so better than alternatives (ordinal competence). There are other dimensions to competence, especially the qualities by which the competence is judged. The three most common are technical, cultural and resources. Overall, institutional reasons are practical, like instrumental ones, but they focus on the process, not on the outcome. They often play a role, perhaps an overstated role, in the framework of remedies across crime and tort. Criminal judges should not be overburdened by deciding civil claims, but the burden is multiplied and shifted to claimants, defendants and civil judges if appropriate claims are not dealt with in the criminal courts. This may have the effect of putting off civil claims, denying justice to many for reasons such as cost, time or effort. At the same time, in many systems, it is often the same judges who could hear criminal or civil cases, so this magnification of effort is particularly strange. Some systems have accepted this reality more than others.

Finally, there are what might be thought *political considerations*, particularly *victim-orientation*. A particularly important issue in the tort/crime remedial framework is the extent of the victim's role in criminal justice. How much should the victim be harnessed, or be allowed to harness, the state's *mechanism* to respond to wrongs? In addition, there is the question whether there should be offences which only a victim can prosecute or trigger the prosecution of. The answers draw on criteria such as the moral or natural description of the wrong; the characterisation of the process of remedying the wrong being of public concern rather than merely private; the presence of 'penalty' or compensation, and on positivist approaches of some kind. Where the victim must consent to or bring the prosecution, the matter is clearly criminal, but it is one in which the private interest is still represented. Such vindication might come formally or informally, such as by prosecutorial practice in the need, in American popular legal language, to 'press charges'. Offences of this kind would have difficulty in being contained, since a victim could always seek to have a veto over, or perhaps even control of, a prosecution. However, such a category is a logical step forward for those who seek to differentiate civil and criminal law: those offences which can be prosecuted without the consent of any victim would be the purest form of criminal law.[83]

These different categories interact and overlap. This makes any one legal system's use of them develop by convoluted iterations. For instance, more recent crime and tort debate in the USA has been a crossroads for different theories and methodological approaches,[84] and has had an impact beyond the USA. It has mixed strong regulatory approaches,[85] the law and

[83] See further eg, RA Duff, 'Torts, Crimes and Vindication: Whose Wrong Is It?' in Dyson, above n 48, 146.

[84] See particularly, the various contributions to: 'Symposium: The Tort/Crime Distinction: A Generation Later' (1996) 76 *Boston University Law Review* 1; 'Crimtorts Symposium' (2007–2008) 17 *Widener Law Journal* 705.

[85] An early example is SH Kadish, 'Some Observations on the Use of Criminal Sanction in Enforcing Economic Regulations' (1962–1963) 30 *University of Chicago Law Review* 423.

economics movement's promotion of efficiency,[86] libertarian views,[87] property and restorative justice centred doctrine,[88] and the role of the state in guaranteeing protection and/or compensation.[89] By the 1990s, a further or counter-movement was evident, seeking to separate crime and tort by clarifying fundamental questions of their purpose and function.[90]

These complications notwithstanding, some patterns of categories and values within them seem to come up again and again. The primary method is to take the criminal justice process as the starting point and add further civil law concerns to it, with the other remedial mechanisms there to incentivise or constrain civil parties to follow the criminal justice model. We have seen two ways in particular by which frameworks are created.

First, we have seen how civil remedies might *piggy-back integration* on the criminal justice system. This process sees the civil rules purportedly applied by a criminal court, and the burden of the would-be claimant carried by the state long enough for him to obtain the appropriate civil order. This is normally accompanied by a rule that the civil claim outside the criminal process is suspended until the prosecution is complete, for reasons of efficiency and sometimes also through fear of contradictory resolutions of the two courts. Once handed down, criminal court decisions are recognised and given effect by such systems within civil procedure. This is a highly pragmatic arrangement, downplaying any instrumental difficulties for the criminal courts in making, or civil courts in abiding by, the prior determinations. There are sometimes artificial limits imposed, such as on the scope of civil matters which can come before the criminal courts, in order to maintain the intellectual cohesiveness of this approach for the simpler cases which criminal justice systems can more easily deal with. Discussion of the unity of the legal system seems to play only a supporting role in this process.

Second, we have seen the *hybrid model*, where some civil concerns are integrated into the criminal law by creating a new object, often criminal in form but typically doing the work of its civil law origins. Thus in the common law the compensation order is a criminal order which provides

[86] Eg, RA Posner, 'An Economic Theory of the Criminal Law' (1985) 85 *Columbia Law Review* 1193.

[87] See, eg, RA Epstein, 'Crime and Tort: Old Wine in Old Bottles' in RE Barnett and J Hagel III (eds), *Assessing the Criminal: Restitution, Retribution, and the Legal Process* (Cambridge MA, Ballinger, 1977) 231, but cf RA Epstein, 'Tort/Crime Distinction: A Generation Later' (1996) 76 *Boston University Law Review* 1.

[88] Eg, RE Barnett, 'Restitution: A New Paradigm of Criminal Justice' (1977) 87(4) *Ethics* 279.

[89] See, eg, the various contributions to: 'Symposium on Governmental Compensation for Victims of Violence' (1970) 43 *Southern California Law Review* 1.

[90] See, eg, JC Coffee Jr, 'Does "Unlawful" Mean "Criminal"?: Reflections on the Disappearing Tort/Crime Distinction in American Law' (1991) 71 *Boston University Law Review* 193; Simons, above n 3.

compensation for the victim of a crime, enforced by the state, but reducing any tortious claim for compensation by the value of the order the victim receives. Parallel proceedings were historically blocked to prioritise the state's interest in the enforcement of the criminal law (both in respect of the crime and originally in respect of the forfeiture of the felon's property). This system may well prioritise compensation over fines, but since the compensation order will only be granted to the amount that the defendant can pay, this priority is somewhat illusory. It is even more illusory where the defendant is imprisoned, depriving him of many means of legally earning money. Interestingly, English law allows private prosecutions though in practice they are not unfettered[91] and are relatively rare. One of the most significant limits today is that the Director of Public Prosecutions (DPP) has a power under section 6(2) of the Prosecution of Offences Act 1985 to take over the conduct of any prosecution initiated by a private prosecutor and either prosecute the case herself or discontinue it. As of June 2009,[92] the same test has been applied to a Crown Prosecution Service (CPS) decision to prosecute as much as to the DPP's decision to take over a private prosecution.[93] This 'Full Code Test'[94] requires a reasonable prospect the defendant will be convicted of the offence it is proposed to charge him with and that it is in the public interest to prosecute. Once taken over, the prosecution could be closed or continued. This Code test, along with judicial discretion in blocking abusive or vexatious prosecutions, has been a significant limitation on private parties using the criminal courts to force sanctions. There has been a particular growth in specialised commercial prosecutions, such as in Intellectual Property, and some in respect of bad business deals and the underlying constitutional reasons for allowing private prosecution have thus far been felt to require its continued availability.

V. CONCLUSION

From the perspective of its users, every legal system should have a remedial framework across crime and tort. It is the state's obligation to provide that framework, though it might well leave certain details to be developed by other legal actors. The framework must cover certain vital questions

[91] See generally, Law Commission's Report '*Consents to Prosecution*' (LC 255, 1998), subject to some later reforms.

[92] www.cps.gov.uk/legal/p_to_r/private_prosecutions. This followed a recommendation of Lord Justice Auld's *Review of the Criminal Courts of England and Wales* (September 2001), available at: http://webarchive.nationalarchives.gov.uk/+/http://www.criminal-courts-review.org.uk/, ch 10, para 50.

[93] *R v Director of Public Prosecutions, ex parte Duckenfield* [2000] 1 WLR 55.

[94] Issued pursuant to the Prosecution of Offences Act 1985, s 10.

whether directly, or by its overall structure making a particular question unimportant or avoidable.

Many different remedial frameworks are possible across crime and tort. The choice of how to address the issues tends to be conditioned primarily by practical concerns, though some underlying values of the system are also represented in the answers. The only way to assess these different frameworks is to compare across the different values *and* across the practical implications of doing otherwise. There are some paradigmatic answers which appear most commonly, such as the *piggy-back integration* model of the civil compensation vehicle and the *hybrid* model. The presence of such paradigmatic answers suggests combinations of responses which are thought to work best in practice, but 'working best' itself is subject to the same qualifications about underlying values. Merely suggesting that certain rights should exist for victims of crime misses the depth of the remedial frameworks that already exist: the real importance is in the detail of how remedial questions are framed and answered, both individually and as a group.

However, the focus on the victim also reminds us that practical effectiveness is one of the simplest ways to achieve law reform. Threading conceptual clarity through the law takes time, resources and luck, which typically make it unlikely. Discrete answers and simple focus points can provide more likely reform prospects. Questions about whether tort and crime use the same concepts, such as 'harm', 'property', 'fault' or 'wrong' might be very difficult to answer properly if their conceptual development has not been attempted once a legal system is up and running. On the ground, legal actors at the whim of a legal framework without such conceptual clarity need at least remedial effectiveness. Through very different means, and with different normative driving forces, the legal systems examined here each offer insight into how that framework works and perhaps how it could be improved. The roles individuals and the state perform within this framework is just one nexus of the role of the state in criminal law; as this book amply demonstrates there are many others. The breadth of these points of contact reminds us of the multi-faceted functions of a state's criminal law. One particularly important conceptual issue is whether the private party's interests are the starting point for the law, or whether the state's interest in punishment to fulfil its obligations to those same private parties should be where we start. Whatever our answer, there are important consequences for how the law reflects it, in substance, in procedure and evidence, and certainly, in remedies.

9

Punishment as an Inclusionary Practice: Sentencing in a Liberal Constitutional State

ANTJE DU BOIS-PEDAIN

THE QUESTION WHY the state ought to punish people who have violated certain kinds of norms is one of the oldest concerns of political philosophy. Practices of punishment long preceded the evolution of state authority, and even in contemporary liberal societies some punishment practices persist (quite legitimately) outside state structures, such as the disciplining of children within families. The state's interest in punishing certain norm violations arose from the consolidation of public power, and from the linking of punishment to the overarching task and concern of maintaining public peace. Yet the forms and functions of state punishment have arguably changed significantly since state punishment first became the norm in the late Middle Ages.[1] This is due both to a change in the conception of who we punish, and in our understanding of what we may seek to do by way of punishment. In liberal constitutional states, we think of state punishment as something that the state does on our behalf to an equal, a fellow citizen (used here in the wide sense of someone rightfully present or rightfully living in our society), and moreover someone whose rights are not subject to forfeiture by reason of what he or she has done.[2] Both of these developments suggest and support a particular conception of state punishment, and more particularly of the sentencing decision: it is a decision that

[1] Compare the literature cited in nn 8 and 13 below. For an interesting interpretation of the historical material, suggesting that the civilisation of punishment in Europe resulted from an extension to everyone of the respectful treatment originally accorded only to high-status prisoners, see JQ Whitman, *Harsh Justice: Criminal Punishment and the Widening Divide between America and Europe* (Oxford, Oxford University Press, 2003).

[2] From an historical perspective, see Whitman ibid. From a philosophical perspective, see RA Duff, 'A Criminal Law for Citizens' (2010) *Theoretical Criminology* 293; C Brettschneider, 'The Rights of the Guilty. Punishment and Political Theory' (2007) 35 *Political Theory* 175.

should be understood (in this regard, not unlike parental or familial punishment) as setting the terms of our continued relations with the perpetrator of a crime in light of his deed.

This chapter puts forward a conceptualisation of the sentencing judgment appropriate for a liberal state:[3] one that matches the rights-respecting and common weal-oriented foundations of modern state punishment. The criminal law's justification rests on the contribution it makes to upholding the conditions of equal freedom. According equal concern and respect at the sentencing stage means that, notwithstanding the commission of the crime, severance of relations with the offender is not an option. He remains a member of the polity. The task of the sentencing judge is to define how, in our public lives, we move forward from here. A punishment that sets the terms of future relations is inherently reintegrative. This conception of state punishment places rehabilitation at the centre of a liberal justification of state punishment. Our foundational constitutional commitments also suggest a particular understanding of the proportionality of a penal response: a proportionate punishment is one that has an inclusionary orientation, seeking to respond to the offender not just qua perpetrator of this crime but also as a fellow citizen whose prospects and interests still matter. These commitments are sometimes difficult to sustain in the reality of social relations. But a state committed to equal freedom has no choice but to uphold them.

My argument proceeds in three steps. Part I introduces the term-setting conception of punishment through a critique of standard definitions of state punishment and the example of parental punishment. Acknowledging that it remains an open question whether this reintegrative perspective on punishment fits punishment as practised through our shared public institutions, Part II turns to punishment as practised in the offender-state relationship. Here I set out how state punishment forms an integral aspect of the liberal-constitutional project of upholding the conditions of equal freedom. By drawing on the writings of Johann Gottlieb Fichte, who saw punishment as a 'way back' we offer to each other as members of the same polity, I defend and develop a reintegrative conception of state punishment. What this means for the sentencing decision of the trial court is addressed in Part III of the chapter, where I argue that a constitutionally legitimate proportionality assessment must be 'bifocal'—focused not just on the seriousness of the offending behaviour but also on the question what undergoing the punishment will mean for and do to the offender. Humanity and welfare in

[3] I use the term 'liberal' to denote a political order that is committed to tolerance and to the protection of individual rights, but whose conception of the common weal includes a broad role for the state in instantiating and maintaining conditions of life conducive to human security and equal freedom. This notion of liberalism reflects the self-understanding of the liberal welfare states of modern Europe. In its acceptance of a wide remit for legitimate state activity, it is closer to what some writers label 'republicanism' than it is to a libertarian conception of the state.

sentencing requires that we, the polity, take responsibility for what we do to a person whom we punish. A thicker conception of constitutional proportionality mandates moderate and non-destructive punishment.

I. THE TERM-SETTING CONCEPTION OF PUNISHMENT

A. The Standard Definition

A fairly standard definition of state punishment would highlight the following features of the practice: 1. an intentional infliction of harm or hardship on a person, imposed 2. in order to reproach that person for a criminal wrong that the person is found to have committed 3. by someone entitled to make this wrong his business and to perform the punishing act.[4]

This undoubtedly captures central aspects of state punishment.

First, by classifying the penal sanction as a harm, a form of hard treatment, a setback to the punished person's interests, a deprivation of some of her rights, and so on, the standard definition reminds us of what many consider the main issue in the justification of punishment: that punishing someone involves doing something to the recipient that is typically experienced as unpleasant and that (in a state context) we would otherwise view as a violation of her rights. If what is inflicted on the punished person is not recognisably a setback to (at least) their liberty-based interests in some appreciable way, then we are not dealing with a core case of punishment.

The standard definition, second, reminds us of the way in which punishment is necessarily backwards-looking and communicative: it is a response to something the person being punished has done, more specifically a response whose point it is (perhaps among others) to censure the punished individual for what she has done. What is done is an act of reprobation. It signifies that hard treatment is inflicted by reason of the punishee's having behaved badly, and in order to bring it across to her that her earlier behaviour is disapproved of.

Third, the definition makes it clear that the punisher claims for herself a certain kind of standing: in the very act of punishing another, the claim is implicit that one is entitled to make the offender's misbehaviour, and hence his punishment, one's business. Such standing arises from the relationship between punisher and punishee. Given that punishment involves

[4] See, eg, D Boonin, *The Problem of Punishment* (Cambridge, Cambridge University Press, 2008) ch 1; HLA Hart, *Punishment and Responsibility: Essays in the Philosophy of Law* 2nd edn, edited by J Gardner (Oxford, Oxford University Press, 2008) 5ff; RA Duff, 'Legal Punishment' in E Yalta (ed), *Stanford Encyclopedia of Philosophy* (revised entry dated 13 May 2013), available at http://plato.stanford.edu/entries/legal-punishment/.

the actual or potential use of force against the punishee (it is not optional for the individual who is being punished to undergo his punishment; he does not undergo it by agreement) this relationship must be asymmetrically structured—in other words, it must be an authority relation: the punished person is subject to the authority of the punishing agent in respect of the behaviour for which punishment is inflicted.[5]

B. A Gap in the Standard Definition?

For all its strengths, the standard definition misses a pivotal feature of punishment. To see this, it helps to take a step back from state punishment and to enter another very familiar penal setting: parental punishment.

Why do parents sometimes punish their children? What I have in mind here are not trivial occasions where children disobey their parents and suffer mild consequences (such as being deprived of ice cream after failing to heed the parental warning that 'If you don't put that smartphone aside now, you will not get any ice cream for dessert'), but instances of fairly serious misbehaviour—say, when a teenager is found to have taken a not insignificant sum of money from his mother's purse to buy himself a desired item that she refused to buy for him. The mother then faces the uncomfortable realisation that she cannot just let this sort of behaviour go, even though she might feel tempted to do just that. Moreover, she realises that her response must have the features identified by the standard definition of punishment. Why? Because her response will set the terms for her continued future existence with her son, and these terms must be set so as to make it clear to him that this sort of behaviour by him will not be tolerated. Let's imagine that the mother decides that her son will be 'grounded' for four consecutive weekends and that he also has to do household chores such as cleaning the bathroom and the kitchen for her until the value of his cleaning work equals the sum of money he has taken. It will undoubtedly take some effort from her to see this through. What will motivate her to make that effort is the knowledge that she and her son will have to continue to live together and that they cannot do so on terms where he gets away with stealing her money. She needs to establish a durable and satisfactory basis for their future interactions.

The important feature which the parental punishment scenario shares with state punishment, and which the standard definition of punishment

[5] But see L Zaibert, *Punishment and Retribution* (Aldershot, Ashgate, 2006) for a sustained challenge to definitions of punishment that build (state) authority into the definition. Thom Brooks, in his review of Zaibert's book, perceptively points out that on Zaibert's definition, the conceptual distinction between punishment and revenge may be lost, and it becomes more difficult to develop the grounds for normatively distinguishing between legitimate and illegitimate punishment: (2007) 10 *New Criminal Law Review* 311 at 313–14.

merely alludes to by highlighting the reprobative element, is this: typically, we engage in punishing a person because we assume that a 'life in common'[6] will somehow have to continue with that person. There is little point in going to the trouble of punishing someone if we will never see them again (though we can, of course, quickly do something to them to 'get even' before they disappear from our lives). Punishment is integral to social practices that teach individuals how to live together.[7]

As a general social practice, then, punishment does not merely mark out the punishee's actions as wrong and blames him for engaging in this wrongful act. It also defines how both punishee and punisher will move forward from here. The penal agent lays down the terms of his or her future co-existence with the offender in a shared social world. Because this is punishment's central social function, there is a reintegrative momentum inherent in punishment that gives the offender himself an interest in being punished. Far from threatening or challenging an offender's membership in the community, punishment reasserts and reinforces it.

C. Punishment and Exclusion

But isn't there an obvious challenge to this conceptualisation of the point of our penal practices? Doesn't punishment sometimes consist in the *severance* of relationship? Isn't permanent exclusion on the cards as something like 'the ultimate sanction', whether in informal, interpersonal or in public and state-administered penal interactions?

Historically it is of course undeniable that some of the things that were done to people by way of sanctioning them for past misbehaviour amounted to their permanent exclusion from their communities.[8] One of the sharpest punishments practised by Germanic tribes was to declare the miscreant

[6] This is the expression used by Timothy Macklem for a shared communal life governed by norms; see T Macklem, *Law and Life in Common* (Oxford, Oxford University Press, 2015).

[7] MK Stohr, A Walsh and C Hemmens, *Corrections: A Text/Reader* (Thousand Oaks, Sage, 2009) 3, summarise the findings of evolutionary biologists as establishing that '[p]unishment (referred to as moralistic or retaliatory aggression) … is an evolutionary stable strategy … for the emergence and maintenance of cooperative behavior' (original emphases omitted). Psychologists have developed more nuanced accounts of the functions of punishment and reward in education. See generally A Bandura and RH Walters, *Social Learning and Personality Development* (New York, Holt, Rinhart and Winston, 1963). The 'moral education' theory of punishment developed by J Hampton ('The Moral Education Theory of Punishment' (1984) 13 *Philosophy & Public Affairs* 208), by contrast, relies on a normative account of moral education and does not build on sociobiological understandings of punishment.

[8] Sanctions aimed at expelling individuals from communities coexisted with a raft of sanctions that were practised on those expected to remain—mostly, sanctions involving public humiliation, shaming and exposure. For the historical development, see CL von Bar, *A History of Continental Criminal Law*, translated by TS Bell and others (London, John Murray, 1916)

vogelfrei, literally 'free as a bird'—effectively an outlaw. This declaration rendered him rightless. He mattered no more than a wild animal to which anyone could do what they liked.[9] In later ages, transportation arguably amounted to something similar to permanent exclusion even though it was often technically imposed for a limited time period, the transported criminal being in theory free after its expiration to return to his home land.[10] And insofar as the death penalty is still practised its point also appears to be to destroy any possibility of a future life in common—not even the life in common that exists between free members of the polity and those incarcerated in prisons or otherwise institutionalised.[11]

These observations may lead us to doubt that, conceptually, punishment is necessarily a reintegrative institution. The communicative dimension of penal practice reminds us that someone may inflict a response by way of punishment that in effect consists in expelling the individual from the community. While such penal dispositions are unlikely to be (at least in practice) a frequent penal response, they are arguably still recognisably cases of punishment.[12]

A long line of legal historians have, however, defended the view that the difference between expulsion and non-expulsion provides us with the conceptual boundary of punishment, and in developing this point their argument invariably turns on the authority relation that genuine punishment appears to require. Some have stressed that being expelled from a community means that one is no longer under the authority (and, of course, the protection) of the law that governs this community, and that those outside our legal sphere of concern are not fit subjects for the exercise of legal authority over them (since they are not legal subjects)—whereas punishment

chs 2 and 4; E Schmidt, *Einführung in die Geschichte der deutschen Strafrechtspflege* 3rd edn (Göttingen, Vandenhoeck & Ruprecht, 1965).

9 On outlawry, see von Bar ibid at 62–66 and Schmidt ibid.

10 On transportation, see JM Beattie, *Crime and the Courts in England, 1660–1800* (Oxford, Oxford University Press, 1986) ch 9; S Devereaux, 'In Place of Death: Transportation, Penal Practices, and the English State, 1770–1830' in C Strange (ed), *Qualities of Mercy: Justice, Punishment and Discretion* (Vancouver, UBC Press, 1996) ch 2; C Herrup, 'Punishing Pardon: Some Thoughts on the Origins of Penal Transportation' in S Devereaux and P Griffiths (eds), *Penal Practice and Culture, 1500–1900: Punishing the English* (Basingstoke, Palgrave Macmillan, 2004) 121.

11 Even before the humanisation of imprisonment, brought about, inter alia, through prisoner rights litigation, the nature of imprisonment as a regime under which legal relations are continued rather than severed cannot be in doubt. On contemporary relations of imprisonment, see D Van Zyl Smit and S Snacken, *Principles of European Prison Law and Policy: Penology and Human Rights* (Oxford, Oxford University Press, 2009). On the history of imprisonment, see T Krause, *Geschichte des Strafvollzugs. Von den Kerkern des Altertums bis zur Gegenwart* (Darmstadt, Primus, 1999).

12 At least where the motivation behind their infliction is retributive rather than preventive.

is centrally the exercise of lawful authority.[13] At least in Western Europe, punishment developed as a practice by which one deals with those under one's government—and was thus not how criminal wrongs were dealt with among free men (suggesting that outlawry marked the end of peaceful relations between equals rather than an authoritative exercise of penal power within a hierarchical relationship).[14]

One indication that relationship-severing reactions may indeed mark the conceptual boundary of punishment can be found in the exact message that relationship-severing dispositions send. Arguably, their communicative meaning is not exhausted in the simple message that 'this is what I do to you in response to your crime'. It is, more specifically, that: 'Because of your crime, I wash my hands of you. I will have nothing to do with you any more. I will make no effort on your behalf. The world in which I live no longer includes you.' Relationship-severing reactions thus come across not as punishments but rather as reactions to transgressions we are no longer prepared to punish.[15] They signify a refusal to affirm the continuation of the relationship by punishing. Recall that punishing a person may require

[13] See already von Bar, above n 8 at 57–66, 71–76, 95ff. For modern analyses, see H Nehlsen, 'Entstehung des öffentlichen Strafrechts bei den germanischen Stämmen' in K Kroeschell (ed), *Gerichtslauben-Vorträge. Freiburger Festkolloquium zum fünfundsiebzigsten Geburtstag von Hans Thieme* (Sigmaringen, Jan Torbecke, 1983) 3. On the evolution of a public criminal law generally, see D Willoweit (ed), *Die Entstehung des öffentlichen Strafrechts. Bestandsaufnahme eines europäischen Forschungsproblems* (Cologne, Böhlau, 1999); H Schlosser, R Sprandel und D Willoweit (eds), *Herrschaftliches Strafen seit dem Hochmittelalter. Formen und Entwicklungsstufen* (Cologne, Böhlau, 2002); K Lüderssen (ed), *Die Durchsetzung des öffentlichen Strafanspruchs. Systematisierung der Fragestellung* (Cologne, Böhlau, 2002); and J Weitzel (ed), *Hoheitliches Strafen in der Spätantike und im frühen Mittelalter* (Cologne, Böhlau, 2002).

[14] German legal historians have convincingly suggested that outlawry was distinct from state punishment, since outlawry, as Mireille Hildebrandt explains, was practised between freemen and 'placed [the offender] outside the community of freemen and outside the grasp of its peace' (M Hildebrandt, 'Radbruch on the Origins of the Criminal Law' in MD Dubber (ed), *Foundational Texts in Modern Criminal Law* (Oxford, Oxford University Press, 2014) 219 at 232). State punishment, by contrast, emerged from the essentially hierarchical and unequal relationship between serfs and their overlords; see G Radbruch, 'Der Ursprung des Strafrechts aus dem Stande der Unfreien', in G Radbruch, *Elegantiae Juris Criminalis: Vierzehn Studien zur Geschichte des Strafrechts* (Basel, Verlag für Recht und Gesellschaft, 1950) 11, of which Hildebrandt's essay is a fascinating discussion and evaluation. A translation of Radbruch's essay is available at www.oup.com/uk/law/foundational-texts.

[15] Hannah Arendt famously suggested that there are crimes of such enormity that we reach a limit to our ability to respond to them meaningfully by way of punishment. She then went on to suggest that, for this reason, we would also reach a conceptual barrier to forgiveness (H Arendt, *The Human Condition* 2nd edn with an introduction by Margaret Canovan (Chicago and London, University of Chicago Press, 1998) 241). While, with Pumla Gobodo-Madikizela, I doubt that our ability to forgive is conceptually tied to our ability to punish, the question how we should respond to persons who have committed crimes that we feel we simply cannot respond to through a mechanism that offers them a way back, remains both acute and unsolved. For an incisive reflection on Arendt's position, see P Gobodo-Madikizela, 'Radical Forgiveness: Transforming Traumatic Memory beyond Hannah Arendt' in F du Bois and A du Bois-Pedain (eds), *Justice and Reconciliation in Post-Apartheid South Africa* (Cambridge, Cambridge University Press, 2008) 37.

considerable commitment and continuing effort on the part of the punisher, an investment of sorts, something that the punisher must consider worth her while. From the punisher's perspective the effort is worthwhile because it will (in her expectation) re-establish the terms of their communal existence.

The pressing question, then, is whether the term-setting conception of punishment introduced in this section through the analogy of parental punishment provides us with a viable perspective on state punishment. Parental punishment is, after all, quite different from state punishment in that it is (ideally at least) a constructive form of discipline linked to a child's upbringing through parental guidance within the family. That said, as Thorburn rightly stresses in his contribution to this collection, something that parental and state punishment have in common is the relationship of authority from which the penal standing of the punishing agent flows. We must therefore look at the nature of the relationship between members of a polity and its public authority to see whether the term-setting conception of punishment is also applicable to the sentencing judgment of a criminal court. The next part of this chapter analyses this relationship, arguing that the humanistic and political commitments on which life in a liberal political community is based require a reintegrative conception of punishment that rules out the severance of relationship as a response to crimes.

II. PUNISHMENT AND THE OFFENDER-STATE RELATIONSHIP

A. State Punishment and the Conditions of Equal Freedom

What is distinctive about modern constitutional states is a certain conception of the rights of members of the populace. Most importantly in the present context, they consist in our guaranteeing to each other the most extensive personal freedom that is compatible with equal freedom exercised by others, and to do so through public institutions that provide equal protection to the (normatively conceived) interests of all. Even if there were no philosophical knock-down argument as to why people have certain fundamental rights, and why these rights (including the right to membership in the polity) should be inalienable, there would be ample grounds for saying that a political order based on the recognition of such rights is preferable to one which is not so structured. This is because an order committed to the recognition and protection of such rights fosters actual security (it does not do to people what would be destructive of their most important interests) as well as perceptions of security (people expect that the actions of those who hold positions of power will not be destructive of their interests).[16]

[16] See also Zedner's chapter in this volume.

It is therefore an order in which the answer that can be given to members who make what Bernard Williams memorably calls the 'basic legitimation demand'[17] is likely to be a satisfactory one: 'I exert power over you (among others) because my doing so is in your interest'.[18]

When we think of the criminal law as helping to instantiate and preserve the conditions of equal freedom, we will first focus our minds on how to preserve freedom at the legislative stage. This will give us some guidance as to what behaviours we need to address through criminalisation. But already at this stage we need to be sensitive to the question how an 'order of freedom'[19] would address those whose freedom is to be secured—as moral agents, not as tigers to be controlled.[20] And—at least to some extent—we will also think about the question how our enforcement mechanisms should, concretely, interact with those we suspect of having violated this order of freedom, and then how they should respond to those who are found to have violated it. But these matters remain rather abstract at the legislative or (from an enforcement perspective) ex ante stage of the criminal law. At this stage, criminal law does the job it is meant to do if it only criminalises behaviour that can be legitimately criminalised as being inimical to the preservation of an order of freedom, and (to the extent that this order is preserved by addressing us as potential law-breakers) by offering us—in form of threats of punishment—an additional prudential disincentive to desist from criminal law-violations. As Andreas von Hirsch has correctly highlighted, this means that not just any punishment can be threatened by the law. The punishment must be measured, otherwise it risks drowning out

[17] See B Williams, *In the Beginning was the Deed: Realism and Moralism in Political Argument,* edited by G Hawthorn (Princeton NJ, Princeton University Press, 2005) 5. The notion of the 'basic legitimation demand' is interpreted and explored by Bottoms and Tankebe, who explain it as the 'demand by subjects that the power-holder should provide adequate justification of his/her claim to rule' (Bottoms and Tankebe, in this volume). I am grateful to them for drawing my attention to Williams' essay.

[18] This possible answer to the demand remains fairly abstract. What meeting the basic legitimation demand entails concretely in the interactions between representatives of state authority and members of the public, is the focus of Bottoms' and Tankebe's chapter in this collection.

[19] Note that by speaking of an 'order of freedom' or 'the conditions of equal freedom', I do not mean to nail my flag to the mast of any particular political theory of what the preservation of freedom entails, and conversely rules out. Rather I use this phrase here as a placeholder for a convincing account. Personally, I lean towards a Hegelian-inspired (sometimes called republican) understanding that conceives of freedom 'not so much [as] a matter of being left alone as it is "the condition of citizenship in a free society"' (R Dagger, 'Republicanism and Crime' in S Besson and JL Martí (eds), *Legal Republicanism: National and International Perspectives* (Oxford, Oxford University Press, 2009) 147 at 154 (quoting J Braithwaite and P Pettit, *Not Just Deserts: A Republican Theory of Punishment* (Oxford, Clarendon Press, 1990) 57)). For a sustained Hegelian account of what makes a free society, see A Honneth, *Freedom's Right: The Social Foundations of Democratic Life* (Cambridge, Polity Press, 2014).

[20] See A von Hirsch, *Censure and Sanctions* (Oxford, Oxford University Press, 1993) 13–14.

the moral message that is respectful of a legal subject's moral agency and personality even when it is telling the subject what not to do.[21]

Respect for offenders as moral agents matters again—and in a somewhat different way from what we have already set out above—when the criminal law stands to be applied to a particular person in respect of a particular incident. Viewed simply from an ex ante perspective, the criminal law might well restrict itself to conduct rules pure and simple. Effective conduct guidance needs to presuppose, and would therefore import, a certain extent of mens rea considerations—enough to differentiate between agency and non-agency, but no more.[22] Yet it is generally not doubted that the criminal law should contain rules of evaluation that address a law-breaker's culpability in a more comprehensive sense.[23] The constitutional reason for wanting blameworthiness and exculpatory defences to matter at the adjudication stage is that relating to each other as moral agents (as opposed to something like harm-causing automatons) requires us to be responsive to the reasoning processes and the motives of the other person—to her culpability, above and beyond the kinds of mental states that made her conduct a token of the exercise of her agential powers in the world.[24] 'All that matters to me is that you did it; your beliefs, attitudes and motives at the time and the pressures

[21] Ibid. For an interesting challenge to the empirical plausibility of the drowning-out objection to harsh penalties, see M Matravers, 'Is Twenty-first Century Punishment Post-desert?' in M Tonry (ed), *Retributivism has a Past. Has it a Future?* (Oxford, Oxford University Press, 2011) 30 at 38–39. For a defence of the 'prudential disincentive' perspective on legal sanctions, see Z Hoskins, 'Deterrent Punishment and Respect for Persons' (2011) 8 *Ohio State Journal of Criminal Law* 369 at 382–84.

[22] For discussion of this point, see Mark Dsouza, *A Theory of Rationale-based Defences* (PhD thesis, University of Cambridge, 2014) ch 2, drawing on Meir Dan-Cohen's well-known article 'Decision Rules and Conduct Rules: On Acoustic Separation in Criminal Law' (1983–1984) 97 *Harvard Law Review* 625, where Dan-Cohen distinguishes between conduct rules (addressed to the citizen) and rules of adjudication (addressed to officials). When applied to the criminal law, rules of adjudication are not (as one might otherwise think) only procedural rules. Rather, they include what one might perhaps label 'rules of evaluation'—certain provisions and concepts of the substantive criminal law that tell adjudicators how to evaluate a breach of the criminal law rather than telling a member of the polity prescriptively how to avoid committing a crime. Broadly speaking, substantive rules that go towards the blameworthiness of defendants (giving rise to incapacity or to non-justificatory exculpation) belong to this group.

[23] On these two senses of culpability, see J Dressler, *Understanding Criminal Law* 6th edn (Albany NY, LexisNexis, 2012) 118–19. For the reasons given in the text, culpability in this wider sense is relevant not just for those who (to paraphrase Douglas Husak) 'dream the retributivist dream'; a point that is overlooked by D Lefkowitz, 'Blame and the Criminal Law' (2015) 6 *Jurisprudence* 451 in his otherwise very interesting rebuttal of D Shoemaker, 'Blame and Punishment' in DJ Coats and NA Tognazzini (eds), *Blame: Its Nature and Norms* (Oxford, Oxford University Press, 2013) 100.

[24] On the culpability principle and its roots in a commitment to engaging with offenders as moral agents, see T Hörnle and MD Dubber, *Criminal Law: A Comparative Approach* (Oxford, Oxford University Press, 2014) 108–09 (quoting a decision by the German Federal Supreme Court, BGHSt2, 194 (200)). For an historical analysis, see S Stübinger, *Schuld, Strafrecht und Geschichte. Die Entstehung der Schuldzurechnung in der deutschen Strafrechtshistorie* (Cologne, Böhlau, 2000).

which may have been exerted upon you are irrelevant to me' would be tantamount to saying 'I refuse to see you and relate to you as a moral agent, I see you and relate to you merely as a cause of harm'. This is a stance we reject in our political constitution.

At the sentencing stage we yet again need to ask the question what our fundamental political commitments mean for how we should go about things at this point. The generalised ex ante aim of all good governance, to provide a system of rules conducive to human freedom and security, to a well-lived life in common, does not as such provide us with direct guidance as to how state authority should act in the particular, ex post case of responding to a situation where its ex ante prohibition has failed to prevail. One of the first philosophers to see this clearly was Johann Gottlieb Fichte, and although his answer is given in the context of a social contract theory that has not attracted many followers, it pays to look at how he sets up and resolves the problem of justifying the infliction of punishment in concrete cases.[25]

Fichte thinks that what obligates people towards each other is a social contract under whose terms they recognise each other as holders of rights. The commission of a crime signifies, for Fichte, that the contract is breached, in consequence of which the contract is terminated and all rights that the offender had under the contract are lost.[26] This, however, is not the end of the matter, nor is punishment yet anywhere in sight. Building the familiar historical notion of outlawry into his theory, Fichte at this point assumes that the crime pushes relations between the offender and the polity into a state of rightlessness—as our brief discussion in Part I intimated, a perilous situation for the offender since he is no longer connected to others through relations of right and anything might be done to him with impunity.[27]

The interesting step in Fichte's account follows on this. Most of the time, he points out, it is neither in our communal interest nor in the interest of the offender himself that he remains in a condition where no rights are recognised between him and us. Therefore, instead of now simply treating

[25] Fichte's discussion of state punishment can be found in § 20 of his *Grundlage des Naturrechts nach Principien der Wissenschaftslehre* Vol 2 (Jena and Leipzig, Gabler, 1797). I quote here from the English translation: JG Fichte, *Foundations of Natural Right According to the Principles of the Wissenschaftslehre*, edited by F Neuhouser and translated by M Baur (Cambridge, Cambridge University Press, 2000) 226–48. Fichte's theory of punishment receives a brief but excellent treatment in von Bar, above n 8 at 424ff. Valuable recent discussions include A Lazzari, '"Eine Fessel, die nicht schmerzt und nicht sehr hindert": Strafrecht (§ 20)' in JC Merle (ed), *Johann Gottlieb Fichte, Grundlage des Naturrechts* (Berlin, Akademie-Verlag, 2001) 173 and R Zaczyk, *Das Strafrecht in der Rechtslehre J G Fichtes* (Berlin, Duncker & Humblot, 1981).

[26] Fichte, ibid at 226.

[27] See esp Fichte, ibid at 241–42. Whatever we may do to a former member of our polity who, through his crime, has forfeited his rights, is not punishment.

the offender as an outlaw, the state will usually offer him a way back—and *this way back* is through punishment.[28] State punishment is thus conceived of in terms of an *Abbüßungsvertrag*[29] (contract of atonement), from which (as von Bar explains Fichte's argument) 'the criminal derives "the important right" that he is not declared absolutely without rights but is to be punished'.[30] Fichte effectively treats the criminal law itself as a general-anticipatory contract of atonement—in the punishments it threatens (with the immediate purpose of preventing violations of the law), it also anticipates the terms on which a future contract of atonement will be struck.[31]

Fichte's starting point that an offender loses all his rights through the commission of the crime and has to be allowed back and regain his rights through a 'contract of atonement' is not one that we need to accept—in fact, we have to resist it because our foundational political commitment is to accord each other rights that are inalienable, including the right to membership. But the difference this makes is unimportant in the context of the present discussion. What matters here is Fichte's realisation that the purpose we pursue ex ante with a penal prohibition that *threatens* punishment (to protect our rights as persons living under a social contract) does not *carry across* to the imposition of punishment. At this point, the deterrent threat of punishment has failed in the individual case, the prudential appeal has not been heeded. If we identify the function of the criminal law at the ex ante stage with (broadly speaking) rights-protection and preventive regulation, then the *imposition* of punishment does (and must necessarily) serve a different function.

B. The Reintegrative Orientation of State Punishment

What, then, is the function of the imposition of punishment?

> [A]ll citizens promise to all others that they will give them the opportunity to make themselves fit to live in society once again, if in the present they are found

[28] Fichte, ibid at 227 and 236.

[29] Fichte's own exposition is more complicated, in that he presupposes not one but two contracts of atonement. The first one deals only with offences for which 'expiation by adequate counterpoise' is possible (ibid, 227–29). This contract does not cover any crimes arising from an offender's 'formally bad' will, nor crimes committed directly against the state (236). A second contract of atonement (discussed at 236–40) deals with this much larger group of offences—and this is the contract of atonement to which my discussion in the text relates.

[30] Von Bar, above n 8 at 425 (quoting Fichte). Incidentally, it follows from Fichte's position that the death penalty is not a punishment at all, and must be understood rather as something we do to a person who we no longer treat as having any rights and to whom we refuse to offer a contract of atonement. See von Bar, ibid.

[31] Note that this right is not absolute, but premised on the ability of the offender to give sufficient assurance that he can 'make [himself] fit to live in society again'—which, Fichte assumes, those guilty of 'intentional, premeditated murder' will be unable to do (Fichte, above n 25 at 241).

> to be unfit; and (what is also entailed by this contract) that they will accept them back into society, after they have reformed...[32]

is how Fichte explains the terms of the contract of atonement. Punishment thus aims at the 'political reformation' of the offender, which Fichte defined as 'reform of the manners and maxims of a person's actual behaviour' and 'certainly not the *moral* reform of one's inner disposition'.[33] Fichte insists that the time an offender spends in an institution of rehabilitation (which is Fichte's conception of the prison) must be subject to a 'peremptory term for reform, in accordance with his particular crime'.[34] The overall orientation of punishment towards reformation does not however permit us to set open-ended terms of indefinite punishment, with successful reformation of an offender a condition of his release. Reasonable contractual terms can include the promise that part of the punishment will be waived if things go well. But they cannot consist in saying 'you are going to be punished until at a later time I decide otherwise'.

Fichte's central insight into the nature of state punishment as concerned with an offender's reintegration into the community of the law-abiding, on terms that are (in my reading of Fichte's theory) set within the broad framework provided for by the criminal law and legitimated in the individual case by the offender's ability to provide us with sufficient reassurance of his future law-abidingness, helps us to address the classical freedom-oriented challenge against reformatory punishment: the suggestion that state punishment may not aim to 'better' or 'improve' the criminal.[35] This challenge is based on a certain conception of what respecting freedom means. We should not interfere with people's lives through the criminal law if all we aim to do is paternalistically to interfere with the way they conduct their lives. Legitimate interference must be directed at conduct that properly concerns other members of the polity because it is conduct that oversteps the boundaries of equal freedom—centrally, because it is harmful to others and violates or endangers their rights, or significant communal interests (say, the preservation of the environment, or road safety).

32 Fichte, ibid at 236.

33 Fichte, ibid at 237.

34 Fichte, ibid at 240. Note, however, that for Fichte this 'peremptory term' for reform also functions as a deadline—the offender will be released, indeed, but if unreformed he will be denied re-entry into society and will be excluded from the polity after all. For discussion see Zaczyk, above n 25 at 115ff.

35 See, generally, M Matravers, 'Political Neutrality and Punishment' (2013) 7 *Criminal Law and Philosophy*, 217 at 219, discussing 'possible tensions ... between (impartialist) liberalism and aspects of a system of criminal law and punishment', arising in particular when state penal policies are based on rejecting some conceptions of the good, or on promoting others. Even if punishment does not aim to reform morally but only politically (in Fichte's sense), it clearly aims to inculcate in the offender skills and a work ethic conducive to a different way of life.

But this argument has force mainly at the criminalisation stage. Assuming a properly restrained reach of the criminal law, it is the violation of the conditions of equal freedom that authorises the penal response by the state. What makes this response legitimate, however, is not (again) that it does not set itself a paternalistic objective. Quite the contrary: what legitimates punishment is that the offender is prepared for living in the conditions of equal freedom. A state that respects the basic entitlement of all members of its population to the conditions of equal freedom has a duty to help those of its inhabitants who cannot respect these conditions to acquire the capacity to do so.[36] And—as Fichte himself clearly sees—offenders cannot be prepared for a responsible life in freedom through an experience of animal-like captivity in which their ability to lead a self-directed life is dulled instead of furthered.[37] He calls for regimes of imprisonment that further responsible agency by allowing prisoners significant self-governance in prison.[38] Prison life should thus inculcate the values, dispositions and habits essential for a law-abiding life post-release.[39]

As for the appropriate level of penal severity, Fichte has this to say:

> The primary rule in this regard is that one should neither despair of [the prisoners'] reform, nor cause them to despair of it—and furthermore, that they should have some degree of satisfaction with their condition, as well as the hope to improve it.[40]

This view does not commit us to purely reform-oriented punishment across the board. To see this, consider how the duties we have towards young offenders (and the consequent offender-orientation) in the context of youth justice differ from the recognition of an adult offender's non-forfeitable status of equal political membership. As individual human beings, many adult offenders may well be rather similar to young offenders when it comes to social and individual dysfunctionalities that are generative of criminal

[36] Compare EN Yankah, 'Republican Responsibility in Criminal Law' (2015) 9 *Criminal Law and Philosophy* 457.

[37] Fichte, above n 25 at 240.

[38] Fichte, ibid at 239.

[39] A politically reformed offender is one whose 'dissoluteness has been replaced by a love of diligence and order, [his] savagery replaced by a milder sensibility' (Fichte, ibid at 240). What Fichte means by this concretely becomes clear from his sketch of reformatory practice discussed in the text: offenders should acquire the skills and habits that give them a stake, and reasonable prospects of self-maintenance, in mainstream society.

[40] Fichte, ibid at 238. One should, however, avoid the impression that Fichte offers on this topic what we would nowadays regard as a coherent and fully worked out liberal position. Fichte's own exposition is somewhat meandering and on occasion veers wildly between what modern readers would consider calls to unreasonable harshness and moderate suggestions. Moreover, the steps in the argument are often open to question. Fichte's own vision of constructive prison life (in something akin to an island community of prisoners) betrays a certain degree of disconnection from common sense.

behaviour. They may have low levels of skills, bad anger control and generally underdeveloped abilities at self-management. They may also struggle with addiction and with mental illness. There is certainly a line of continuity here (which is also unsurprising, given that many young offenders continue offending into (at least) early adulthood).[41] Yet the objectives of sentencing—also the communicative objectives—change when we move from youth to adult cases. They change with the community's overall relationship with the offender. What we owe (as a community) to under-age members (whether they have come in conflict with the law or not) is in two important ways defined by that person's status as being under-age: this supplies both a ground and justification for paternalistic intervention, and an obligation to educate and protect.[42] And it is accepted that doing these things in the interest of young people imposes certain additional burdens on other members of the community—and that it is distributively appropriate that they should be shouldered by the community. It is a shared obligation to help young people get a sufficiently good start in communal life—and to the extent that the young person is failing at that, part of the responsibility for making things right rebounds on those who are generally responsible for helping the young get a reasonable start. It is thus our duty towards the young offender that mandates the educational or reform-orientation of youth justice.

The sense that we have obligations towards offenders does not evaporate when offenders reach adulthood. But the nature and extent of the obligations change. The sentencing judgment speaks to the offender, the victim and the community, and what it communicates are the terms that we—a political community that governs itself under the ideal of equal freedom—believe are appropriate to impose on a member of our polity who has violated the terms of equal freedom. We believe that some hardship is necessary to mark the seriousness of what he has done. Proportionate punishment is therefore the

[41] See generally AAJ Blokland and P Nieuwbeerta, 'Life Course Criminology' in SG Shoham, P Knepper and M Kett (eds), *International Handbook of Criminology* (Boca Raton, CRC Press, 2010) 51; M Rocque and BC Welsh, 'Offender Rehabilitation from a Maturation/Biosocial Perspective' in M DeLisi and MG Vaughn (eds), *Routledge International Handbook of Biosocial Criminology* (Abingdon, Routledge, 2015) 501.

[42] Compare eg the German Juvenile Justice Act, s 2 (Aims of the Juvenile Justice System): '(1) The main aim of the application of criminal law to young people is to counter renewed offending by young persons. In order to achieve this goal, procedure and disposals … shall be chosen primarily with educational objectives in mind.' See also Sentencing Guidelines Council, *Overarching Principles: Sentencing Youths: Definitive Guideline* (November 2009), para 1.2: 'When sentencing an offender aged under 18, a court must have regard to: a) the principal aim of the youth justice system (to prevent offending by children and young persons); and b) the welfare of the offender.' See also (with individual contributions analysing juvenile justice policies and policy shifts in various jurisdictions) J Junger-Tas and SH Decker (eds), *International Handbook of Juvenile Justice* (New York, Springer, 2006).

first and foremost objective—it is the way in which we mark the seriousness of the offending conduct (and treat each other as equals in doing so). But we also believe that the offence is not the end of relations between us and the offender. Punishment does not sever legal or societal links. The offender is here to stay, and he or she is (at least in principle) also here one day to return to a life in freedom. For that reason, proportionate punishment must also be constructive—constructive in the sense that a successful life in freedom must be a real possibility. We must not (as Ashworth once put it) 'de-socialise' the offender,[43] and we may have to (as Yankah argued) provide active assistance to those who once released would otherwise not stand much of a chance of building law-abiding lives for themselves.[44]

The sentencing decision marks the moment where the criminal law moves from threatening people with certain consequences for breaches of its rules to doing burdensome things to particular individuals who have transgressed these rules anyway. When this stage is reached, the conceptually dominant goal becomes rehabilitation.

To see why this is so, we need to recall what justifies the state in actually punishing an offender: the offender's interest in partaking again in a life in common committed to the preservation of the conditions of equal freedom. His interest in succeeding in such participation—in leading a coercion-free life in the future—provides the justification for a penal imposition that has his reformation as its goal (and realistically possible outcome).

Based on our discussion thus far, more can be said about how this goal may be pursued. Punishments aimed at an offender's personal reform run the risk of overstepping the 'licence' given to the state, which is only to preserve conditions of equal freedom, not to make people better people as such.[45] To place rehabilitation within the licence, we have to connect it to the understanding of the sanction as setting out the terms for future existence in a shared social world—conditions bounded by the focus on securing the conditions of equal freedom for all. Rehabilitation is a legitimate goal of the criminal justice system when it is based on acknowledging that it serves the interests of offenders as well, in that it is meant to make it more likely that they will be able to conduct themselves in future as members of society who respect the conditions of equal freedom for all.

[43] A Ashworth, 'European Sentencing Traditions: Accepting Divergence or Aiming for Convergence?' in C Tata and N Hutton, *Sentencing and Society: International Perspectives* (Aldershot, Ashgate 2002).

[44] Yankah, above n 36 at 473. This is why it is entirely right that liberal constitutions such as the Italian one mandate that the objective of punishment is rehabilitative, and link this to the state's respect for the dignity of offenders.

[45] Compare also A von Hirsch and A Ashworth, *Proportionate Sentencing: Exploring the Principles* (Oxford, Oxford University Press, 2005) ch 7 (critiquing the penance perspective developed by Antony Duff).

The most important aspect of the trial court's sentencing judgment is that, in determining what should happen to an offender in respect of the crime, the judgment holds out the promise that this is what will settle the matter; it defines how we move forward from here. The sentence is part of an interaction that is irreducibly not merely past- but also future-oriented: future-oriented in the sense that it is aimed at creating the conditions under which full equality and full community with the perpetrator is re-established. This conception of the sentencing judgment is the only one appropriate to the criminal justice practices of a constitutional state. In such a state, exclusion is not an option; rights are not forfeitable—they cannot be lost or denied as a consequence of a crime; they can merely be limited or interfered with in certain ways. Legitimate state punishment punishes offenders on the assumption that a way of life that includes both the punisher and the punishee continues for the duration of and also after the punishment—the assumption is one of a shared social world, in which punisher and punishee both remain. If we break the law, terms of atonement must always be offered to us.

III. CHOOSING THE SENTENCE: HOW TO PUNISH PROPORTIONATELY

A. Proportionality and Individualisation

If one treats the perspective on the sentencing judgment put forward here as 'the basis of a sentencing system',[46] then certain parameters emerge as necessary or desirable features of the system. Some leeway to individualise sentences is constitutionally required because the legitimacy of the individual sentence hinges on the defensibility of setting precisely *these* terms for continued relationship with *this* perpetrator in respect of *this* crime. Proportionality and individualisation of punishment are thus hard-wired into the criminal justice practices of states founded on the ideal of equal freedom[47]—arguably, all modern constitutional states. Far from proportionate and discretion-based sentencing being contrasting ideals potentially in tension with each other, proportionality in sentencing emerges, as one Irish judge put it, as 'the manner in which judicial discretion should, as a matter of principle, be exercised within particular proceedings'.[48]

[46] Ashworth, above n 43.

[47] For judicial recognition of this point, see the jurisprudence of the Supreme Court of Canada, which held in *R v Ipeelee; R v Ladue* [2012] 1 SCR 433 (SCC) that 'proportionality in sentencing could aptly be described as a principle of fundamental justice under s 7 of the Charter', and has stressed that the duty of the judge is to 'impose a sentence that both speaks out against the offence and punishes the offender no more than is necessary' (*R v Nasogaluak* [2010] 1 SCR 206 (SCC) para 42 (LeBel J)).

[48] Murray CJ in *Whelan and Lynch v Minister for Justice, Equality and Law Reform* [2007] IESC 34, [2012] 1 IR 1.

This does not however help us much in resolving the question how proportionate sanctions should be identified in particular cases. Lacey and Pickard argue that it is a mistake to think that 'appealing to proportionality as an abstract ideal can deliver limits to punishment'; rather, such limits 'need to be grounded in substantive judgments about fair and proportionate penalties which are meaningful to, and regarded as legitimate by, the populace in whose name they are imposed'.[49] They are surely right about this. The notion of proportionality as such does not give us much substantive guidance (although it can, and does, supply us with the three-step methodology familiar from constitutional adjudication). We need to know what values and aims underpin the decision we are about to make.[50]

Matravers also believes 'that an entitlement to proportionality in sentencing is not an independent principle, but is—as with all entitlements—determined by the wider theory of justice'.[51] Regarding the latter, Matravers himself has pursued the connections that may exist between a Rawlsian notion of distributive justice and retributive justice concerns—particularly the question whether we can draw a parallel between natural talents and dispositions such as intelligence, discipline, perseverance that Rawlsians understand as supplying no 'desert basis' in distributive justice, and (in our society) unfortunate individual 'constitutions' (dispositions and personality traits) that tend to bring a person in collision with the criminal law.[52] I want to ask that same question, starting however with a different conceptual framework: the wider theory of justice implicit in a constitutional order founded on equal concern and respect, and on inalienable rights.

Of course, one conclusion has long been drawn explicitly in many a constitutional document: the prohibition of 'unusual or degrading' punishments. But even after we rule out sanctions that humiliate offenders

[49] N Lacey and H Pickard, 'The Chimera of Proportionality: Institutionalising Limits on Punishment in Contemporary Social and Political Systems' (2015) 78 *Modern Law Review* 216 at 219.

[50] It is not clear to me that scholars promoting proportionate sentencing would (have reason to) disagree. Andreas von Hirsch explicitly recognises that the anchoring points of any penalty scale are fixed through a political process that is responsive to cultural notions of severity and to political ideals (of which penal leniency may well be one). The overall defensibility of the system is only assured if the anchoring points are set so as not to violate the injunction against threatened sanction levels that strike fear rather than appeal to moral agency. Ordinal proportionality, which involves parity between crimes of comparable seriousness, rank-ordering of types of crimes according to seriousness, and spacing of penal responses so as to reflect these different degrees of seriousness, operates within this cardinal setting. (See von Hirsch, above n 20 at 12–19 and 36–46.) To my mind, then, in von Hirsch's model proportionality is (quite in line with what Lacey and Pickard, ibid, call for) precisely not 'a naturally existing relationship, but a product of political and social construction, cultural meaning-making, and institution-building'.

[51] Matravers, above n 21 at 42 (original emphases omitted).

[52] M Matravers, 'Mad, Bad, or Faulty? Desert in Distributive and Retributive Justice' in C Knight and Z Stemplowska (eds), *Responsibility and Distributive Justice* (Oxford, Oxford University Press, 2011) 136.

and/or inflict suffering for suffering's sake as violations of our constitutional order, we still have to confront the question how heavily the human interests and prospects of the person we punish should weigh with us in deciding upon their punishment. Do we have a warrant—perhaps even an obligation—to look any further than the seriousness of the offending behaviour (its gravity and the offender's degree of culpability) in determining the severity of the response? In some jurisdictions the courts have taken this stance. Irish courts have long stressed that '[s]entences must be proportionate first of all to the crime but also to the personal circumstances of the offender', because '[t]he accused person has a *constitutional right* which guarantees that his trial [does] not shut out a sentence appropriate to his degree of guilt and relevant personal circumstances'.[53] In Canada, one commentator recently concluded that the constitutional jurisprudence on sentencing has arrived at a point where

> it would now be an error ... for a judge to speak of proportionality without emphasizing the individualized nature of the sentencing process and then wrestling with the real effects of the criminal process and proposed sentence on the life lived by the offender.[54]

In this section, I want to defend this 'bifocal' proportionality assessment, where the sentencer must (as part of her task of setting reasonable terms for re-entry) look not just at the gravity of the offending behaviour, but also consider the effect of the contemplated punishment on the offender considered as a socially embedded human being. Unlike others who defend this position, I will not base my argument on giving mercy (or some other concept employed to loosen the strictures of a purely deeds-based sentencing approach) its due.[55] My position is a different one: a constitutionally legitimate proportionality assessment, I argue, must *include* considerations pertaining to the person of the offender, above and beyond what matters to an assessment of his culpability in respect of the crime. This argument relies on two interconnected constitutional values—humanity and welfare.

[53] *Pudliszewski v Judge Coughlan* [2006] IEHC 304 (MacMenamin J) (emphasis added), referring to *The People (DPP) v M* [1994] 3 IR 306 (Denham J) and *Director of Public Prosecutions v Stephen Kelly*, judgment of 5 July 2004 (CCA) (unreported) (Hardiman J). The same substantive point is already made in earlier judgments, see, eg, *The State (Healy) v Donoghue* [1976] IR 325 (Henchy J); *The People (Attorney General) v O'Driscoll* (1972) 1 Frewen 351 (Walsh J).

[54] BL Berger, 'Sentencing and the Salience of Pain and Hope' (2015) 70 *Supreme Court Law Review* 337 at 361. For a review of developments in the case law, see also M-E Sylvestre, 'The (Re)Discovery of the Proportionality Principle in Sentencing in *Ipeelee*: Constitutionalization and the Emergence of Collective Responsibility' (2013) 63 *Supreme Court Law Review* 461.

[55] See, eg, J Tasioulas, 'Punishment and Repentance' (2006) 81 *Philosophy* 279; B van Stokkom, 'Tempering Justice with Compassion: Rationales of Personal Mitigation in Sentencing' in DJ Cornwell, J Blad and M Wright (eds), *Civilising Criminal Justice: An International Restorative Agenda for Penal Reform* (Sherfield-on-Loddon, Waterside Press, 2013) 255.

B. Humanity and Welfare in Sentencing

If punishment responds to what *this person has done*, that also means that it responds to *this person who has done it*. Refusing to see this person as a full, three-dimensional, human being with a biography and a future would be to disregard and thereby disrespect his humanity. Such a shutting out of questions concerning who it is we punish—treating him as entirely defined (for our purposes) by the crime he has committed and the mindset with which he committed it—would be a kind of disrespect. By considering how a sentence will affect a convicted person's life more generally, a sentencer shows that she is prepared to treat the offender as a potential source of value—not just of 'intrinsic value' as a human being, but as importantly connected to others—of value as a socially embedded agent who cares about, and is cared about, by other people, for reasons pertaining to him and how he leads his life if one casts one's eye wider than the crime. In other words, she does not reduce the person to the crime. Ideally, perceiving the offender concretely as a socially embedded individual whose existence brings value to some other people's lives, will push the sentencer towards a better understanding of how the sanction she has in mind to impose will affect that person, and she will make an effort to avoid gratuitous infliction of harm.[56] Sentencing is also a human interaction. Once the 'you' is seen more clearly for who he is, the question 'what should I do to you' becomes more arduous. Proportionality as

> an intrinsically individualized concept … denies escape to the comfort of cool metrics and abstract guidelines for the judge faced with the harrowing moment of intervening in the shape of an individual's life through the infliction of suffering. Ethically, that is as it should be, because this demand for sympathetic engagement with the particular person standing before the court invites modesty and caution about the use and effects of state violence as a response to social breakdown.[57]

As the sentencer understands better what is at stake for the person being sentenced, moral responsibility for the sentence can no longer be hived off to the impersonal command of the law that authorises the decision.[58]

For some, such individualisation of sentencing decisions is itself a cause for worry. What is at the heart of this worry has perhaps been captured best in Thorburn's defence of a 'strong proportionality principle'—the term

[56] On the risk that such human emotions may also backfire against particular offenders, and the consequent need to have sentencers who are self-aware and calm enough to control against their own visceral reactions of disgust and contempt, see JQ Whitman, 'Making Happy Punishers' (2004–2005) 118 *Harvard Law Review* 2698 at 2713–14, 2720 and 2723–24.

[57] Berger, above n 54 at 361.

[58] A similar point is made by Whitman, above n 56 at 2713 and by H Müller-Dietz, 'Probleme der Strafzumessung—Sanktionsauswahl, -bemessung, Prognose' in E Wadle (ed), *Recht und Gesetz im Dialog* (Cologne, Carl Heymanns, 1982) 43 at 76.

coined by Michael Tonry[59] for the proportionate sentencing model developed and defended by Andreas von Hirsch and Andrew Ashworth[60]—over a 'limiting retributivism' that allows sentencers to take different sentencing goals into account in shaping the outcome of their decision. Thorburn asserts that desert-based sentencing 'ties the structure of judicial reasoning in the process of determining sentences to the grounds of the state's role in imposing criminal punishment'[61] in that it keeps the sentencing judge within the bounds of considerations it is constitutionally appropriate for a sentencing judge to engage in: it ensures that the judge will 'provide *the right sort of justification* for the sentence she imposes in the particular case'.[62]

Thorburn's objection to inviting judges to consider the life history and personal characteristics of the offender, and to adjust a sentence in light of how the judge expects the sanction to affect the future life course of the offender, rests on a divergence between state punishment and parental punishment when it comes to 'the normative ground of the authority the punisher holds over the punishee'.[63] Whereas 'parents are legitimately charged with ensuring the welfare of their children, broadly understood', the remit of the state's authority over the individual citizen qua offender is both 'different in kind and much narrower in scope'.[64] By implication this appears to exclude a welfare orientation from state punishment, given that welfare-oriented decision-making presupposes a legitimately paternalistic stance which, in turn, only exists when the grounds of authority are essentially fiduciary in nature.

There is considerable truth in that contrast. Yet it becomes in my view overdrawn when it appears to rule out a welfare-oriented dimension to state-imposed punishment. Thorburn is sensitive to this, hinting that it might be possible to justify 'deviat[ions] from the proportionate sentence on grounds of rehabilitation … [as] part of a larger argument concerning the necessary conditions for ensuring the independence of the offender'.[65] My

[59] M Tonry, 'Proportionality, Parsimony and Interchangeability of Punishments' in RA Duff, SE Marshall, RE Dobash and RP Dobash (eds), *Penal Theory and Practice* (Manchester, Manchester University Press, 1994).

[60] For von Hirsch's classic account, see his *Censure and Sanctions*, above n 20 and the later and fuller treatment together with A Ashworth, in von Hirsch and Ashworth, above n 45.

[61] M Thorburn, 'Proportionate Sentencing and the Rule of Law' in L Zedner and J Roberts (eds), *Principles and Values in Criminal Law and Criminal Justice: Essays in Honour of Andrew Ashworth* (Oxford, Oxford University Press, 2012) 269 at 271.

[62] Ibid at 271 (emphasis added). Note that, like von Hirsch and Ashworth, Thorburn does not mean to rule out judges ever responding to other considerations pertaining to the interests of an offender. His view is merely that the sentencing judge 'must give proportionality what Rawls calls "lexical priority"', which leaves 'some (very limited) room for sentencing judges to consider other factors' (ibid).

[63] Ibid at 283.

[64] Ibid at 283–84.

[65] Ibid at 284.

main argument here is that we should not think of rehabilitative considerations as leading to 'deviations' from a punishment that would otherwise be warranted at all—instead, we should recognise that considerations concerning the offender's humanity and personal interests are integral to the notion of proportionate punishment in the constitutional state.

Our fundamental constitutional values commit us to treating each other as creatures of intrinsic value. This gives rise to a concern for the welfare of every member of the polity. At the most general level, this commits us to shaping our institutions of public life such that they will not be harmful or disadvantageous to individual members of the polity but will rather help them in leading productive and fulfilling lives.

Insofar as we act with a welfare orientation, we treat fellow members of the polity as entitled to a certain degree of support simply because they are fellow citizens, and not because of any factors about them as individuals that make them particularly deserving of support. Thus, we do not make access to healthcare conditional upon a person having done nothing to put their own health at risk: we treat mountain climbers, smokers, drinkers, drug addicts, and the sexually adventurous, just like everyone else. This is not, I take it, because we wouldn't be prepared to judge such behaviours morally (and, in the context of such moral judgement, disapprove of some behaviours on the basis that the person not only lets herself down, but indirectly us as well, given that we promised to provide each other with a certain level of basic services without enquiring whether a person's need to access these services was avoidable or not, and that they knew this as well as we do). Of course, part of the reason why we refrain from allowing such moral judgements to register in our public settings of access to services is the practical concern that it would be very difficult to make such judgements reliably. But the larger part of the reason pertains to our political morality—we think that the kind of society in which access to basic social support depends on judgements of individual moral deservingness is one that imports too much personal moral judgement into the public domain, which is ultimately not conducive to our common good.

This is not a commitment that evaporates when a member of the polity commits a crime. The welfare orientation of all state action must also register in how we design our criminal justice system. The offender remains a member of this polity, and a concern with his legitimate interests—including the interest to one day to return to a common life in freedom—is integral to what may be done to him by way of state-imposed punishment.[66] In short, constitutionally appropriate sentencing considerations must seek to assess

[66] This duty is recognised (as an upshot of the state's basic welfare obligation towards each citizen) in German constitutional law; for discussion, see T Hörnle, 'Strafzumessungslehre im Lichte des Grundgesetzes' in E Schumann (ed), *Das strafende Gesetz im sozialen Rechtsstaat* (Berlin, De Gruyter, 2010) 105 at 124ff.

not just culpability related matters but also the reality of this offender being made subject to this punishment.

If I am right, we are now in a position to see why Thorburn is wrong to assert that strong proportionality is the only position compatible with the grounds of state authority. The state's authority partly rests on its commitment to welfare—this does not give it an entitlement to 'forge ahead making people better in their own interest' but it does need to be factored into how we run our penal system—and if we do so, responsiveness of the system to the person of the offender becomes a necessity.

C. Towards a Thick Conception of Constitutional Proportionality in Sentencing

The view I defend reflects sentencing principles that are widely accepted and practised elsewhere as well.[67] What makes the Irish courts' position noteworthy is that what I have described as a 'bifocal' approach to proportionate sentencing is drawn directly from the constitution, and while the judgments do not spell out from which specific provisions in the Irish constitution this interpretation is drawn, it is at least plausible that some notion of the state's concern for the humanity and welfare of each member of the polity underlies it.[68]

The Irish courts' approach leads to a thicker notion of 'constitutional disproportionality' than the traditional approaches to constitutionally disproportionate punishment, where it is the extreme disconnection between the overall severity of the penal response and the gravity of the underlying crime that drives the investigation.[69] It also pushes sentencing outcomes towards moderation. By accepting that the punishment, quite independently

[67] See, eg, the German Criminal Code, s 46 (Principles of sentencing): '(1) The guilt of the offender is the basis for sentencing. The effects which the sentence can be expected to have on the offender's future life in society shall be taken into account. (2) When sentencing the court shall weigh the circumstances in favour of and against the offender.' [A list of aggravating and mitigating considerations follows, which includes not just crime-related factors but also reference to 'the offender's prior history', 'his personal and financial circumstances', 'his conduct after the offence, particularly his efforts to make restitution for the harm caused as well as the offender's efforts at reconciliation with the victim'.]

[68] Compare the Irish judgments cited above at n 53. In Canada, the courts have nestled their proportionate sentencing jurisprudence under s 7 of the Canadian Charter of Rights and Freedoms (protecting the right to life, liberty and security of the person and permitting infringements only in accordance with 'the principles of fundamental justice'). See Sylvestre, above n 54 at 464ff.

[69] I discuss the limitations of a 'classic' understanding of constitutional disproportionality in sentencing in A du Bois-Pedain, 'The Place of Criminal Law Theory in the Constitutional State' in AP Simester, A du Bois-Pedain and U Neumann (eds), *Liberal Criminal Theory: Essays for Andreas von Hirsch* (Oxford: Hart Publishing, 2014) 305 at 310–13 and 317ff.

of the severity of the offending behaviour to which it is a response, also has to be proportionate to 'the personal circumstances of the offender', it links proportionality with respect for the humanity of the offender. It recognises the value of the offender's life in a substantive rather than a merely formal sense. But perhaps the most important implication of the injunction to consider whether the sentence is appropriate not only to the offender's 'degree of guilt' but also to his 'relevant personal circumstances'[70] is that we have to consider the effects of the imposition of punishment on the offender as a human individual *as something that we have to take responsibility for* when punishing him, and not simply as something that we can, indeed should, shrug off with a 'he brought it all upon himself'.

Earlier in this chapter I mentioned Matravers' exploration of a Rawlsian approach to retributive justice. Matravers observes that:

> The tendency to act aggressively, and the tendency to work hard, are not only 'influenced by … natural abilities and skills', but are also both related to certain kinds of outcomes only because of arbitrary circumstances that converted one into an advantage and the other into a handicap.[71]

Extending the benefit of a constitutional welfare commitment also to offenders is one way of making concrete 'Rawls' vision of justice as an agreement "to share each other's fates"'—Matravers emphasising that 'the reasons we have to endorse prejusticial egalitarianism apply equally to the retributive case'.[72] This is not, Matravers stresses, because individual offenders are not responsible for their actions. They are. Holding people to account for their violations of our order of equal freedom is quite compatible with recognising that living one's life successfully on the terms set by that order is harder for some than for others, and that this in itself gives us reason to consider only a welfare-oriented criminal law distributively just.

The practical import of the stance I take varies with the overall level of sanction severity prevalent in a given penal system. The humanistic proportionality approach endorsed by the Irish courts makes a real difference when compared to deed-proportionate approaches in sentencing systems which resort with greater frequency to sanctions with inherently destructive effects on the lives of those who undergo them for significant periods of time. The significance of the contrast I have drawn here between a sentencing decision that is responsive in its own right to what a particular sanction will do to an offender as a person, to his selfhood and life prospects more generally, and a sentencing decision that restricts its attention (except in exceptional cases) to an effort to respond to the gravity of the offending behaviour under sentence, will fade as sanctions themselves become less fearsome

[70] See the case citations given above at n 53.
[71] Matravers, above n 52 at 149 (quoting Rawls).
[72] Ibid (again quoting Rawls).

and destructive. In penal systems where curfews, weekend imprisonment, electronic monitoring, open prisons and the like are standard ways of serving even fairly long prison sentences, the offender still has ways of engaging in 'almost normal' personal and work relationships. These types of restrictions on the offender's free movement are, unlike traditional confinement in prison, pared down to their pure freedom-restricting effects. They do not restrict life-chances to a degree comparable with traditional incarceration. In such a sanctioning system judges will have less cause to be troubled by the effects that a sanction will have on the person of the offender—as these effects are unlikely to be destructive of the life prospects of released offenders. Against the backdrop of sanctions that are in themselves already moderated compared to present levels of penal severity, apportioning punishment along the lines advocated by von Hirsch and Ashworth will lead to much the same result as an explicit instruction to judges to consider how the punishment imposed will affect the punishee as a human being. But we should not forget how far many penal systems are from such a situation.[73]

It ought to be clear now that the reintegrative conception of the criminal court's judgment does not demand that judges be given an almost unfettered sentencing discretion. Setting appropriate terms for a polity's continued relations with the perpetrator, as a practical task and a normative ideal, does not require the absence of any restrictions on the court's ability to carve out a response. The perspective on the trial court's sentencing judgment developed here is intended to give shape and unity to the court's task by identifying the overarching framework of assumptions and purposes in which this task is necessarily performed. The model I defend differs from both of the two main scholarly positions on the exercise of sentencing discretion, limiting retributivism and desert-based sentencing. Against limiting retributivism, it maintains that the sentencing stage of criminal justice must be oriented towards one particular goal pursued by criminal justice systems over others: the goal of reintegration. It is not open to sentencing judges to pursue what are in effect policies of deterrence of certain kinds of conduct (of which the defendant's crime is taken to be a typical instance) by imposing a heavier sentence on a defendant than they otherwise would. Against desert-based sentencing, it argues that the sentencing decision legitimately should—indeed, must—consider the person of the offender and his situatedness in the social world (his subjectivity) quite apart from his mental state and other criteria going to his blameworthiness when he was

[73] Compare the analysis of the effects of imprisonment in J Jacobs, 'From Bad to Worse: Crime, Incarceration, and the Self-Wounding of Society' in S Farrall et al (eds), *Justice and Penal Reform: Re-shaping the Penal Landscape* (Abingdon, Routledge, 2016) 3 at 23ff (warning against the 'erosion of agential capacities' through contemporary imprisonment regimes, especially but not only in the United States). On 'supermax' prisons, see esp Z Hoskins, 'Punishment, Contempt, and the Prospect of Moral Reform' (2013) 32 *Criminal Justice Ethics* 1.

committing his crime. Such attention to the offender's social self is not incompatible with proportionate sentencing practices. To the contrary: this is how, in a sentencing system oriented towards reintegration for the very same constitutional reason that animates proportionality, the constitutional promise to treat each other with respect for our humanity and welfare can be fulfilled.

There is, of course, a possible wide divide between the normative ideal of being a criminal defendant (and later convicted offender) whose entitlement to equal concern and respect as a fellow member of the polity is acknowledged throughout, and the lived reality of being a criminal defendant and later a convicted offender. The real terms of interaction may well be status-reducing, dignity-sapping and expressive of a perception that the punished individual is less than equal and not entitled to full citizenship rights. This can be true both for the legal regimes that govern individuals with some types of criminal records (collateral consequences of conviction, post-release reporting duties and reduced privacy protections are cases in point)[74] and of informal social consequences of, particularly, prolonged periods of imprisonment—the de-socialising effects of prison being well known and researched.[75]

Two further points should be made in this regard, though. First, the normative ideal of equal membership in the polity can (and already does) inform critiques and reform efforts directed at current penal realities, whether these strive to replace imprisonment with alternative sanctions or to reform imprisonment such that it avoids alienation and de-socialisation.[76] Second, we must distinguish between commitments we make in our political constitutions about how we will relate to each other through the powerful institutions of collective self-governance, on the one hand, and how we interact with each other in our private social encounters, on the other hand. Notwithstanding that the line between public and private matters is difficult to draw (employment discrimination against ex-convicts being a case in point), there is a difference between upholding the normative political ideal of equal freedom and the moral ideal of treating everyone with equal concern and respect in our interactions as private individuals. It is not illegitimate in our private lives to seek to distinguish between persons by their differing moral worth, nor is it the point of our political constitution to disallow people from doing that. In this sense, the promise of treating each other with equal concern and respect will always be partial.[77] It binds us only in the part of

[74] See, eg, Z Hoskins, 'Ex-offender Restrictions' (2014) 31 *Journal of Applied Philosophy* 33.

[75] See, eg, S Besemer and J Murray, 'Prison as an Environmental Pathogen' in DeLisi and Vaughn, above n 41, 622.

[76] See, eg, H Müller-Dietz, *Menschenwürde und Strafvollzug* (Berlin, De Gruyter, 1994).

[77] This not to deny that the boundary between public and private morality is blurry here in another way. If people generally 'maintain hostile, unsupportive attitudes' to released offenders

our lives that is structured through our public political institutions. It is a personal choice for each one how far we commit ourselves to living according to that ideal also in our private lives.

A generally non-reintegrative, exclusion-based vision of criminal justice is, however, *not* one by which our criminal justice system can claim to implement the basic commitments on which our political constitution is founded. Assuming that the ideology which informs the penal practices of modern constitutional states rests on the inclusionary, rights-respecting vision of political membership and limited power that I have developed in this chapter, questions can and must be asked about the legitimacy of 'life-thrashing sanctions' of which very long terms of imprisonment and whole-life sentences imposed to meet punitive objectives alone are pertinent examples. If our entitlement to punish each other for criminal wrongs through our collectively created penal institutions is, as I have argued, grounded in a non-negotiable commitment to equal concern and respect premised on equally non-negotiable membership, and if—as I have also argued—we are for this reason committed to a reintegrative conception of state punishment, then some punishments are so obviously destructive that, qua punishments, they are beyond this account of legitimation.

IV. CONCLUSION

A penal system needs what Loader has called 'a coherent public philosophy—a story about why and whom, and how and how much, "we" punish that connects with, and re-articulates, sentiments that have some purchase within ... society'.[78] When examining the legitimacy of trial justice, Henham similarly claims that we need to focus 'on the extent to which sentencing outcomes reflect a "shared morality" about the appropriateness of punishment and its impact'.[79] What I suggest here is that this 'shared morality' is not a shared conception of punishment but a shared vision of legitimate public authority—a constitutionally grounded vision of how we must treat and what we may and may not do to each other.

This vision of political morality might well be a contested one. Hutton observes that one reason why sentencers are increasingly exposed to negative press reaction and to political intervention in sentencing through mandatory

that betray their 'unwillingness to adopt a civil disposition' towards them (Jacobs, above n 73 at 24), one's personal refusal to engage with an ex-prisoner may amount to participating in a 'public culture' of rejection such that one's actions stand to be assessed under our public morality.

[78] I Loader, 'For Penal Moderation: Notes Towards a Public Philosophy of Punishment' (2010) 14 *Theoretical Criminology* 349 at 351.

[79] R Henham, *Sentencing and the Legitimacy of Trial Justice* (London, Routledge, 2012) 97.

sentencing laws appears to be a weakening of the 'social justice paradigm' that underpinned, among other things, trust in judges as representatives of a societal interest common to all—what Garland (whom Hutton cites) has called 'the ideas and values of the solidarity project which emerged in the postwar years'.[80] One consequence may be that 'the public may no longer be convinced by the discourse of justice used by courts', giving rise to a 'need for a "replacement discourse" for sentencing'.[81] This connects to Lacey and Pickard's hypothesis that 'contemporary societies which have managed to sustain stable limits to punishment have done so ... through institutions and attitudes that foster reconciliatory dispositions between citizens', and to their further claim that 'cultural and institutional arrangements which foster high "Associational Value"—in other words, greater expected benefits of continued cooperation between individuals and groups—also foster reconciliatory dispositions'.[82] For Lacey and Pickard, societies that invest heavily in the education and skills development of their members will be more reluctant than others to render such members unproductive—hence their preference for shorter sentences and for non-incapacitating sanctions.[83]

The replacement discourse that is suggested by the conception of the sentencing decision that I put forward in this chapter reminds the public of the offender's common membership in this political community; of the reasons why such membership ought not to be forfeitable, and why exclusion from the shared social world is not a coherent objective of punishment. It is true, of course, that even this commitment may crumble, that societies stop believing in extending recognition and rights to all. But loudmouthed calls for extreme punishments are often made in the abstract, with the recipient of such punishment being conveniently imagined as less than human. When

> criminals are viewed as recognizable members of the community ... and the criminal acts portrayed are more mundane, the kinds of things respondents might imagine themselves doing in certain circumstances, an alternative discourse about the nature of crime and punishment becomes possible.[84]

My sense is that penal moderation may not so much emerge as a quasi-automatic upshot from empirical conditions of high associational value as that it requires *associational commitment*, a political commitment towards continued association—which, in turn, can be read as a commitment to a (possibly counterfactual) assumption of high associational value. That said,

[80] N Hutton, 'Reflections' in Tata and Hutton, above n 43, 575 at 585.
[81] Hutton, ibid.
[82] Lacey and Pickard, above n 49 at 221.
[83] Ibid at 234–37.
[84] BK Crew et al, 'Crisis and Contradictions in a State Sentencing Structure' in Tata and Hutton, above n 43, 184–85.

it may be true that for *this political commitment* to be upheld, Lacey and Pickard are right to suggest that 'the key to penal moderation lies not only in reintegrative criminal justice policy, but in social policy and in political arrangements and institutional structures which maximise expected Associational Value among citizens'.[85]

[85] Lacey and Pickard, above n 49 at 239.

10

Why Privatisation Matters

ALON HAREL

THE TRADITIONAL ARGUMENTS opposing privatisation are based on the view that privatised entities are less likely to realise certain goals: accountability, impartiality, due process etc. In contrast, advocates of privatisation argue that private entities are as capable as public entities to realise such goals. There is nothing that necessitates the conclusion that private entities are less accountable or less likely to reason on the basis of what is traditionally classified as 'public reasons'. The advocates of privatisation argue therefore that private entities can reason (or even are likely to reason) in a publicly-oriented way as a result of their 'publicisation'.[1] This term refers to a process in which private entities come to be guided by public reasons and modify their decisions accordingly. Thus, while advocates and opponents of privatisation reach different conclusions, they use a similar mode of reasoning—instrumental reasoning. The only justification for or against privatisation is that private entities are more (or less) capable than public entities of reasoning properly and reaching the right decisions.

The primary aim of this chapter is to challenge this approach. Even when private entities are moved by the right reasons, they are still inferior in some respects to public entities. Hence, publicisation does not remedy the problems resulting from privatisation. It cannot do so because the concern underlying the opposition to privatisation is not that private entities are incapable or unlikely to reason fairly or impartially or to act justly; it is that private entities do not speak 'in the name of the state' with the result that their decision cannot be attributed to citizens. It is therefore not *the reasons underlying the decisions* that count but, instead, *the identity of the agent* making a decision or performing the act.

Part I distinguishes between two conceptions of publicness: reasons-based and agency-based.[2] The former relies on a dichotomy between public and

[1] See especially J Freeman, 'Extending Public Law Norms Through Privatization' (2003) 116 *Harvard Law Review* 1285.

[2] The argument in this section rests partly upon my previous work. See A Dorfman and A Harel, 'Against Privatisation As Such' (2016) 36 *Oxford Journal of Legal Studies* 400. I deviate however in some respects from the claims made there.

private reasons and the latter relies on a distinction between public and private agents. I also show that despite the prevalent view among theorists that what really matters is the reasons underlying the decisions, courts often endorse the agency-based view of publicness. Part II defends the agency-based view. It argues that what ultimately justifies the agency-based view is the fact that only public officials can speak 'in the name of the state' and that the decisions and only decisions and acts of public officials can properly be attributed to citizens. While publicisation may guarantee that private entities act fairly and impartially, the decisions and acts of private entities cannot be attributed to its citizens. I also argue that such an attribution is at times important and necessary for the legitimacy of the provision of the relevant goods.

I. REASONS-BASED AND AGENCY-BASED PERSPECTIVES OF PUBLIC LAW

The question addressed in this part is perhaps the most fundamental question concerning public law: what constitutes publicness. The first section examines the reasons-based hypothesis. Under this hypothesis public decisions are characterised by the reasons underlying them. To the extent that a decision is grounded in concerns for impartiality, due process etc, it should be classified as a public one. In contrast, if the decision is grounded in self-interested or in sectarian ideology, it is a private one. The identity of the agent matters only to the extent that it provides an indication of the reasons underlying the decisions. In contrast, the agency-based view rests on the belief that the very identity of the agent determines whether the relevant decision is private or public. A decision is public only if it is made by a public official. Sections A and B each examine one of these views and provide the background for the normative discussion in Part II.

A. The Reasons-based Perspective

The distinction between 'public' and 'private' is central to any modern legal system. One prevailing view is that a decision is 'public' (and consequently the individual making the decision can claim to be acting in the name of the state) if the decision is grounded in appropriate publicly oriented reasoning. More specifically, it is claimed that a decision is public if it meets certain conditions of equality and impartiality. Malcolm Thorburn defended this view:

> In order for an individual to successfully claim to be exercising a state power, he must meet the accountability standards set out in public law—roughly,

> reasonableness and fairness—in the exercise of his discretionary powers ... but the justification for the state's power turns on its ability to act impartially in the name of all. If it fails to do so it undermines its own legitimacy.[3]

The appeal of this view is self-evident. Arguably, the decision-maker is only an instrument for making a right decision. It follows that what we should care about is not *who the decision-maker is* but *whether the decision-maker is likely to make the right decision or to be moved by the right reasons*. The decision-maker is to be selected on the basis of its likelihood of making the right decision. Under this view, privatisation is merely a technical or technocratic change;[4] it is a change in the identity of the agent who makes the decision but it does not necessarily change the reasons underlying the decision or even the content of the decision. Consequently, a decision made by a private entity can be public in nature as long as the agent is moved by 'public' reasons and decides accordingly.

However, very often the legal system characterises publicness on the basis of the identity of the agents rather than the reasons underlying the decisions. Traditional administrative law employs tests for determining publicness that rest upon the identity of the agent. Perhaps most prominently, statutes often contain restrictions on privatisation that focus on the identity of the decision-maker. For instance, under the United States Federal Activities Inventory Reform (FAIR) Act of 1998, an 'inherently governmental function' is defined as 'a function that is so intimately related to the public interest *as to require performance by Federal Government employees*'.[5] The requirement that only federal employees can perform an inherently governmental function seems to support the agency-based view of publicness. There is therefore an incongruity between the reasons-based view of publicness and the legal definitions used to define publicness.

To address this incongruity, the advocates of the reasons-based view distinguish between the fundamental normative core of publicness (resting on the reasons used by the agent to reach the decision) and the contingent institutional means to guarantee that the agent is guided by these reasons. The reasons guiding the agent are what ultimately determine whether the decision is public or private; it is public if it should be impartial, fair, deliberative, and thereby promote the public interest. To guarantee fairness and impartiality, one needs at times to use public officials, as only such officials are generally or frequently moved by the right type of reasons and therefore

[3] M Thorburn, 'Reinventing the Night-Watchman State' (2010) 60 *University of Toronto Law Journal* 425 at 442.

[4] See S Dolovich, 'How Privatization Thinks: The Case of Prisons' in J Freeman and M Minow (eds), *Government By Contract: Outsourcing and American Democracy* (Cambridge MA, Harvard University Press, 2009) 128 at 145.

[5] Federal Activities Inventory Reform Act of 1998, 31 USC § 501 note (2006) (emphasis added).

are more likely to reach the right decisions. Given the institutional environment and the type of incentives operating on them, public officials or public entities are more likely to be guided by public rather than private reasons. In contrast, the institutional environment characterising private entities is likely to induce them to act partially.

If indeed the only concern underlying privatisation is (as the advocates of the reasons-based view believe) the concern about the reasons for decisions, the question whether to privatise a particular service has both a normative and an empirical dimension. One first has to determine what reasons should govern the decision, and then one has to ask which institution is more likely to act on the basis of these reasons. The disagreement between advocates and opponents can rest either on positing different goals and ends, eg, efficiency versus accountability. Or, it can rest on disagreement concerning the best means to bring about efficiency or accountability. The former is a normative question while the latter is an empirical one.

Yet, as I argued elsewhere, this framework does not reflect the way publicness is understood in legal circles.[6] Publicness is not regarded merely as instrumental to the quality of the resulting decisions. Instead, publicness is to be understood as a feature that hinges upon the identity or status of the decision-makers. Often, transferring powers to private entities offends a sensitivity that is not instrumental in nature. The emphasis upon instrumental considerations concerning the quality of the reasoning or decisions may miss the point, as such an emphasis relies on an understanding of political institutions and procedures that fails to capture what makes such institutions politically and morally attractive.[7] While in the past I provided ample evidence illustrating the incongruity between the instrumental approach and legal doctrine,[8] let me focus here on one judicial decision illustrating that the legal system cares deeply about the identity of the agent, not because public officials are better capable of rendering appropriate decisions but for other more elusive reasons—reasons which will be discussed in Part II.

In its famous decision barring the privatisation of public prisons, the Israeli Supreme Court considered the constitutionality of an amendment to the Prison Ordinance. Under this amendment, the State of Israel was empowered to establish, for the first time, a (single) prison to be operated and managed by a private corporation rather than by the state. The constitutionality of this amendment was challenged by the petitioners on several grounds. Among these grounds, it was claimed that the amendment

[6] See Dorfman and Harel, above n 2.

[7] A Harel, *Why Law Matters* (Oxford, Oxford University Press, 2014) 4.

[8] See A Dorfman and A Harel, 'The Case Against Privatization' (2013) 41 *Philosophy and Public Affairs* 67 at 89–102; Dorfman and Harel, above n 2; and A Harel and A Porat, 'Commensurability and Agency: Two Yet-To-Be-Met Challenges to Law and Economics' (2011) 96 *Cornell Law Review* 749 at 772–74.

disproportionately violated the rights of prison inmates as a result of the actual transfer of imprisonment powers to a private enterprise.[9]

There were two major arguments supporting the view that establishing private prisons violate the inmates' rights: an empirical-contingent one and a principled one. In her concurring opinion, Justice Procaccia argued that private prisons are likely to violate rights 'to a greater extent than is permitted under the limitations clause in the Basic Law: Human Dignity and Liberty'.[10] Justice Procaccia believed that a private enterprise is unlikely to internalise the doctrine of balances in the exercise of sovereign power, in all of its particulars and aspects. It further suffers from a conflict of interest and therefore it is inapt to perform the necessary task. Thus, as a *contingent conjecture*, Justice Procaccia concluded that privatisation is detrimental to the protection of human rights and therefore that the amendment is unconstitutional.

This argument was rejected by the majority of the Court and, in particular, by President Beinisch. President Beinisch agreed with Justice Procaccia that the privatisation of prisons is wrong as it violates the dignity provision in Basic Law: Human Dignity and Liberty. But to her, unlike Justice Procaccia, the violation is not contingent; it is an inevitable by-product of the privatisation, as the publicness of the institution *in itself* is a necessary prerequisite for protecting the dignity of prisoners. Under her view:

> In Israel the power to punish someone who has been convicted under the law and to imprison him in order that he may serve his sentence is, therefore, one of the most significant powers of the state, and under the law the body that is responsible for carrying out this function of the state is the Israel Prison Service. This power, as well as the powers of the other security services, is an expression of a broader principle of the system of government in Israel, according to which the state—through the government and the various security services that are subordinate to it—has exclusive authority to resort to the use of organized force in general, and to enforce the criminal law in particular.[11]

President Beinisch reiterates this point and says:

> We have already discussed the fact that according to the basic values of society and the system of government in Israel, the legitimacy for exercising powers that involve a serious violation of the constitutional right to personal liberty derives from the fact that these powers are exercised by and on behalf of the state, after the person with regard to whom they are exercised has been tried and convicted by the legal system of the state. Imprisoning a person is the culmination of the criminal proceeding initiated against that person by the state on behalf of the entire public. The power of imprisonment and the other invasive powers

[9] See HCJ 2605/05 *Academic Centre of Law and Business v Minister of Finance* 63(2) PD 545, 612–17 [2009] (Isr). A translation can be found at www.privateci.org/private_pics/Israel_Ruling.pdf. References below to page numbers are to the English translation.

[10] Ibid at 127.

[11] Ibid at 65.

> that derive from it are therefore some of the state's most distinctive powers as the embodiment of government, and they reflect the constitutional principle that the state has a monopoly upon exercising organized force in order to advance the general public interest.[12]

In my terminology, President Beinisch here defends the agency-based view of publicness. She believes that certain tasks ought to be performed by public institutions not because public institutions are more likely to render right decisions, but simply because the identity of the agent matters as such. President Beinisch defended her position on the ground that the view that the state is in charge of performing certain tasks is at the foundations of the Israeli legal system.

B. The Agency-based Perspective

Assume now that a theorist believes that private entities are as capable as the state or even more capable of running prisons in an impartial way and in a way that respects human rights and provides sufficient protection to the public. Assume, for instance, that the state operates public prisons and pays for the operation of private prisons and also assume that both public and private prisons provide identical conditions for prisoners. The directors of both private and public prisons are moved by public concerns, such as the concern to promote prisoners' welfare, protect their rights and provide opportunities for rehabilitation. Should we not conclude (as the reasons-based view of publicness requires of us) that in an important respect both prisons are 'public', as in both public values have been used to dictate the decisions?

I believe the answer is negative. There is a sense that is clearly reflected in the prison case that the *mere fact* that the prison is run by a private entity gives rise to a grievance on the part of prisoners. It is this fact rather than the contingencies resulting from the institutional structure which gives rise to the grievance. The nature of this grievance will be examined in Part II. Let me here only provide a more general framework preparing the grounds for that analysis.

Some agents are chosen to perform a task because of their excellence in doing so, when excellence in executing the task is understood and evaluated independently of the agent's identity. At other times excellence (or even competence) in executing an enterprise is inseparable from the identity or status of the agent. The latter enterprises are 'agent-dependent enterprises', namely enterprises whose success hinges (conceptually rather than contingently) on the agent performing them.[13]

[12] Ibid at 68.
[13] Harel, above n 7 at 69.

To illustrate such a case, I have previously used the example of blood feuds.[14] Blood feuds are ritualised ways of seeking vengeance for a wrong by killing or punishing a person belonging to a tribe or a clan of the original perpetrator who committed the wrong. Anthropologists found that only a male relative of the deceased is capable of performing a blood feud. Of course, any person can kill a person who belongs to the relevant tribe or clan. But, such a killing constitutes a 'blood feud' only if it is performed by the right agent. A killing by the wrong agent is not merely an impermissible blood feud; it simply does not constitute a 'blood feud' and is characterised as a mere killing. The agent performing the killing in this case is not an instrument for the performance of an enterprise whose success is independent of its identity; instead, its identity is a prerequisite for its success. Male relatives of the deceased are the appropriate agents to make public decisions *simply because of their status*.

Similarly, in the context I am discussing, the legitimacy of the decision hinges on the 'public' status of the agent not simply because the agent is more or less likely to be guided by public reasons but because of that very status.[15] More generally such a view was also expressed in the context of punishment by John Locke. Locke argues that:

> To justify bringing such evil [ie, punishment] on any man two things are requisite. First, that *he who does it has commission and power to do so*. Secondly, that it be directly useful for the procuring of some other good ... Usefulness, when present (being but one of those conditions), cannot give the other, which is a commission to punish.[16]

Locke believes that in addition to the fact that the punishment is 'directly useful for the procuring of some other good' the agent must also have 'commission and power' to inflict it. It should in other words be the 'right' agent to perform the task. This raises the question of who the right agent is and what makes an agent the right agent.

The Israeli Supreme Court's decision in the prison case reflects a similar sentiment. The Court believes that imprisonment may be necessary to guarantee public order. Prisons also have to promote and protect the welfare of

[14] A Harel, 'Why Only the State May Inflict Criminal Sanctions: The Case against Privately Inflicted Sanctions' (2008) 14 *Legal Theory* 113 at 121.

[15] In her comprehensive historical survey, Sarah Percy illustrates that there is a persistent opposition to mercenaries in European history. Yet, the reasons provided for this opposition shift and change in time. Percy's survey indicates that while most reasons provided for this opposition are instrumental, the sense of discomfort is deeply entrenched and cannot easily be explained in instrumental terms. This provides support for the conjecture that the instrumental reasons are mere rationalisations of a much deeper resistance to privatisation which this chapter aims to explicate. See S Percy, *Mercenaries: The History of a Norm in International Relations* (Oxford, Oxford University Press, 2007).

[16] J Locke, *A Second Letter Concerning Toleration* in R Vernon (ed), *Locke on Toleration* (Cambridge, Cambridge University Press, 2010) 100 (emphasis added).

prisoners. Private prisons can of course guarantee public order and protect the welfare of prisoners. Yet public wardens are not merely means to run prisons that could, in principle, be run by private wardens. Instead, the Court believed that public wardens are necessary for the successful protection of dignity. Let me provide in the next section a more abstract framework that may explain the significance of public provision of goods and services when publicness is understood in terms of the agency-based view.

II. DEFENDING THE AGENCY-BASED PERSPECTIVE

This part challenges the instrumentalism that infects the dominant view concerning publicness. It challenges the view that all goods and services can *in principle* be provided by both public and private institutions. It shifts therefore the type of considerations bearing on the question of 'who the appropriate agent is' from considerations concerning the likely *correctness or justness of the resulting decision or action*, to considerations concerning *the legitimacy of the agent to make the decision or to perform the action*. It also shows that the persistent resistance to privatisation is rooted in an unarticulated conviction—the conviction that at least in some cases, an act cannot acquire its public nature unless it is performed by a public agent. The identity of the agent (public or private) rather than the reasons underlying the decision or the act (or the resulting justness of the decision or the act) determines whether the decision is a public or a private decision. It provides therefore a normative argument supporting the agency-based perspective.

This task is particularly important given the conclusion of Part I. Part I established that sometimes the legal system protects 'publicness' not in order to facilitate better deliberation or high quality decisions. Instead, as the prison case illustrates, the legal system is sometimes concerned directly with the identity of the agent, that is, it insists that the agent be a public agent. Decisions or acts are characterised as 'public' not simply because they serve the public, promote the public interest or are grounded in the right reasons. Instead, as President Beinisch said: '[T]he state—through the government and the various security services that are subordinate to it—has exclusive authority to resort to the use of organized force in general, and to enforce the criminal law in particular.'[17] This observation raises the normative question: why should the legal system care about who the agent is? Should we regard the agent (as the reasons-based view advocates) as a mere instrument designed to reason properly and decide justly?

I shall argue that what makes such decisions or acts public is the fact that they are made or performed by public officials because only such decisions are made *in the name of citizens*. More specifically, only decisions made by

[17] *Academic Centre of Law and Business v Minister of Finance* above n 9 at 65.

public officials can be attributed to citizens and be regarded as decisions that have been made by citizens. In contrast, a private entity, I shall argue, can often promote the public interest, but it can never speak in the name of citizens and its decisions can never be attributed to citizens. I shall also argue that at times it is very important for a decision to be made in the name of citizens. To see why, let us examine first the character of the decisions made by public officials and then turn to examine in what ways they differ from decisions made by private entities.

Every act or decision of a public official is potentially subject to the accusation that it does not serve the public interest. Such an accusation, if sound, implies that the decision should not have been made. The only valid justification for a decision of a public official is one that rests on the public interest and establishes that the decision promotes the public interest. Any justification that rests on the private interests of the official or on her ideological commitments cannot justify the decision. Further, the public interest that should guide the public official is not simply her own judgement as to what the public interest is. The official's view as to what the public interest is has no relevance; instead, she ought to pursue the perspective of the sovereign. The public official cannot justify her decision on the grounds that *she believes* that the decision promotes the public interest. She can however argue that her decision reflects the policies pursued by the elected representatives, namely that her decision reflects their vision of what the public good is. In the modern state, this observation implies that politicians as representatives of the sovereign have a significant role in guiding decisions of public officials. Let me elaborate more on the role of public officials.[18]

Public officials are typically engaged in a practice. The execution of their task depends on there being an ongoing framework or coordinative effort in which participants immerse themselves *together* in formulating, articulating and shaping a shared perspective from which they can approach, systematically, the implementation and execution of decisions, thus tackling questions such as how one should proceed in general and in the particular instance. The process takes a coordinative form in the sense that participants are responsive to the intentions and actions of one another as they go along with the execution of government policy and decisions.

Yet public officials do not control their practice. A practice of public officials does not merely operate among bureaucrats (with politicians taking the backseat), but rather includes among its engaging participants both politicians (representing the sovereign) and bureaucrats. Thus, the integration of the political offices into the community of practice does not limit the role of politicians to that of setting the practice of bureaucrats in motion by determining the basic rules of conduct and the boundaries of the framework within which bureaucrats deliberate toward action. Nor does it limit their

[18] This section is based on Dorfman and Harel, above n 2.

role to that of monitoring and supervising the participants (either directly or indirectly through other state officials). Rather, integration enables political officials to guide, within the limit of their legal powers, the ongoing deliberations and everyday actions performed by bureaucrats. In that, political officials can exert their influence on the other participants directly.

Note that this claim does not focus on how much, and to what extent, politicians make actual use of their power to influence the practice. In some cases and with respect to some spheres of state action, politicians seldom use their powers. That said, it is the combination of the potential for intervention in and guidance of the practice, on the one hand, and the readiness of politicians to intervene whenever they are dissatisfied with the ways in which the practice operates, on the other, that counts. Accordingly, the realisation of this potential, namely de facto intervention on the part of politicians, is not in and of itself crucial to determine whether the political offices are sufficiently integrated into the practice. Instead, what is crucial is the participants' Hohfeldian liability to the power of political officials to place them under a duty to act in certain ways and the willingness to exercise this power whenever they are dissatisfied with the ways in which the practice operates. It is this involvement of politicians in the practices of public officials that gives rise to the claim that public officials speak in the name of the state and in the name of its citizens.

This is not the case however with a private entity. The private interests or the ideological commitments of the private entity can at times justify a decision or an act of the private entity. Privatisation typically involves a contract between the state and the private entity. Such a privatisation agreement sets usually in general, underspecified terms, the desired ends and the basic constraints on the means that the private executor can deploy in pursuit of these ends.[19] It then makes some room—*an arena of permissibility*, as it were—for the private entity so that the latter can meet the designated ends with whatever means it chooses, provided that they are consistent with the basic constraints set out by the contract in accordance with the government's guidelines.[20]

A defined arena of permissibility is just an authorisation for private contractors to act according to their own views as to what the public

[19] As with statutory provisions, the vague and underspecified content of the contract is not coincidental. It reflects different considerations (such as uncertainty and the bounded rationality of the parties) that render it natural to leave the language of the contract sufficiently airy to accommodate foreseeable and unforeseeable future events.

[20] This typical scenario can accommodate a case where state officials are authorised by the state to renegotiate the terms of the agreement with the other party insofar as circumstances change and modifications become necessary. These modifications (if accepted by the private entity) merely change the *scope* of the arena of permissibility, but do not eliminate it. The only way to eliminate it (or even to come close to its elimination) is to require the private entity to defer to state officials in all matters. However, this will be tantamount to converting the participants in the practice to public officials properly conceived.

interest requires—that is, to pursue the general interest as filtered through their own viewpoints of what impartial concern for this interest requires. Further, what I label 'an arena of permissibility' is not an accidental feature of privatisation—a feature which may be dispensed with. It is a prerequisite for realising the goals that privatisation is designed to bring about, in particular, efficiency. As one commentator has noted:

> The emphasis on outcomes gives private service providers latitude to develop their own strategies for achieving the desired results. If all tasks were specified in the governing contracts, there would be little room for the beneficial effects of competition to operate.[21]

Insofar as privatisation involves 'an arena of permissibility', private entities participate in a practice that takes a separatist form. The participants in a private community of practice do not incur an obligation to engage the relevant political offices deferentially. Unlike public officials participating in an integrative practice, no such deference to political officials is required from private entities (in typical cases) simply by virtue of being in charge of performing government functions. Were they required to display the requisite deference, the participants would in essence become public officials, regardless of their formal title (eg, private contractors). In contrast to public officials, private actors possess a valid claim-right against state interference insofar as they act within the designated arena of permissibility. In other words, instead of being liable to the power of the state to direct their conduct, private agents enjoy a form of immunity on the basis of which they can invoke their *right* not to follow the demands of the public interest (as viewed from the polity's point of view). Agents of public institutions, by contrast, enjoy no such immunity. Accordingly, they have no valid claim of their own against state intervention whenever the polity determines that the judgments of these agents fail to serve the public interest.

Let me illustrate these observations by using the private prison case. A private prison can operate for profit; consequently, it can justify some of its decisions on the grounds that the decision is conducive to its financial interests. Other non-profit private entities often operate to promote a sectarian view. A non-profit private prison can justify a decision on the ground that such a decision is necessary to promote its ideological convictions, eg, the eternal salvation of prisoners, which may be the ultimate concern of a non-profit entity. Such considerations can be justifiably taken into account by private entities as long as the resulting decision does not conflict with the contract between the state and the private entity. Naturally, neither private profit nor sectarian ideological commitments can be attributed to the polity

[21] See M Diller, 'Form and Substance in the Privatization of Poverty Programs' (2002) 49 *UCLA Law Review* 1739 at 1745.

as a whole. They reflect legitimate ends of private entities but they are not constituents of the public interest. It follows therefore that while the private entity can at times promote the public interest to a greater degree than a public entity, it cannot claim to act *in the name of* the public. Some of its decisions, namely decisions made within the arena of permissibility are not done in the name of the state. A citizen who resents a decision of the private entity may urge it to change its position, but she cannot claim that the decision is illegitimate simply because it does not promote the public interest, as not all decisions of the private entity are designed to promote the public interest. Contrast this with the case of a public prison. Assume that the state operates prisons in a way which is perceived by a citizen as inappropriate. The citizen has large stakes in fighting against this mode of operation. As she is a member of the polity, the decision of how to operate public prisons is attributed to her. Citizens after all are responsible for decisions made by their state and consequently their voice ought to be considered by public officials.

The citizen can of course protest a decision of the private entity. She can argue that it is unjust. But, her protest can be addressed not only (as in the case of the public entity) by providing reasons why the relevant decision serves the public interest. It can also be answered by claiming that this decision promotes private interests, eg, the financial interests of the entity, or that it is conducive to sectarian ideological commitments of the private entity. The private entity can claim that the issue is not the 'citizen's business' at all. As long as the decision is compatible with the contract, it is permissible for the private entity to act in this way. Moreover, precisely for this reason, the decision of a private entity cannot be attributed to the citizen and, consequently, she has lesser stakes in it than in public officials' decisions. Citizens who protest against decisions made by private entities cannot maintain that such decisions are made in their name. Consequently, they do not share responsibility for these decisions. It is this feature that underlies the fundamental difference between public officials and private entities: the former act in our name and we are responsible for their decisions while the latter, at best, act for us but not in our name.

These observations have important consequences. Citizens always have good reason to struggle against injustice simply by virtue of being persons who care about justice; however, there arises an additional reason to do so when the injustice in question is the doing of public officials. This is because the latter instance of injustice is done *in their name*—that is, by public officials who act in the name of the polity to which they belong. Hence, the special status of public officials has repercussions concerning the responsibility of citizens, that is, persons acting in their collective political capacity. The citizen's protest against the injustice committed by a public agency differs from mere protest against injustice committed by an individual, private entity or another state. It is a protest against injustice (or some other grievance) that can be attributed to the citizen—someone who should take responsibility for its occurrence.

Our conclusion may raise the following objection. Arguably the polity is the one that decides voluntarily to alienate its powers to a private entity. For that reason, the polity should also be held responsible for the decisions made within the arena of permissibility by virtue of having made the initial decision to alienate its powers. It follows that the private entity operates also 'in the name of the polity' as ultimately its powers are ones that were granted (in the appropriate sense) by the polity.

It is of course true that the polity and its constituents bear responsibility for making the initial decision to privatise a given activity, selecting the appropriate contractor, and monitoring its conduct. That said, none of these could compensate for the loss of control over the manner in which the private entity acts (at least insofar as it acts within the arena of permissibility). Even given that the polity had a specific vision when it privatised the activity, it is barred from reconsidering or changing its course and purpose. Citizens who protest against decisions made by private bodies cannot maintain that such decisions are made in their name and consequently they do not share responsibility for these decisions. It is this feature which underlies the fundamental difference between public officials and private entities; the former act in our name while the latter, at best, act for us. Under this account, the privatising state cuts itself off from the privately executed activities (eg, the infliction of punishment). These privatised activities are not the doing of the state; private entities vested with the formal authority to execute the activities in question cannot speak and act *in the name of the state* as some of their decisions are grounded—appropriately—in their private interests or sectarian ideologies.

This conclusion establishes that there is a fundamental difference between public officials and private entities. This difference does not rest on the reasoning characterising public officials or on the quality of their decisions. Instead, it rests on the fact that public officials speak in our name; their acts are attributed to us as citizens. In contrast, private entities cannot speak in the name of citizens and their decisions should not be attributed to citizens.

Yet, despite the significance of these conclusions, they are not sufficient to provide a case against privatisation. I have not yet provided any reasons why one should care that decisions and acts be performed *in the name of citizens*. Perhaps while this difference is important, it has no practical implications concerning privatisation. To address this concern, let me briefly provide two arguments why some decisions ought to be made such that they could be attributed to citizens.

First, as I have argued in the past, some goods and services can be provided only when they are provided in the name of the state. Supplying such goods and services by other providers is simply conceptually impossible. In the past, I argued that punishment is a good that must be provided publicly.[22] This is because punishment involves condemnation and condemnation must emanate from an entity which is superior to that of the person who is being sentenced. A private entity cannot claim that its judgement concerning the wrongfulness of an act is superior to that of the person whose behaviour is being evaluated. The person who is subject to the condemnation can always argue that her judgement concerning the act is superior to the entity which judges her act to be wrongful. Under this view, punishment must emanate from the state because punishment involves a judgement concerning wrongfulness and such a judgement gains credibility when the judge is the state rather than a private entity.

Further, privatisation has additional costs resulting from the fact that privatisation undercuts the responsibility of citizens. Given that citizens do not bear the same type of responsibility for private decisions as for public decisions, privatisation might undermine an important dimension of our moral practices and in particular responsibility-taking. Privatisation reduces the political dimension of responsibility by partially obviating the distinctive role of *collective undertaking* in discharging the responsibility persons have in virtue of being citizens. The argument is not one of political solidarity; that is to say, it does not turn on the psychology of joint activity and its beneficial effects. Rather, the argument is that political engagement forms a special instance of our moral practices of taking responsibility.[23] The reason for that lies in the collective form that this instance of assuming and discharging responsibility takes.[24]

The effects of privatisation are not restricted to the question of whether a public prison is better or worse qua prison than its private counterpart or whether private forestry is better or worse qua forestry than its public counterpart.[25] They extend to the question of whether stripping the state of its powers erodes public responsibility. For privatisation is not only the transformation of detention centres, trains, tax inquiry offices, forestry operations, and so on, considered one service at a time. It is also the transformation of our political system and public culture from ones characterised by robust shared responsibility and political engagement to ones characterised by fragmentation and sectarianism.[26]

[22] See Harel, above n 7 at 96–99.

[23] A brief discussion of this point appears in IM Young, *Responsibility for Justice* (Oxford, Oxford University Press, 2011) 169.

[24] I developed this view in Dorfman and Harel, above n 2.

[25] For a similar view, see J Gardner, *The Evil of Privatization* (unpublished workshop paper, June 20, 2014) available at http://papers.ssrn.com/sol3/papers.cfm?abstract_id=2460655.

[26] To this extent, the problem with privatisation identified in these pages is not limited to the private provision of the most basic goods and services. Rather, privatisation (at least on a large scale) can be objectionable even when the goods and services do not count as the most basic ones.

III. CONCLUSION

This chapter examined the nature of publicness. It differentiated between two conceptions of publicness: reasons-based and agency-based. I also argued that the legal system seems at times to endorse the agency-based view. The chapter provided normative support to the agency-based view. More specifically, I argued that only public officials can speak in the name of the state and only their decisions are ones that can be attributed to citizens. Finally, I argued that at times it is important that decisions be made in the name of citizens. These observations do not imply that every case of privatisation is wrong; it merely implies that privatisation has costs that are often ignored. The modest ambition of this chapter is to raise to awareness these costs—especially in the context of criminal justice.

Index